Nurse Executive

LINDA THOMPSON ADAMS, DrPH, RN, FAAN, is the dean and professor of the School of Nursing at Oakland University. She brings over 20 years of academic and administrative experience in significant leadership positions. Prior to joining Oakland University she was the associate dean for Policy, Planning & Workforce Development at the University of Maryland School of Nursing and served concurrently as director of the Center for Community Partnerships for Children and Families. Previous to that post, Governor Parris Glendening of Maryland appointed her as special secretary of the Governor's Office of Children, Youth and Families. She served as director of the city of Baltimore's Office of Occupational Medicine and Safety—a cabinet-level position under Mayor Kurt Schmoke. In addition, she has held administrative and teaching positions at the University of Maryland, Johns Hopkins University, Coppin State College, and Hampton University in Virginia. She earned both BSN and MSN degrees at Wayne State University (MI), and masters and doctoral degrees in public health from Johns Hopkins University (MD).

EDWARD H. O'NEIL, PhD, MPA, FAAN, is professor of Family and Community Medicine at the University of California, San Francisco, where he also serves as codirector of the Center for the Health Professions, a research, advocacy, and training institute created to stimulate change in health professions education. Since 1989, he has been the executive director of the Pew Health Professions Commission, which he started as a way of elevating health professional education and health workforce issues in the debate on national health care reform. Prior to assuming his position at USCF, he was assistant dean for Medical Education at Duke University and associate professor in the Departments of Family Medicine and Public Policy. He also served as codirector of the Pew Veterinary Medical and Dental Education Programs, associate dean at the School of Dentistry at the University of North Carolina at Chapel Hill, and program associate with the W. K. Kellogg Foundation. He received his BA and MA from the University of Alabama, and his MPA and PhD in American Social and Intellectual History, Public Policy, and Administration from Syracuse University.

Nurse Executive

The Four Principles of Management

Linda Thompson Adams, DrPH, RN, FAAN
Edward H. O'Neil, PhD, MPA, FAAN
Editors

SPRINGER PUBLISHING COMPANY

NEW YORK

Springer Publishing Company, LLC
11 West 42nd Street
New York, NY 10036
www.springerpub.com

Acquisitions Editor: Allan Graubard
Production Editor: Julia Rosen
Cover design: Joanne E. Honigman
Composition: Apex Publishing

08   09   10   11/   5   4   3   2   1

Library of Congress Cataloging-in-Publication Data

Nurse executive : the four principles of management / Linda Thompson Adams, Edward O'Neil, editors.
      p. ; cm.
   Includes bibliographical references and index.
   ISBN 978-0-8261-1104-3 (alk. paper)
   1. Nursing services—Administration.   2. Nurse administrators.   3. Leadership.
I. Thompson Adams, Linda S.   II. O'Neil, Edward H.
   [DNLM: 1. Nursing—organization & administration.   2. Leadership.   3. Professional Competence.   WY 105 N97133 2008]

RT89.N748   2008
362.17'3068—dc22   2007045876

Printed in the United States of America by Bang Printing.

Contents

Contributors

GAURDIA BANISTER, PhD, RN, FAAN

GAURDIA BANISTER is the new Executive Director of the Institute for Patient Care at the Massachusetts General Hospital in Boston. Before assuming that position, she was the Senior Vice President for Patient Care Services and CNO at Providence Hospital in Washington, DC. She also spent a year teaching in the School of Health Sciences in Sapporo, Japan. She received her PhD and MSN from the University of Texas at Austin. She received her BSN from the University of Wyoming.

SARA BARGER, DPA, MSN, FAAN

SARA BARGER is dean and professor of the Capstone College of Nursing at the University of Alabama. Her prior positions include chair of Northern Illinois University's School of Nursing, and associate dean, department head, and director of the Nursing Center at Clemson University in South Carolina. She has held positions in the public health systems of Maryland, Virginia, and Georgia. She has a BS in Nursing from the University of Maryland, a masters in nursing from Emory University, and a doctorate in public administration from the University of Georgia.

JANIS P. BELLACK, PhD, RN, FAAN

JANIS P. BELLACK is currently the vice president for Academic Affairs/provost and professor of Nursing and Health Sciences at the Massachusetts College of Pharmacy and Health Sciences in Boston. She formerly served as associate provost for Education and professor of Nursing and Health Professions at the Medical University of South Carolina in Charleston. She received her BSN degree from the University of Virginia, master's degree in pediatric nursing from the University of Florida, and doctoral degree in educational policy and evaluation from the University of Kentucky.

SHIRLEY S. CHATER, PhD, RN, FAAN

SHIRLEY S. CHATER is an independent lecturer and consultant to colleges, universities and other organizations on management and leadership development issues. She holds the position of Adjunct Professor at the Institute for Health and Aging, School of Nursing, University of California, San Francisco (UCSF). She previously served as Commissioner of the United States Social Security Administration from 1993–1997. She was President of Texas Woman's University for seven years (1986–1993) after serving as Vice Chancellor of Academic Affairs at UCSF from 1977–1982 and Associate Vice Chancellor for the preceding 4 years. Dr. Chater holds a bachelor's degree in nursing from the University of Pennsylvania and a master's degree in nursing from UCSF. She received her doctorate in education from the University of California, Berkeley and a post-doctoral certificate from the Sloan School of Management, MIT. She was honored in 2000 by the American Academy of Nursing as a "Living Legend." She is the recipient of twelve honorary doctoral degrees and the UCSF medal, the highest honor awarded by the University.

KAREN S. COX, PhD, RN, CNAA, FAAN

KAREN S. COX is currently executive vice president/cochief operating officer of Patient Care Services at the Children's Mercy Hospitals and Clinics in Kansas City, Missouri. She is also assistant dean at University of Missouri's School of Nursing, adjunct graduate faculty in the School of Nursing and senior fellow at the Center for the Health Professions at the University of California-San Francisco. She began as a nurse manager at Children's Hospital of Philadelphia, then she moved to Children's Mercy Hospital in Kansas City to become nurse manager of Hematology/Oncology in the Infant/Toddler Unit.

JEANETTE IVES ERICKSON, MS, RN, FAAN

JEANETTE IVES ERICKSON is senior vice president for Patient Care and chief nurse at Massachusetts General Hospital, a teaching associate at Harvard Medical School, a visiting scholar at Boston College, a senior associate at the Institute for Nursing Healthcare Leadership, and assistant professor at the Massachusetts General Hospital Institute of Health Professions. She is a graduate of Boston University Graduate School of Nursing

GWENDOLYN A. FRANKLIN, MSN, RN

GWENDOLYN A. FRANKLIN is director of Detroit Department of Health and Wellness Promotion's Office of Nursing. She has 17 years of experience in public health nursing. Concurrently, she is the director of the Detroit Childhood Lead Poisoning Prevention and Control Program. She was director of Public Health Nursing from 2000 to 2004.

VALENTINA, GOKENBACH, DM, RN, MBA

VALENTINA GOKENBACH is the vice president, chief nurse executive for William Beaumont Hospital in Royal Oak, Michigan. She possesses a doctoral degree in management and organizational leadership, a master's degree in business administration and a bachelors of science in nursing. Dr. Gokenbach has a true passion for leadership and has been in administrative health care positions for more than 30 years. Over the years she has managed an expansive span of responsibility, which included nursing and several support departments such as radiology, respiratory therapy, radiation oncology, nuclear medicine, oncology services, neurodiagnostic services, employee health, schools of allied health, and the emergency services. Her greatest accomplishment for the organization has been the receipt of our Magnet accreditation awarded on January 14, 2003.

Dr. Gokenbach is also involved in several community initiatives and served as the cocreator of Safety City USA, a nonprofit interactive learning facility for the community, dedicated to the reduction in pediatric trauma. In her spare time she lectures on health and wellness topics and is active on several advisory and leadership boards throughout the community.

MARGARET GREY, DrPH, RN, FAAN

MARGARET GREY, certified pediatric nurse practitioner and certified diabetes educator, is also the associate dean for Scholarly Affairs as well as the director of the Center for Self and Family Management in Vulnerable Populations in the School of Nursing at Yale University. She has also been a part of the Schools of Nursing at the University of Pennsylvania and Columbia University.

JEANNIE K. HANNA, MSN, RN, COHN-S, FAAOHN

JEANNIE K. HANNA is Director of Integrated Health and Productivity at The Hershey Company in Hershey, PA. Her responsibilities include helping to drive business results by furthering the company's strategic approach to employee health and wellness across the globe with the goal of improving productivity and efficiency across the business. She leads the corporate-wide initiatives for health, safety, and productivity with an emphasis on process improvements, cost controls, and case management. She also leads the company's efforts at driving fitness and wellness activities throughout the organization including chairing the Wellness Everyday Team and responsibility for the fitness centers. She has had in-depth experience in design, implementation, and evaluation of strategic global occupational health, wellness, and workers compensation programs at Visteon, Monsanto, & Baxter along with other various health care organizations. She has previously served on numerous local, state, and national offices for AAOHN and was steering committee chair of the Council of Nurse Leaders. She is currently on the AAOHN Education and Awards committees, the AAOHN Election Advisory Committee, the *AAOHN Journal* editorial review board, and is on the ICOH Scientific Committee for Occupational Health. She is a national and internationally recognized lecturer on health and productivity, business skills, wellness, and fundamentals of occupational health nursing. She has spoken numerous times at AOHC, ASE, SEAK, and at ICOH in Singapore and Brazil. She was a chapter contributor in the first edition of the *AAOHN Core Curriculum of Occupational Health Nurses* on health promotion and is a Robert Wood Johnson Executive Nurse Leadership Fellow.

SUSAN R. LACEY, PhD, RN, FAAN

SUSAN R. LACEY assumed a new position as director of nursing workforce and systems research at Children's Mercy Hospital and Clinics in December 2007, leaving a faculty position at the University of Alabama at Birmingham School of Nursing where she began her Fellowship. She was the lead investigator for the development and testing of the new pediatric quality indicators for the National Database of Nursing Quality Indicators (NDNQI) now being used by more than 450 pediatric nursing units across the United States. She has coauthored book chapters on pediatric medication safety, leadership, and workforce collaborations. She serves on the editorial board of the *Journal of Nursing Care Quality*, reviews for four major journals and has published extensively. Dr. Lacey is on the steering committee for the National Nursing Practice Network™, an evidence-based collaborative and holds a patent for decision-support software for frontline and senior managers to monitor adverse events and nurse staffing. She received a BA in communication studies at Mississippi State University, a BS in nursing at the University of Southern Mississippi, an MS in maternal/child nursing at the University of Texas, Austin, and her PhD in family studies from Kansas State University.

PATRICIA REID PONTE, DNSc, RN, FAAN

PATRICIA REID PONTE is the senior vice president for Patient Care Services and chief of nursing at Dana-Farber Cancer Institute and the nursing director of the Hematology/Oncology, BMT Program at the Brigham and Women's Hospital. She is the Cancer Center nurse leader within Dana-Farber/Partners CancerCare, which includes Dana-Farber Cancer Institute, Brigham and Women's Hospital, and Massachusetts General Hospital. She is an associate clinical scientist at the Cantor Center for Nursing Research, a research associate professor in the Department of Nursing at the University of Massachusetts Boston, and an adjunct assistant professor at the University of Massachusetts Amherst. She received both her doctorate of nursing science and masters of science from Boston University. She received her bachelor of science in nursing from the University of Massachusetts, Amherst.

MAXINE PROSKUROWSKI, MS, RN, BSN

MAXINE PROSKUROWSKI is the program manager of Eugene 4J School District Health Services, Eugene, Oregon. She specializes in school health for a school district of 18,000 students, with four school-based health centers, and directs the McKinney Program for the education of homeless children and youth. Previously she has been a school nurse and social worker at the most disadvantaged school in Oregon for 11 years. In the summers she has been an interpreter and counselor for Mobility International in Costa Rica, a community health nurse and health care consultant for the Institute for Latin American Concern in the Dominican Republic, and a nurse for 17 years at a Native American camp. She received her bachelor's degree from Mount Holyoke College, a master's from the University of Stockholm, Sweden, and a bachelor of nursing from Creighton University.

MICHELLE TAYLOR-SMITH, MSN, RN, BSN, CNA-BC

MICHELLE TAYLOR-SMITH is a board-certified nurse administrator with several years experience in chief nurse and executive operation roles in tertiary, community, and teaching health care organizations. Proficient in system-based nursing structures, she codeveloped and implemented a Nursing Workforce Transformation initiative designed to transform nursing care delivery and enhance the patient experience. An advocate of evidence-based practice, Taylor-Smith has participated and been principal investigator in a number of research studies including neonatal developmental care, nurse-managed care access, education transformation, acute care spans-of-control, staffing, and care-model efficiency. Taylor-Smith has been awarded at the local, state, and Congressional levels for her nursing leadership, community partnerships, and health-promotion program designs.

DONNA THOMPSON, MSN, RN

DONNA THOMPSON is chief executive officer, Access Community Health Network. She joined Access Community Health Network (ACCESS) in 1995 as chief operating officer and was named chief executive officer in November 2004. She has 14 years of experience as a staff nurse and manager and previously served as the director of pediatrics at Christ Hospital and Medical Center from 1991–1994.

Foreword

The American health care system is challenged on many fronts. Every day, there are reports of medical errors and patient safety concerns. The nation struggles to provide care for the 15% of the population without health insurance. Costs continue to grow two to three times faster than the cost of living. Consumers leave their costly and risky encounters with less and less satisfaction that they have received the value they feel they deserve and desire. The public health system, strained after years of providing care for a medically indigent population, now faces new challenges in man-made and natural disasters. These occurrences and potentials ranging from terrorist threats to hurricanes and pandemics play out before us as we watch the public health system try to keep up with the enormity of the challenge. Health professional education, for many years the envy of the world, has seemed trapped in the same challenges facing care delivery and public health. Shortages of workers, crowded programs, and research programs that seem out of sync with the needs of the public are just a few of the many challenges facing education.

The major conundrum of health care in the United States is how we can spend so much on health care, over 16% of the gross domestic product, and derive such questionable outcomes. Increasingly, the answer seems obvious—we do not need more resources. But the resources we have are locked away in traditional ways of behaving, jealous institutions, antiquated laws and policies, professional bias, inadequately shared knowledge, misaligned financing arrangements, fear of the unknown, and an absence of vision. In other words, tapping the bountiful resources that exist in the nation today and releasing their energy to unleash the opportunities for a better system of health care is a leadership problem.

But where do we get that leadership? Perhaps the best way to begin to identify the leadership needs of the future is to generally describe where the system of care is headed and see if leadership traits might be matched to anticipate system needs. Today the health care system is focused on acute care delivery; as the population ages there will an inexorable shift of attention to chronic care. Correspondingly, care that today is characterized by delivery in the inpatient or clinic setting will increasingly shift to ambulatory settings with more emphasis on home care, community care, and self-care. This will force a different consideration of patient care needs, reaching beyond the symptoms that present with the patient to the broader context of the psychosocial behavioral web that shapes disease and disability and should inform treatment and management. Learning to live with and manage disease within this context will require better care management skills and improved patient and family education. The complexity of care will only grow in such a world and the team that brings service will be more varied than today's health care team; this will in turn require exquisite group skills and processes. To manage patients, teams, and disease within a system will become the hallmark of good health care in the future.

To scan this future health care landscape in even a cursory manner reveals that one health profession is particularly well prepared to lead these transitions: nursing. Nurses have always been care managers, and as modern professional nursing has defined itself, it has grown to include a rich base of psychological, sociological, and behavioral science in its care model. Nurses have always been about teamwork and managing the various contributions of the varied health professionals that serve the patient's needs. Nurses have also excelled at working as team players within systems, producing the best possible outcomes within the constraints of resources. Public health is a core discipline of every nurse's training, and nurses have been the dominant professionals in many pubic ambulatory settings including the home, school, office, and clinic. This book is about how nurses in the three broad areas of hospital service, education, and public health can bring their birthright of leadership to the reconfiguration of the American approach to health.

The book was inspired by the fellows of the Robert Wood Johnson Executive Nurse Fellows Program and their work in service, education, and public health. The book's organization follows the leadership compass used in that program to organize leadership skill development. The four points of that compass are based on the leadership programs of the Center for the Health Professions at the University of California, San Francisco, which sponsors the Robert Wood Johnson Program. These four points of the compass are:

- Purpose—the vision to lead
- People—the passion to work with others
- Process—the skills to manage change
- Personal—the self-knowledge to thrive

The book begins with an overview of challenges in health care and in nursing by the two coeditors of the book. Following this there are three sections, one each dedicated to service, education, and public health. In each section the four points of the compass will be explored by a different nurse leader, sharing their challenges, struggles, and success to bring about change in health care.

Shirley S. Chater, PhD, RN, FAAN
Chair, National Advisory Committee
Robert Wood Johnson Executive Nurse Fellows Program
President Emerita, Texas Woman's University

Preface

The health care system in the United States is now in considerable peril. The rate of cost increases is simply not sustainable by the rest of society, either as a tax on public expenditures or as private contributions from employees and individuals. But even with these extraordinary costs, the outcomes of this system are suspect. Some now estimate that the fourth leading cause of death in the country is admission to the hospital, not from the ailment that necessitated the admission but because of a medical error, hospital-acquired infection, or faulty discharge. Moreover, our incredibly impressive, but expensive, acute care system is positioned more frequently to deliver care to individuals who are suffering from chronic disease and need quite different interventions. Do we really want to treat the raging epidemic of childhood-onset diabetes with dialysis and amputation followed by an early death? And if all of this were not problem enough, the nation still fails to provide ready access to health care for over 45 million individuals.

Over the next decade, health care in the United States will change dramatically, but to do so in the best possible way will require leadership of an uncommon variety. For the past decade the Robert Wood Johnson Executive Nurse Fellows Program has focused on developing one of the great untapped leadership resources in American health care: the nurse. This book captures many of the leadership stories of these fellows and other nurses who are making for significant change in America's health. The three domains of the program represent the location where much of the action for change must take place. Certainly, the service sector must evolve to respond to needs that are more cost aware, more focused on chronic disease, more oriented to teams, and more committed to serving patients as customers and partners. Much of what must be remade to have a vibrant health sector lies within the domain of public health. Can we reinvigorate this population-based approach to health and well-being, reactivating communities, schools, and families in ensuring their health? If we can, it will be nurses who carry this leadership mantle. Finally, will we have enough nurses for the future and will they have the right skills, expectations, and values to address this leadership challenge? These three domains—service, public health, and education—are where nursing will make its leadership contributions in the coming years.

Each story told here centers on one of four dimensions of leadership. To be an effective leader, knowledge of the environment, vision, and effective strategies must come together to give purpose to our work. But these broad visions must also be carried out in practical ways that attend to budgets, conflict, teams, and effective decision making, so that the processes run smoothly. Nurses are famous for "getting it done," regardless of how much they have had to do by themselves, but one defining element of leadership that is often overlooked by nurses is the need to work through other people, developing and motivating them along the way. Finally, self-knowledge is essential for any leader to be successful, and these personal insights are a part of any leadership journey.

This book offers insight into a new vision of the leadership roles for nurses and provides the practical stories of how some of the nation's best nurse leaders have acted on that vision.

Linda Thompson Adams
Edward H. O'Neil

Nurse Executive

PART I

Introduction

The Leadership Compass: Competencies for Health Care

Edward H. O'Neil

Developing leaders for health care is a challenge. Over the past 14 years, the Center for the Health Professions at the University of California–San Francisco (UCSF) has developed a strategy for developing leaders that has proven itself in clinical, biomedical research, and education settings. All of the Center's work is built around four interrelated core leadership dimensions, each of which has an in-depth set of distinct competences. The art of leadership development is blending these into a program that meets immediate needs of the participants and stretches them to address the longer-term needs of the institution.

PURPOSE

Proverbs 29:18 warns us that without a vision "the people will perish." Direction has always been one of the defining marks of an effective leader and that is what purpose is all about. The task is how to take where we have been, the challenges we face today, the desired future state and translate what we have learned into a vision that appeals to both the heart and the head, motivating others to move forward. This core leadership dimension includes competences in:

- understanding the changing environment both internal and external
- understanding and responding to organizational mandates
- developing and projecting organizational mission

- clarifying and using core values
- embracing a capacity for creativity in vision
- translating vision into effective strategies for action
- moving strategy to action by using short-term objectives, plans, and budgets
- communicating strategy
- developing an awareness of institutional culture and its impact on purpose
- developing and sustaining new partnerships and collaborations

This is a long list, but there is one more essential trait for the competent leader to project around purpose: adaptability and responsiveness. While there will always be some things that one cannot anticipate, purpose prepares the leader to respond to the unanticipated with grace and courage.

PEOPLE

The essential difference between doing a good job and doing a good leadership job is the ability to accomplish work through others. Many people have the technical skills to be an effective physician or nurse and many of these even have a vision of what needs to be done. Fewer have the ability to create relationships that bring others to work in a unified manner. The elements of this core leadership domain are varied but include the following:

- building effective teams
- creating environments for giving and receiving feedback
- managing relationships up, down, and to the side
- motivating and developing others
- building consensus
- gaining and using power
- developing interpersonal communication skills including listening
- having difficult conversations
- working with diverse populations and needs
- building positive work environments

Together, these competencies help create relationship capital, which combined, have the power to align and inspire the contributions of those we seek to lead.

PROCESS

Work still needs to be accomplished and it will fall to the competent leader to possess an array of technical process skills to accomplish these tasks. In all leadership work there is a need to understand the core activity that one is leading. There are more generic organizational skills that need to be a part of every leader's toolkit. These include:

- designing operational plans to enact strategies
- using project management structures for planning, control and evaluation
- using budgeting and financial management principles and techniques
- making a relevant business case for an undertaking
- managing a change process
- managing conflict within the organization
- using negotiation to push a process
- working with and through systems
- using decision-making techniques
- using performance assessments
- developing and using process improvement projects

These competencies must be linked back to the purpose. Much mischief occurs in health care because these core process competencies are not present, which can cause the implementation of any strategy to fail.

PERSONAL

This domain is about the individual as a leader and their personal attributes. Few in leadership roles will have success without adequate attention to this competency. In many ways this core domain is the key to the successful deployment of the other three leadership domains. The skills in this area vary from the most philosophical to the most practical and include:

- developing self-knowledge and awareness
- developing personal learning and development strategies
- managing time and energy
- gaining strategic leadership focus
- using communication skills interpersonally and publicly
- developing a capacity for self-regulation

- maintaining integrity and developing trusting relationships
- demonstrating courage
- valuing leadership style and presence
- achieving work–life balance
- maintaining resilience

The personal is about using the self as an instrument of leadership. The real art of leadership is not only the technical acquisition of these skills and competencies but also the ability to synthesize the right skills in the moment to address a leadership challenge. How and where these skills are taught and reflected upon matters greatly as to how effectively they will enhance the leadership skills of those in our health care systems.

CHAPTER 1

Issues Driving Health Care and Nursing

Edward H. O'Neil

The issues facing the American health care system are large, complex, diverse, and interrelated. Before we begin this discussion of how nurses are confronting their leadership challenges, it is important to gain a common understanding of the nature of these challenges. These concerns range from the growing cost of care to the quality of the system's performance and a set of demographic drivers that will impact every dimension of the system, from the types of care that will be needed to the availability of workers to provide it.

COST OF CARE

There is perhaps no greater issue in health care today than its cost. By 2005, the last year for which we have comprehensive data, the cost of care had risen to slightly over 16% of the gross domestic product. This represents a per-person annual expenditure of $6,700 and over $2 trillion as an aggregate expenditure (Catlin, Cowan, Heffler, Washington, & the National Health Expenditures Accounts Team, 2007, pp. 142–153). At this size, health care in the United States has become the sixth largest economic undertaking on the face of the globe, just nosing out the Chinese economy at $1.93 trillion and only a few billion dollars short of surpassing the French national effort (The Economist Newspapers Limited, 2007). These costs are projected by the Centers for Medicare and Medicaid Services (CMS) to increase to 19.2% of the gross domestic product (GDP) and over $4 trillion by 2016 (CMS, 2007). This increase is a function of the health care segment growing 2.4% faster than the rest of the economy for almost 40 years (CMS, 2007).

Health care in the United States costs more than it does in any other nation. In 2004 the United States spent 15.3% of the GDP on health care, and the closest nation to this spending was the Swiss at 11.6% (Anderson, Frogner, & Reinhardt, 2007, pp. 1481–1489). Most of the Organization for Economic Cooperation and Development (OECD) nations that the United States competes against in the global market spend in the range of 8% to 10% of their GDP on health care. All of the other nations represented at this level of expenditure provide some universal health benefit to their citizens.

In 1960 the U.S. health expenditures represented only 5.5% of the GDP. The expansion to over 16% of GDP represents an enormous transfer of wealth to the health care sector. The cost increases in health care strongly correlate with decreases in the rate of health insurance coverage (Chernew, Cutler, & Keenerr, 2005). Expenditures in health care at this level mean that other public investments in areas such as transportation infrastructure or education are short-changed. Over the next decade, if health care continues to expand twice as fast as the rest of the economy, it will likely endanger the long-term economic health of the nation (McKinsey and Company, 2004).

For nursing leaders in public health, care delivery, and education this economic reality has several important consequences. First, new expenditures will come under closer scrutiny, and the economic or business case for any new investments will need to be made prominently by any leader needing new capital for growth. In education, this added scrutiny comes at a time when new capacity is needed to meet rising workforce needs. Public health investments often leverage significant contributions to reducing health care costs and expanding life, but they take a longer period to demonstrate return (Bunker, Frazier, & Mosteller, 1994, pp. 225–258). Care delivery organizations will require the most focused justification for new expenditures. Much of the work here will need to address why the cost of a unit of care in the United States is so much more than the cost in other health systems.

DEMOGRAPHY

Although costs will dominate the health care system's concern for the next decade, demography will be an interrelated factor contributing to a part of the cost pressures. The most important, but often overlooked, demographic phenomenon will be the simple fact of growth itself. The nation passed the 300 million mark in population in 2006 and is on track to pass 336 million by 2025. This is a function of increased longevity and of immigration

(Motherhood, the Fertility of American Women, 2007). This growth will not be even across the nation, as large parts of the middle of the country; particularly rural areas, struggle to sustain their populations, while urban centers, particularly in costal areas, continue to expand. Discussed in more detail below, the growth will also have different racial and ethnic makeups in various regions.

As the Baby Boom generation ages toward retirement and moves onto the Medicare system they will, because of increasing disability and access to a universal coverage, begin to consume more health care resources (Yang, Norton, & Stearns, 2003, pp. S2–S10). If the health system was operating in an efficient manner it would have a significant challenge in meeting these demands. However, as the cost figures illustrate, this is not the case and the challenges for cost containment will only grow as the population ages and requires and demands more care. The median age in the United States in 2005 was 36.4 years, relatively young when compared to Japan at 42.9 and the United Kingdom at 39. But the over 65-year-old population will grow in the United States considerably over the next decade, reaching over 17% by 2040.

In addition to an aging population, the United States will also continue on its pathway of becoming more diverse. Fueled by immigration, both legal and illegal, the United States will become a nonwhite majority country around mid-century. Most of this growth will come in the Latino or Hispanic population, but there will be significant change in the Asian population. African-American, white, and Native American populations will grow, but this growth will not be fast enough for them to become a larger percentage of the overall population. The population changes will be uneven across regions, with the West Coast experiencing the most growth in Asian population, the Sunbelt from California to Florida experiencing most of the Latino Hispanic growth, and the southern states experiencing the largest growth in African Americans.

These changes will have a profound impact on health care and nursing. The growth in population will demand a corresponding growth in the capacity of every part of the health care system or a significant change in the practice models of service, public health, and education. The combination of more people and older people will drive a part of the coming crisis in the nursing workforce. This impact will be compounded, of course, by the retirement of the Baby Boom generation, which has already started in nursing. These demands will not be limited to the workforce but will also create new demands for care delivery capacity and educational institutions. Both of these will require nursing leadership. As the population becomes more diverse it will create significant new challenges for public health nursing both to understand the needs of a more diverse society and to respond accordingly.

EPIDEMIOLOGY

The disease patterns that cause disease, disability, and death cannot be divorced from the demographic trends, but it is important to highlight how these will change over the next few decades. At the broadest level the nation, and really all nations in the postindustrialized world, have moved over the past century from an epidemiology driven by acute disease, particularly those driven by infection, to one in which people live longer and die from chronic disease. In 1900, stroke, heart disease, and cancer accounted for barely 15% of deaths in the United States, but today they represent more than 60%. A host of other chronic diseases including chronic obstructive pulmonary disease (COPD) and diabetes now challenge the nation's health.

The unfortunate development around this transition is that the health care delivery system is dominated by the tools to treat acute disorders, not prevent and manage the chronic diseases that now are an increasing part of the population's disease burden. These acute care treatments for chronic disabilities, such as end-stage renal dialysis for diabetes patients, are very expensive and often have poor promise for return to a high quality of life. Most other countries have moved their health care delivery system to a more primary or community-based orientation, which allows them to do a better job of preventing and, even more importantly, managing chronicity once it appears. A part of this accommodation will move the point of delivery of care from highly acute inpatient settings such as hospitals to the ambulatory settings of home and community. This transition will be driven by consumer demand and availability of new technology, discussed later in this chapter, and the unremitting cost pressures addressed earlier.

Well over half of the nation's nurses remain employed in hospital settings, and their employment will be under pressure to change and move to other settings. This threat to much of traditional nursing will be matched by the recovery of demand for the traditional role of ambulatory-based nursing in the community, home, and school. To meet these challenges, nursing leadership will be needed in education to reorient the curriculum and training locations, public health to rebuild the long tradition of the community-based nursing professionals, and service to lead the changing strategies as hospitals balance their focus on inpatient and ambulatory needs.

TECHNOLOGY

Technology is a double-edged sword in health care. Many of the lifesaving benefits of contemporary medicine are mediated by the complex array of biomedical and information-based technology. But most health economists point to the proliferation of technology as the principal driver of health care costs. Over the past three decades, information and communications technology has remade the American workplace, delivering an impressive array of productivity gains. Unfortunately, these changes have not found their way into health care settings, and the complex exchange of knowledge that is the basic fabric of health care is still carried out in an antiquated manner in most settings. The transactions associated with these exchanges are not merely costly in terms of revenue, but are at the heart of much health care quality failure as well.

The technological revolution looming just beyond the horizon is in the world of biomedicine. In many ways biomedicine is still in the discovery phase and yet to move into the era in which the new knowledge around basic biological science will find its way into technological application. As it does it will create the opportunity to match designer drugs to the makeup of an individual's genome. The efficacy of such interventions will be unsurpassed in the history of medicine, as will the cost of the care.

These developments in biomedical technology have already begun to combine with the capabilities of information technology. As they continue they will create a new generation of care management technology that will provide tools that will enable care to move more quickly out of the hospital, allow individuals to provide more of their own diagnosis, treatment, and management, and create new roles for nursing as they help facilitate the use of these new technologies with patients.

CONSUMERS

A decade ago the consumer would not have been recognized as a strategic consideration of which nursing leaders would need to be mindful. However, the general lack of consumer or service response by the health care system is now motivating new entrants to the delivery of health care to base a part of their business plan on their ability to provide customer satisfaction through convenience, price, availability, and friendliness. Although many of these new health care players are emerging from the private sector, some public institutions are recognizing the need to respond to their customers as a part of their overall strategy.

It seems likely that as health care costs increase, purchasers in both the public and private domains will attempt to press more and more responsibility for decision making and financial contribution onto individual consumers. This is likely to make the satisfaction of those individuals as customers a key to the marketing of all dimensions of health care. This arena of responding to consumer service and satisfaction desires is a foreign province for most health care institutions.

As the largest and most diversely deployed of all health professionals, nurses will find themselves in a particularly good position to respond to these demands. It will often be nurses who will be the face of the organization, and their ability to understand and take on these service missions will be of critical importance. To do so will mean that the education of nurses will need to address this topic and incorporate this value in the way in which all student nurses come to understand their roles. In a similar vein, public health nurses will carry this value into community-based delivery systems.

INTEGRATION OF CARE

The U.S. health care system remains a crazy quilt of different professionals, in- and outpatient institutions, private and public health, specialists and generalists. Much of the cost and poor performance of the system can be attributed to this lack of integration. In part this discordance is driven by a lack of the technology to integrate the enormous amount of information that is generated by the health care system on each individual. But it is also a function of misaligned financial incentives that often reward work at cross purposes.

Teamwork is also a vital, but often missing part of the overall integration of care for individuals. As demands for more efficiency and better outcomes grow there will be more pressure on all of the sources for integration.

Nurses represent one of the great untapped leadership resources around the issues of integration. Across the continuum of education, public health, and service they have opportunities to use their patient advocacy skills, organizational perspective, and care management concepts to drive the ways teams form and integrate their work.

Nursing leaders will need to use these changes in the health care environment to leverage the reforms in institutions, practice, and policy that will be needed as we move forward. Understanding these trends and mastering their consequences will be essential for any successful leadership pathway in health care.

REFERENCES

Anderson, G., Frogner, B., & Reinhardt, U. (2007). Health spending in OECD countries in 2004: An update. *Health Affairs, 26*(5), 1481–1489.

Bunker, J., Frazier, H. S., & Mosteller, F. (1994). Improving health: Measuring effects of medical care. *The Milbank Quarterly, 72,* 225–258.

Catlin, A., Cowan, C., Heffler, S., Washington, B., & The National Health Expenditures Accounts Team. (2007). National health spending in 2005. *Health Affairs 26*(1), 142–153.

Centers for Medicare and Medicaid Services (CMS). (2007). *National Health System: Facts and Figures, 2007 edition.* Retrieved December 31, 2007, from http://www.cms.hhs.gov/The Chartbook_2007-2007-pdr.pdf_2007-10-27

Chernew, M., Cutler, D., & Keenerr, P. S. (2005, September). *Increasing health insurance costs and the decline in insurance coverage. ERIU working Papers 8.* Retrieved June 16, 2006, from http://www.umich.edu/-eriuu/pdf/wp8.pdf

The Economist Newspapers Limited. (2007). *Pocket World in Figures.* London: Exmuth House.

McKinsey and Company. (2004, September). Will health benefit costs eclipse profits? *The McKinsey Quarterly Chart Focus Newsletter,* 1–29.

Motherhood, the fertility of American women, 1900–2000. U.S. Census Bureau. Retrieved December 31, 2007, from http://www.census.gov/population/pop-profile/2000/chap04.pdf

Yang, Z., Norton, E., & Stearns, S. (2003). The real reasons older people spend more. *The Journals of Gerontology Series B: Psychological Sciences and Social Sciences, 58,* S2–S10.

CHAPTER 2

Nursing Leadership

Linda Thompson Adams

Never doubt that a small group of committed citizens can change the world.
Indeed, it is the only thing that ever has.

—Margaret Mead

Health care in the United States is a major concern for business and civic leaders, policy makers and consumers. The United States spends almost $2 trillion annually on health care, and costs continue to escalate to levels approaching a national crisis (Porter & Teisberg, 2006). Rising cost, mounting quality problems, and increasing number of citizens without health insurance are not only unacceptable but unsustainable. One strategy to reform health care is to invest in nursing leadership to design solutions for current problems in all areas of nursing including health services administration, education, and public health. Nursing executives in education, service, and public health must lead change by redefining strategies, practices, and structures to unleash stunning improvements in the value and quality of the care delivered to the general public.

WHY NURSING

The size and complexity of the health care crisis in the United States today is daunting. But it also creates an enormous opportunity for nurses to respond as leaders with solutions. Nurses are a natural group to provide health care leadership if only due to their numbers. According to the Bureau of Labor Statistics, nurses who constitute the largest part of the health care workforce with

2 million jobs in 2006 are considered the backbone of the health care system (Bureau of Labor Statistics & U.S. Department of Labor, 2008). Furthermore, nurses are educated to provide patient care in a holistic, comprehensive way and in a variety of roles across the life span from birth to death, providing support in labor, consultation on care of the infant and child, care for the acute and chronically ill and elderly, and care for the dying and support for the family. Patients and families seek advice from nurses to translate information imparted by physicians.

Nurses have responded to changing economic, technological, and social forces in the U.S. health care system by advocating to support a system that is just, equitable, and effective for the health of the public. According to Aiken (2005), nurses have advocated for some of the most significant innovations in modern health care resulting in a more humane and patient-centered approach to care. Innovations led by nursing include demedicalizing normal births, liberalizing visiting hours, family participation in hospital care, and providing alternatives to invasive medical intervention at the end of life such as hospice care. This advocacy for quality care for patients has influenced the public's trust and respect for nursing allowing its influence to lead change in the health care system. In fact, history has shown that nurses have always been consistently in the group of committed citizens on the front line of change (Adams, 2006).

Today, nurses have an opportunity to reshape, rebuild, and redefine how health care will be delivered in the 21st century. As nurses transform health care, they will also redefine the nurse's role and influence on the health of the public. Yet, how do we develop nurses who can lead this transformation of the health care system? Are there resources nurses can use to assist them in finding their voice, strategic direction, and focus that others will embrace?

HOW TO LEAD CHANGE

Few people ever feel confident to lead change. Leaders such as Harry Truman, Florence Nightingale, Martin Luther King Jr., Helen Keller, and Harriet Tubman did not set out to make history. These inspirational leaders did believe, however, that there was a need for change and that someone had to do it. This is where they each took their first small steps to establishing leadership roles.

Leadership springs from the pursuit of purpose. Discovering purpose is simply a matter of paying attention to what our life has been telling us. Bennis (1989) reports that all of the leaders he interviewed agreed on the following points: leaders are made, not born, and made more by themselves than by any external means. No leader sets out to be a leader, but rather to express him or herself freely and fully. First and foremost, leaders find out what it is you're about.

The discovery of purpose is central for leadership development. It is the first step along the way to the leadership journey, which requires paying attention to that inner voice. Nurses who choose to listen to their inner voice about the surrounding external world will follow their own path to leadership by articulating their vision and empowering others to transform health care.

To be successful in leadership, nurses must be informed. For example, nurses need access to every kind of information available such as health care, health policy, health disparities, and health professional workforce issues. The nurse must also have the skill to see relationships and interconnections that are outside of their typical organizational environment. Recognizing and analyzing a broad range of information allows the nurse leader to step outside the professional box and see how the world is changing. Not all that is going on in the transition of health care is pleasant, but all of it must be seen and understood for leaders to begin to know how to plan and how to act. But knowing is not enough; leaders must also develop the skills for action. Health care has been a heavily regulated industry that neither valued nor needed entrepreneurial-type action. This is no longer the case. Entrepreneurship will be a critical element of nursing leadership in the emerging future. Finally, nursing leadership must be integrated across all areas of nursing including education, service, and public health.

Education, health services, and public health have organizational systems with a life of their own. That is, they act as any living organism does when change is introduced: they resist change and ensure survival (Senge, 1990). Only when leaders have the courage to meet the challenge of structural change head-on do they have a chance of seeing their vision become reality.

Leaders, like nurses, come in a myriad of shapes and sizes, with various kinds of upbringings, educational backgrounds, and motivating factors. The passion that drives one to become a nurse is the same passion that enables a nurse to lead. Most nurses have a passion to serve and to heal people by developing their knowledge, skills, and abilities to achieve results. Clearly, combining the efforts to serve and to heal carries the potential for leadership.

To lead change in a positive direction, nurse leaders must inspire others with a purpose or vision. Further, leaders must develop a passion to get things done through other people. They must learn how to cope with change, adapt to it or even exploit it. Finally, nurse leaders must develop the self-knowledge to thrive in situations of uncertainty.

Closing the leadership gap within nursing involves developing a clear understanding of the internal and external forces influencing the profession.

These forces include: the demographics of the patient population; how to educate and retain the future workforce; nursing's influence on patient care outcomes; embracing technology to improve safety and quality of care; managing complex health care environments; and, using research to build evidence-based practice. The responsibility to lead nursing into the future requires a systematic approach to develop nurse leaders from a variety of positions that they know best: comforting patients in the hospital; mentoring of the next generation of nurses in the classroom; preventing disease and disasters in the community; and conducting research to discover new ways to manage disease and promote the health of the public.

LEADERSHIP DEVELOPMENT PROGRAM

Emergence as a leader is a developmental process in which capabilities, insights, and skills gained through one's experience or at one's level serve as the basis for further growth. Leaders go through progressive stages in their development as a leader, which is a lifelong process. As nurses progress through their careers, they will face challenges. The need for change will always exist and groups will need leaders to help them weather the forces of change. Conflict will always exist and require leaders to manage it. As the circumstances of our lives are altered, our leadership skills also need to be refined, renewed, and further developed. Kouzes and Posner (2002) suggest that leadership is an observable, learnable set of practices. Given the opportunity for practice and feedback, nurses with the desire to make a difference can develop and improve their ability to lead.

Examples of leadership challenges are illustrated in this book by some of the leading nurse executives in the country. Each author is a nurse who has excelled in their career and received national recognition by being invited to participate in the Robert Wood Johnson (RWJ) Nurse Fellows Program. The RWJ Nurse Fellows Program was developed by the Center for the Health Professions at the University of California, San Francisco. Beginning in 1998, the Nurse Fellows Program has tested and evaluated which competencies would be most effective.

The RWJ Nurse Fellows program seeks outstanding applications from nurses in executive roles from health services (including patient care service, integrated delivery systems, health plans, and other health organizations engaged in organizing and delivering health care), public/community health, and nursing education who, along with their employing institutions, are willing to make a three-year commitment to the program. The fellowships are intended to offer participating nurses the experiences, insights, competencies, and skills necessary to achieve or advance in executive leadership positions in a health care system undergoing unprecedented change.

The fellowship is an in-depth and comprehensive leadership development program that is structured to acknowledge the unique education and life experiences of experienced executive nurses. The fellowship extends beyond the scope of traditional executive programs by focusing on five core leadership competencies (i.e., self-knowledge, inspiring and leading change, strategic vision, risk taking and creativity, and interpersonal and communication effectiveness). Each fellow engages with a leader from within and outside health care, combined with a mentor experience designed to provide significant exposure to a top-level executive outside the health care system. Each fellow is expected to develop an individual learning plan that will be used as a guide for the fellow's self-directed learning activities throughout the program (Robert Wood Johnson Foundation, 2007).

These nationally renowned nursing leaders share their experiences in nursing leadership roles in hopes of inspiring nurses and nursing students to take on the leadership challenge. Each nursing leader incorporates the leadership core competencies to anticipate, create, and act to make the future a reality.

With movement, momentum, and a new wave of enthusiasm and energy, nursing can create the vision and change needed to create a reformed health care system responsive to health needs of the American public. One of the most famous nurses of all time, Florence Nightingale, said, "Unless we are making progress in our nursing every year, every month, every week, take my word for it we are not going forward, we are going backward" (Rivett, 1998). I challenge you to take that step forward toward leadership and follow the passion you have as a nurse.

REFERENCES

Adams, L. Thompson. (2006, March). Keynotes of note, Terrance Keenan nursing leadership lecture: Pathway to leadership. *Online Journal of Issues in Nursing*. Retrieved January 24, 2008, from www.nursingworld.org/ojin/keynotes/speech5.htm

Aiken, L. (2005). Improving quality through nursing. In C. Mechanic, L. Rogut, D. Colby, & J. Knickman (Eds). *Policy challenges in modern health care*. New Brunswick, NJ: Rutgers University Press.

Bennis, W. (1989). *On becoming a leader.* Cambridge, MA: Perseus Books.

Bureau of Labor Statistics & U.S. Department of Labor. (2008). *Occupational outlook handbook, 2008–9 edition*. Registered Nurses. Retrieved January 24, 2008, from http//www.bls.gov/oco/ocos.083.htm

Kouzes, J. M., & Posner, B. Z. (2002). *The leadership challenge: How to keep getting things done in organization*. San Francisco: Jossey-Bass.

Porter, M., & Teisburg, E. O. (2006). *Redefining healthcare: Creating value-based competition on results.* Boston, MA: Harvard Business School Press.

Rivett, G. (1998). *From cradle to grave: Fifty years of the NHS.* London: King's Fund. Retrieved January 1, 2006, from www.nhshistory.net/1860-1889.htm#Nursing

Robert Wood Johnson Foundation. (2007). *Home page.* Retrieved December 8, 2007, from http//rwjf.org

Senge, P. (1990). *The fifth discipline: The art and practice of the learning organization.* London: Random House.

PART II

Issues in Public Health

Current Issues in the Public Health Industry

Linda Thompson Adams and Edward H. O'Neil

It is cheaper to promote health than to maintain people in sickness.
—Florence Nightingale

HISTORY

This quote by Florence Nightingale traces the roots of public health nursing to England in the 19th century. At this time, Florence Nightingale assisted in organizing nurses to be responsible for the health of people living in their neighborhoods. This type of organization finds its echo today in many public health departments, where public health nurses organize their work by groups of census tracts called districts and the nurse is known as the district public health nurse (Public Health, 2007).

Public health nursing was started in the United States by Lillian Wald in the late 1800s. She established the Henry Street Settlement in New York City, where nurses lived in the neighborhoods where they worked. The initial focus of public health nursing was to provide health care services to individuals in their homes who were sick. Lillian Wald recognized that sickness found in the home had origins in larger societal problems such as conditions of employment, sanitation, recreation, and education. Lillian Wald coined the term *public health nurse* (JWA, 2007).

What is public health? What are the challenges facing modern day public health nursing leaders interested in health promotion and disease prevention for the population? What are the strategies used by public health nurse leaders to influence health outcomes? This section describes the complexity of health problems in the United States today and the importance of the public health approach in influencing the determinants of health and disease. This section includes case studies of challenges faced by contemporary nurse leaders and their approach to seeking solutions to public health problems.

DEFINITION OF PUBLIC HEALTH

Public health is the science and art of preventing disease, prolonging life, and promoting health and efficiency through organized community effort for: sanitation of the environment, control of communicable infections, the education of the individual in personal hygiene, the organization of medical and nursing services for the early diagnosis and preventive treatment of disease, and the development of the social machinery to insure everyone a standard of living adequate for the maintenance of health, so organizing these benefits as to enable every citizen to realize his birthright of health and longevity.

(Winslow, 1920)

This definition by Winslow is the classic definition of public health, which implies the concept of enhancing the quality of life of the public. More recently the Institute of Medicine (1988) defined the mission of public health, as "assuring the conditions for people to be healthy." This mission is pursued by governmental agencies, public and private health care organizations, academic institutions, and community-based organizations using the public health or population-based approach. The population-based public health model is characterized by concern for the health of a population in its entirety and by awareness of the linkage between health and the physical and social ecological environment. Public health focuses not only on the traditional areas of diagnosis, treatment, and the etiology of disease, but also on the epidemiological surveillance of the health of the population at large, health promotion, disease prevention, and access to and evaluation of services (Encyclopedia of Public Health, 2006). While governmental public health agencies exist at federal, state, and local levels, the broadest powers, and most fundamental responsibility for securing the public's health, rests with state government (IOM, 1988).

The public nature of public health practice means it must depend on social values and popular support for both its ends and its means. This makes public health practice inherently political in that different values and perspectives exist in various communities as to what needs to be done about important public policy problems. These sentiments and viewpoints change over time and, as a result, the problems to be addressed by public health professionals have changed over time as well. The ever-changing agenda of what is important to public health leaders reflects the dynamic nature of its two most influential forces: science and social values. While public health is grounded in science, what we choose to do with that scientific knowledge is determined by social values. Public health leaders understand that health and disease are influenced by societal factors including where we live, work, and play.

ISSUES AND CHALLENGES

The interface between public health science and social values is illustrated by the interest of the general society and other health professionals in public health. Health leaders concerned with public health were limited to a few policy makers and leaders working in the public sector of health care until the appearance of AIDS, anthrax, SARS, West Nile virus, and a range of other infectious threats of which we are now keenly aware. Civic and community leaders are increasingly conscious of how chronic diseases such as diabetes, hypertension, and asthma take an even greater toll on our health, although some of the causes, like smoking and obesity, are largely preventable. Population-based health care is clearly essential in keeping us all healthy and safe.

The first public health departments functioned at the state and local levels. They were confined largely to treating infectious diseases, with some attention to maternal and child health. Today's public health system is a national network with a broad focus that cuts across all levels of government. It addresses an array of issues and challenges, including chronic diseases, mental health, substance abuse, violence and crime, traumatic injuries, environmental and occupational health, health disparities (IOM, 2003), and, more recently, bioterrorism (McGinnis & Foege, 1993; World Health Organization, 2007). There is a tremendous opportunity for nurse executives to address theses issues and lead change in the public health sector by developing processes to create the infrastructure required to respond to these challenges. In addition, nurse leaders must develop and inspire a highly skilled workforce who can use sophisticated information and data systems to influence financial support of public health programs.

The challenge to public health leaders and policy makers is great. Beyond these immediate challenges to public health policy, there is a looming threat that may dwarf them all. With increased life expectancies, older Americans will consume an ever-growing share of health care dollars, but with a smaller proportion of working-age Americans to provide financial support (Magee, 2007). Population-based prevention of chronic illnesses that are characteristic of older adults, rather than individual treatment, is the only approach to maintaining the health of large numbers of Americans into their later years that will be economically viable. The scientific, demographic, and economic forces that are converging could well lead public health to preempt clinical medicine in the decades ahead as the primary focus of American health care (Magee, 2007). The sooner public health leaders begin to frame issues, needs, and concerns, the better society can meet the challenges ahead.

REFERENCES

Encyclopedia of Public Health. (2006). In Wikipedia, the free Encyclopedia. Retrieved January 24, 2008, from http://en.wikipedia.org/w/index.php?title=Encyclopedia-of-Public-Health&oldid=94716636

Institute of Medicine (IOM). (1988). *The future of public health*. Washington, DC: National Academies Press.

Institute of Medicine (IOM). (2003). *Unequal treatment: Confronting racial and ethnic disparities in healthcare*. Washington, DC: National Academies Press.

Jewish Women's Archive. JWA—Lillian Wald—Public Health Nursing. Retrieved January 24, 2008, from http//www.JWA.org/exhibits/wov/wald/w3.html

Magee, M. (2007). *Home-centered health care*. New York: Spencer Books.

McGinnis, J. M., & Foege, W. H. (1993). Actual causes of death in the United States. *Journal of the American Medical Association, 270*(18), 2207–2212.

Winslow, C. (1920). The untilled field of public health. *Science, 51*(1306), 23–33.

World Health Organization. (2007). *The world health report 2007: A safer future: Global public health security in the 21st century*. Retrieved December 31, 2007, from http://www.who.int/whr/2007/whr07_en.pdf

CHAPTER 3

Purpose

Maxine Proskurowski

If we don't stand up for children, then we don't stand for much!
—Marian Wright Edelman

ISSUES IN PUBLIC HEALTH: CHILDREN'S HEALTH

Marian Wright Edelman, founder and president of the Children's Fund, an agency that advocates for the poor, minorities, and disabled children, calls for adults to vote for children, and to champion education, health, and housing programs so that children can grow up in safe, healthy, and nurturing environments. Her call to action is found in the words: "Investing in children is not a national luxury or a national choice. It's a national necessity."

Even though she and many others call for public health programs to address children's needs, the reality is that many children continue to live in poverty and as a result are more likely to suffer from ill health and conditions like obesity, mental health problems, and learning disabilities.

Our nation's children are the stewards of our future. If children lead healthy lives, they will be healthy adults. This growing recognition that we are responsible for our children's health has led to the establishment of state insurance programs, yet there are millions of children who are eligible and not enrolled in these programs, and millions who do not qualify because of their immigrant status, or other qualification criteria.

The key findings released by the Campaign for Children's Health Care in September 2006 are the following:

- There are more than 9 million uninsured children—ages 0–18 years.
- One out of every nine children is uninsured.
- One out of every five uninsured people is a child.
- The majority of uninsured children—88.3%—come from families where at least one parent works.
- 71% of uninsured children come from low-income families, with the income at or below two times the federal poverty level, $33,200 for a family of three in 2006.

Currently, 18% of American children live in poverty. Researchers Paul Newacheck, Neal Halfon, Anne Case, and data from the 2001–2005 National Health Interviews Surveys (NHIS) show that poverty is linked to ill health. These studies indicate that

- 70% of poor children are reported by their mothers to be in excellent or very good health, compared with 87% of higher-income children.
- 33% of poor children have at least one of these conditions—mental health issues, hearing and speech problems, vision difficulties.
- Poor children miss more days of school as a result of illness and/or injury than nonpoor children. (Halton N., DuPlessis, H., and Inkelas, M., 2007)

Most importantly, children who lack access to health care are more likely to have unmet needs for care, such as

- The likelihood of not having seen a doctor in the past year is more than three times greater for poor children.
- Less than half, 46%, of uninsured children had a well-child visit in the last year, compared to 75% of the more affluent children.
- Many uninsured children with asthma are hospitalized for acute asthma attacks that could have been prevented.

Poor children carry many burdens. They are at increased risk for ill health, for missing school, for low educational attainment. Jocelyn Elders, former surgeon general of the United States, stresses the importance of developing a universal health care plan for all Americans. She states: "The American health care system has become a very expensive 'sick care system.' Our public health care system is in disarray. It costs too much, delivers too little, and is not cost effective, not affordable and certainly not universal." For children this means, as Jocelyn Elders states: "You can't educate people if they're not healthy. And you certainly can't keep them healthy if they're not educated" (Elders, 2006).

To resolve this conundrum, school health programs can play important roles in promoting children's health care so that children, especially the uninsured, can come to school healthy and ready to learn.

INITIATIVE: SCHOOL HEALTH PROGRAMS

Child health professionals at schools across the nation are providing care to children. These include 99,000 counselors, 56,000 nurses, 30,000 school psychologists, and 15,000 social workers who work daily to help resolve children's psychological, economic, social, and health problems. In many instances, the schools are becoming the default physical and mental health care system for children who otherwise cannot access health care.

To understand how schools have become public health providers, it is important to review the social and economic changes that have prompted schools to assume social justice responsibilities.

Historical Issues

Schools and Immunizations

Historically, schools have been assigned the guardian, or police role by the state governments to see that children are properly vaccinated. When registering, children must show proof of vaccination; without adequate documentation, children are barred from attending school. To avoid this, especially for low-income and immigrant children, schools around the country offer vaccination clinics. As new vaccines are introduced, schools publicize the need for the vaccines, encourage families to vaccinate their children, and when the vaccines become required, again often offer special clinics. The results are that in the 1980s schools nationwide did mass vaccinations for measles shots, in the 1990s for Hepatitis B, and currently for Hepatitis A and HPV vaccines.

Schools and Contagious Diseases

Schools have also historically been responsible for screening students for infectious diseases. Tuberculosis testing routinely occurs in schools, especially for immigrant and homeless children. When children test positive, schools often arrange for chest X-rays and administer the prophylactic medications to ensure compliance and proper care.

School nurses have traditionally screened for conjunctivitis, impetigo, head lice, and scabies, and excluded children until symptoms disappeared. Now that the American Pediatric Association and Public Health Departments declare that head lice is not a public health issue, and that many diseases are viral in origin, schools are relaxing their "police role" in screening and excluding children from schools.

Current Issues

Nurses concentrate on new areas for care that have emerged as a result of:

- medical advancements that allow children with multiple medical issues to survive
- a rising incidence of diseases with life-threatening implications
- an increase in mental health disorders
- an increasing number of children who are living in poverty, are homeless, migrants, immigrants, or refugees

Medical Advances Bring Changes to School Health Programs

Children with multiple medical issues who previously died at early ages are now students at schools and require skilled nursing care. The main advancements:

- the ability to have tubes in children's bodies that safely provide liquid nutrition and a way to deliver multiple medications
- tracheostomies that allow children to be suctioned
- specialists in many different medical fields

All assure that medically fragile students can attend school, provided there is adequate nursing care. School nurses must either perform skilled nursing tasks, or use their professional judgment to decide if the tasks can be delegated to persons who are willing and capable of assuming these responsibilities, and then provide adequate support and supervision. The nurses become consultants, case managers, and supervisors as they juggle different physician orders, coordinate home and school care, and train bus drivers, teachers, and assistants to handle emergencies.

Increasing Incidence of Diseases With Life-Threatening Implications

In the last 10 years there has been a dramatic increase in health conditions that require nurse supervision and have life-threatening implications, including:

- diabetes management
- seizures, especially uncontrolled ones
- potential severe allergic reactions, especially peanut allergies
- asthma
- bleeding disorders
- genetic and hereditary diseases

Depending on the severity of the illness, and the child's understanding, willingness, and ability to do self-care, a nurse must decide the level and intensity of care that is needed for the child to safely be in school.

An example illustrates what schools and nurses face every day. A diabetic kindergarten-age child with an insulin pump needs at least three people in a building who are trained to assist the child to calculate carbohydrate intake and insulin dosages, supervise administration of insulin, and be prepared to handle diabetic emergencies. The bus driver also needs training, and if the child is going on field trips, someone familiar with the diabetes management should accompany the child. This scenario can be replicated for children who have other illnesses with life-threatening implications.

Increasing Incidence of Mental Health Disorders

The last 10 years have also seen a dramatic increase in mental health disorders, including:

- rising incidence of autism and related neurodevelopment disorders, with which approximately 1 in 160 children born are now being diagnosed
- increase in youth gambling, alcohol and drug use, smoking and other addictive behaviors
- increase in youth with eating disorders, anxiety, depression, and suicidal ideation
- increase in bullying, harassment, and violent behaviors at schools

In the United States, about one in 5 children have some type of mental health disorder, and one in 10 suffer from a mental health disorder severe enough to cause impairment socially, academically, and emotionally (U.S. Department of Health and Human Services, 1999). However, among youth suffering from a mental illness with some level of impairment, only about one in five, or 20%, are receiving the treatment they need (National Institute for Health Care Management, 2005).

Nurses, social workers, and counselors attempt to provide calm, nurturing environments so that these children can feel safe in the schools. However, the reality is that most school districts do not have enough financial resources, or skilled experts, to handle the mental health emergencies that occur daily.

Increasing Number of Children Who Are Homeless or Runaways

In 2001, the National Coalition for the Homeless declared that homeless youth are the fastest growing segment of the homeless population. The Federal Administration on Children and Families statistics show:

- 1.5 million youths run away from or are pushed out of their homes annually; approximately 200,000 of these youth are homeless and live on the streets.
- Every day 400,000 children in the nation's schools are homeless.
- 800,000 homeless children are under the age of 6 years.

Homeless children are more likely to have worse health than their peers who have stable housing. The National Association for the Education of Homeless Children and Youth estimates that homeless children are:

- twice as likely to be sick and to be hospitalized than children with stable homes
- four times more likely to have asthma
- six times more likely to have speech problems
- more than twice as likely to have mental health problems

These children face daily stresses as they try to survive. They usually have low math and reading scores, limited social skills, and every time they change schools they regress academically by 4–6 months.

Increasing Number of Immigrant, Migrant, and Refugee Children

In the decade 1990–2000 the population grew by the biggest 10-year numerical leap in U.S. history, mainly because of immigration. Fifty-six million Americans, or one in five, are foreign-born or children of foreign-born parents. For the first time the biggest minority group, and also the largest immigrant group, are Latinos. The name Jose is the number one name for baby boys in Texas, number two in Arizona, and number three in California.

Although Smith remains the most common surname, the top 50 names include Garcia, Martinez, Rodriguez, Hernandez, Lopez, Gonzalez, and Peres (Roberts, 2004).

The challenges faced by many immigrant families are:

- less educated parents
- low-wage work with no benefits
- language barriers
- discrimination and racism—racial profiling
- poverty and multiple risk factors
- lack of social supports
- ineligibility for public assistance programs, including food stamps, Special Child Health Insurance Program (SCHIP), and Medicaid.

The health profile of immigrant children shows that the first generation children do well at early ages. The babies are born healthy and have high immunization rates, but as they reach their teens, adolescent well-being declines. Many immigrant adolescents suffer from dental decay and pain, prolonged periods of sadness, and although the majority of teens in immigrant families attend school, they are more likely to be behind grade level and not to graduate (Fuligni & Hardway, 2004; Hernandez, 2004).

RESPONSES TO AND RESULTS OF THE CURRENT ISSUES

School Nurse Programs

Amy Garcia, executive director for the National Association of School Nurses, states that "about 20% of students today have medical issues that require regular encounters with a school nurse" (Zaslow, 2006). There are no reliable historical statistics regarding school nursing and duties, but the consensus nationwide among nurses is that the burden for providing minimum health and safety standards for the nation's children has increased dramatically in the last 10 years. Previously, nurses concentrated on health screenings, vision and dental referrals, immunizations, and contagious diseases; now there is, as nurses call it, "selective abandonment" of historical duties to focus on the children with multiple medical, emotional, social, and economic needs.

In past decades, most schools had a school nurse. Now, school nurses are becoming a dinosaur of the past—few nurses go into this area of public health, and when they do they often leave frustrated by constant juggling of responsibilities and despair over not being able to adequately address the children's needs. As school districts face budget cuts nationwide, school nurses are often the first to lose their jobs. This is especially true in states that do not mandate school nurses. The federal government requires that children who have health impairments need to have a connection with a school nurse, but in many school districts this may mean contracting for a few hours of nursing service.

The national federal guidelines for school nurses are a ratio of one nurse to 750 students. Only 12 states comply with this ratio—Vermont has the lowest ratio, Utah the highest.

A sample (National Association of School Nurses, 2001) shows the nurse-to-student ratio as:

Florida: one nurse for 2,639 students
Oregon: one nurse for 2,000 students
New Jersey: one nurse for 601 students
New York: one nurse for 1,008 students
Michigan: one nurse for 3,611 students
Utah: one nurse for 4,952 students
Vermont: one nurse for 305 students

The current nurse-to-student ratios means that nurses cover multiple schools and as a result run from one emergency to another. Their cars become their offices. They do not have time to know the needs of the majority of students, or to form relationships with parents and families or with staff at the schools. Robin Wellwood, a school nurse in Eugene, Oregon states "A successful year for me is when no one has died under my watch." To address the current inadequacies—in which the nurses face work overload, and have too many duties—school nurses, parents, children, and communities must raise public awareness about the need for school health programs.

Everyone needs to view the nation's classrooms through the eyes of a child who is hungry, tired, sad, and crying for support and stability. Jocelyn Elders speaks about the only club that poor children belong to—the 5 H club, which stands for hungry, helpless, hopeless, hugless, hurting club. To break this cycle of poverty and allow low-income children to fully participate in school and life activities, they need to be well-fed, nurtured, well-educated, and have access to health care.

The real problem is how we treat the nation's children and how we limit ourselves in coming up with creative approaches to helping them succeed. This calls for leadership, for the nurses to speak up, speak out, and do everything in their power to make a difference. If public health nurses truly believe the saying, "It is far easier to build strong children than repairing adults" by Frederick Douglas, they need to become advocate leaders.

School-Based Health Centers

The other school health programs that are addressing children's health needs are the school-based health centers (SBHCs) located at the schools. The SBHCs are primary care clinics that provide developmentally appropriate physical, emotional, behavioral, and preventive health care to students regardless of their ability to pay.

SBHCs are staffed like a local pediatrician or family practice office, with a secretary or receptionist, nurse, nurse practitioner, and at some sites, a mental health therapist. They incorporate the school and student surroundings with student artwork on the walls, beanbag or colorful chairs in the lobby, and kid-friendly music or videos in the waiting area. Students are encouraged to drop by or make appointments when they need medical attention or want to learn more about a health issue.

Currently 1% of the nation's schools have school-based health centers—1,500 SBHCs. The SBHC movement celebrated its 20th year of existence in 2006, a movement that started as a way to help resolve the rising number of teenage pregnancies and sexually transmitted diseases. The founding leaders and the health foundations that first sponsored school health centers hoped to start a nationwide movement in which health centers would exist in every school. This has not occurred, mainly because of funding issues, confusion about the role that health centers play, and controversies on providing family planning services.

SBHCs are funded in a myriad of ways. Usually schools provide in-kind support including space, telephones, electricity, and janitorial services; the clinics partner with other entities such as a hospital, a public health department, or a Federally Qualified Health Center System to help pay for operating costs and provide administrative oversight. The clinic managers must also find other local and state funding sources to keep the centers solvent. As a result, nurses have become business leaders as well as public policy advocates.

Every time there is a potential budget cut, school health nurses initiate publicity campaigns, which can include taking students to testify at state legislatures, arranging for public meetings, and gathering supporters to influence policy by writing letters and visiting politicians. Nurses have been forced to respond reactively to crises; now the challenge is to react positively and build a strong community support base to avoid continual financial and political crises.

Although health care is expensive, SBHCs are recognized by state and local insurance companies as an important and effective partner for health care delivery. They are also cost effective—three to four additional dollars are leveraged through local public-private partnerships for every one dollar invested by state programs (Oregon, 2007).

Most importantly, health centers provide the following positive impacts:

1. SBHCs are prevention and wellness oriented.
2. SBHCs see children who otherwise would not get care.
3. One in four adolescents who are at risk for adverse health outcomes such as teen pregnancies, suicide, and substance abuse can easily and readily access services in a setting where they spend the majority of their days.

Nationwide satisfaction surveys indicate that 97% of the students appreciate and value the care they receive at the SBHCs, and 60% report they would not have received health services without the health centers (Schlih, 2007).

The SBHC model is one solution for children to access health care; the challenge is how to keep this model alive and strong, and it includes finding strategies to:

1. convince communities to adopt SBHC
2. secure adequate financial resources, including diverse revenue streams
3. build consumer-centered care where local communities, including youth, shape the content, quality, delivery, and financing of health care

School nurses and employees of SBHCs around the country are currently analyzing and implementing strategies to strengthen the school health center movement. Thanks to a Kellogg Foundation grant, a $15 million dollar nationwide initiative in which nine states and the National Assembly of School-Based Health Care are collaborating to improve and sustain access to quality services for children, there have been many successes in the last 3 years. Among them are:

- New Mexico opened 200 new SBHCs in 2006.
- California called for health centers as a solution to children's health problems.
- Oregon earmarked an additional $3.2 million to open 16 new SBHCs in six counties that have never had health centers.
- Michigan leveraged Medicaid moneys to help finance their health centers.
- Maine and Massachusetts are developing reimbursement plans with private insurance companies.

These successes are a direct result of people championing health care solutions and joining forces. The Kellogg Foundation's mission "helping people to help themselves" has brought national visibility to these issues and has empowered local communities to promote and sustain quality health care.

The Kellogg Foundation grant results show that nurse leaders are emerging to inform policy and share best practices nationally. Nurse leaders must continue to use their energy and expertise to become advocates for school health programs, like the SBHCs, by

- bringing one's strengths and resources to the cause
- bringing other supporters along
- becoming proactive by initiating or encouraging legislation or policy that will advance the cause
- being acknowledged publicly by others for their work on behalf of school-based health care

This requires a strong vision for a better future, and dedication to encourage others to find solutions, even if mistakes are made along the way.

> Destiny is not a matter of chance;
> It is a matter of choice.
> It is not a thing to be waited for;
> It is a thing to be achieved.

> —William Jennings Bryan

School nurses cannot wait and see their jobs disappear or be forced to juggle added responsibilities. They must make choices and take action.

Richard Rothstein, a researcher at the Economic Policy Institute, and author of "Class and Schools: Using Social, Economic and Educational Reform to Close the Black-White Achievement Gap" (2004) calls for three programs:

1. early education programs
2. after-school programs
3. fully staffed health clinics in schools serving low-income children

These programs, focusing on education, health, and social benefits, all can improve children's lives. By forming productive partnerships with other public and private agencies, nurses can participate in designing and implementing innovative programs that allow children to grow and thrive.

PERSONAL EXPERIENCE/LESSONS LEARNED

The Minnesota Department of Health, the Henry Street Consortium (Minnesota Public Health Department, 2003), lists the following personal characteristics that contribute to effective public nurse health practice:

1. passion, care, and compassion
2. creativity, risk taking, resourcefulness
3. courage, confidence, persistence
4. adaptability, flexibility, independence
5. positive attitude
6. being a lifelong learner
7. self-care

As I look at nursing leaders, these characteristics are always present.

The Robert Wood Johnson Foundation Executive Nurse Fellowship (Robert Wood Johnson Executive Nurse Fellows Program, 2003) outlines five core competencies for nurse leadership:

1. self-knowledge and self-renewal
2. strategic vision
3. interpersonal and communication effectiveness
4. risk taking and creativity
5. inspiring and leading change

Combining the public health characteristics with the nurse leadership competencies, the following emerges for a strong public health nurse leader:

- strategic vision: passion, care, and compassion
- risk taking and creativity: creativity, risk taking, and resourcefulness
- interpersonal and communication effectiveness: adaptability, flexibility, and independence
- inspiring and leading change: courage, confidence, persistence, and positive attitude
- self-knowledge and renewal: lifelong learning, self-care

In my own career, I have focused on developing these competencies as I have striven to improve health care for children.

Strategic Vision: Passion, Care, and Compassion

It is in the shelter of each other that the people live.

—Irish Proverb

The Irish proverb illustrates that together, as communities, we can protect and nurture America's youth. Once an overlying vision exists, then the mission for the work becomes clear. Marian Wright Edelman states, "Service is the rent we pay to be living. It is the very purpose of life and not something you do in your spare time."

Everyone should contribute, in time, money or energy, to make the world better than what we currently have.

My vision for building strong healthy communities comes from my life experiences in three different cultures. As a child growing up in Mexico City, I was surrounded by extreme poverty. Children and their families came daily to our house to get the leftover food from our meals. Extra pencils, papers, and clothes all went to the neighborhood children.

I wondered while I was growing up—how did I become fortunate to have two working parents, a home, and an excellent academic school where I studied in two languages and received an International Baccalaureate degree before this degree became popular in the United States, while others all around me did not have the same opportunities? As I could not find an answer, I decided to come to the United States, hoping the wealthiest country in the world would provide an answer.

I studied at Mount Holyoke College in Massachusetts. The college was situated in a scenic, rural area, yet the closest city was suffering from textile and paper mill closures. Yes, the women at the college were encouraged to think independently, and strive for excellence, yet local young women had no hope for the future. I then decided to continue my search for answers to why social and economic disparities exist by studying and working in Sweden. I earned a master's degree from the University of Stockholm and interned for the United Nations Food and Agriculture Organization to plan projects that eradicate hunger in the developing world.

I could now compare three cultures—Mexico, a developing country, but where children are better immunized than many American children; the United States, a wealthy country that has many social injustice issues; and Sweden, where everyone is taken care of from the cradle to the grave. Although I had a comfortable life in Sweden, I decided to return to the United States, because I welcome change over security, and adventure over residing in a safe, predictable place.

I then studied at Creighton University in Nebraska for a nursing degree, because I wanted to diminish health disparities. I have dedicated my entire nursing career to addressing social inequalities by first becoming a school nurse at the poorest school in the state of Oregon. I have had many opportunities to work with immigrants, migrants, refugees, and homeless children.

The first migrant family to arrive in Eugene, Oregon from a small town in Michoacan, Mexico enrolled their five children at the school on my first day of work. Every year more family members have come, and now the original children are having their own families. The result is that one family in a span of 17 years now has 215 members living in the city. This family growth is replicated in immigrant communities around the entire country.

These immigrants grow and tend the fruits and vegetables we eat, clean the houses we live in, and take care of our children while we work. As long as we want to pay reasonable prices for the products we purchase, and as long as there is hope for a better future, immigrants suffering from poverty in their home countries will continue to come to the United States, just as they have for the last 300 years.

As a bilingual/bicultural nurse I can relate to these families and help them navigate through school, employment, immigration, and health issues. From my youth I had experience in bilingual education; I could now use that expertise to write federal and state grants for educational programs. I have also become the spokesperson for the Latino community and joined the boards of several community agencies so that I can help both the Americans and Latinos understand each other, and build a strong, diverse community.

The other major societal change has been the growth of the homeless population. In 1990 there were children who were homeless for a few months; now I know children who have been homeless their entire lives—12 to 14 years. These children move from hotels, to cars, to shelters, to friends, to other states, and then start the cycle all over again. I call these children the "lost generation," as they do not have opportunities to bond with teachers, make friends, join sports activities, or pursue enrichment programs. They do not have routines, or regular meals, or a place to hang their jackets, or a place to study. These children need advocates—someone to speak for them, to demand that they have access to housing, to good schools, and to adequate health care.

When I meet with my Swedish friends and discuss my daily activities— finding a dentist who will treat a child's abscessed tooth, or buying medications for a child who has been wheezing for days, or delivering a food box for a family who has not eaten in 2 days—they look at me in wonderment. Their response is, "This sounds like Sweden in the nineteenth century." That statement fires me up, gives me the passion to find solutions for the twenty-first century. We are becoming an increasingly stratified society, where the rich are becoming increasingly richer, and the poor continue to fall desperately behind, and we must reverse this trend.

Creativity, Risk Taking, Resourcefulness

The people who are crazy enough to think they can change the world are the ones who do.

—Apple computer commercial

Once the vision exists, a leader must align with other supporters and find funds to further the cause. This requires creativity, resourcefulness, and willingness to take risks. As a school nurse for 11 years I learned these skills. A yearly budget of $300 and one person's commitment could not resolve poverty. To raise public awareness about the children in this area I spoke at community gatherings, visited political and community leaders, appeared on radio and television shows, and wrote op-ed pieces for the newspaper. The results were positive: one donor, a retired history professor, yearly contributes $15,000; churches, service clubs, and individuals volunteer and lead fundraising projects; dentists and physicians see children for free.

Now that I could mobilize the community, I felt I could expand my horizons. I helped children in one school, but what about the entire district—350 children versus 18,000 children? I accepted the supervisor position for Health Services for the school district. In the year 2000 I walked into a department that had a $12,000 deficit, a staff that had too many responsibilities, dealt with too many problems, and needed to be reenergized. As Sheldon King, retired CEO from Stanford Medical School recommends, I decided to "seize the moment, articulate the vision and my values, and then people as they are aligning with me, will understand that I am a leader."

I had a community base of support, now I needed to strengthen and expand this base by collaborating with foundations and businesses, convincing the school board and superintendent that we needed more staffing, and starting new programs that addressed critical children's needs in mental and oral health care. By being courageous and arranging meetings, writing proposals, and volunteering for community committees, I again saw results. I managed to turn the deficit into a strong budget with $600,000 in reserves, added more nurse time, hired four mental health therapists, and organized a community oral health project to provide free dental care to 700 children yearly.

Now that children in one community had more access to health care, I could once again move to a higher commitment level. The Oregon School-Based Health Centers faced a serious crisis in 2003 when the state legislature voted to eliminate funding for adolescent health programs, and 9 of the 40 health centers closed. A small group of volunteers from around the state had previously formed the Oregon School-Based Health Care Network (OSBHCN) to advocate statewide for the advancement of school health care and now had the overwhelming responsibility of providing oversight to the remaining health centers, and finding solutions to the fiscal uncertainties.

To assume these responsibilities, I as the president, together with the other volunteers, embarked on strengthening the OSBHCN by seeking outside help and funding. I applied for a Robert Wood Johnson Executive Nurse Fellowship, and to the Pacific Source Foundation for matching funds, both of which I received.

Now that I had start-up funds, could hire part-time help, and had many mentoring advantages through the Robert Wood Johnson Fellowship, I could leverage other funds by obtaining a Kellogg Foundation grant for $1.25 million for Oregon. These funds continue to leverage other funds with new foundations, and the work that previously had been done by volunteers is now performed by a full-time executive director, a development director, an administrative assistant, and a half-time policy director. The combined advocacy efforts of many individuals around the state, plus having paid staff members who assumed leadership responsibilities, have resulted in the following successes:

- The Oregon governor and legislature reinstated funds in 2003–2005 to the original $2.7 million, increased funds to $3.2 million in 2005–2007, and increased to $5.5 million in 2007–2009 for school health centers.
- Sixty youth from around the state attend a School-Based Health Care advocacy day at the state capital; 14 youth participate in a year-long Teen Advocacy Council, videotape their experiences, do local and national presentations, and pursue fund-raising activities.
- Oregon sponsors a national conference that brought 600 attendees in June 2006, and yearly leads an annual institute.

All these accomplishments have occurred because I searched for opportunities to find and nurture allies so that a collective voice could speak for children's health. Bill Hewlett's philosophy that "creativity is nurtured by being receptive and encouraging" means always looking for ways to obtain results, and building from one success to another.

Interpersonal and Communication Effectiveness: Adaptability, Flexibility, Independence

Leadership is all about relationships, learning that everyone is talented.
—Shirley Chater, previous director of Social Security

Mary Wakefield, a nurse leader and consultant, declares that, "you can gain a lot by giving a little" (Wakefield, 2006). She encourages nurses to serve on committees and in elected positions. A lot of what can be accomplished depends on who one knows. It is therefore imperative to develop relationships within the profession and with public and private agency leaders with an interest in health care. As she states, "You have to get off the porch to run with the big dogs." This may mean attending long meetings for the opportunity to talk with others at the breaks; of volunteering on a committee to learn from others and develop friendships. By stretching, taking on added responsibilities, I improve my skills and expertise, at the same time that I become known as an energetic leader and make friends before I need them.

I have volunteered to lead many committees. I respond quickly to community leaders' requests. I support others in their endeavors, and in turn they support me. In this way, champions emerge—the mayor, the governor, a county commissioner, and a state representative all speak strongly for school health centers.

Two other leadership skills, adaptability and flexibility, require a nurse leader to continue with a mission, despite fiscal and political crises. The futurist Thorton May discusses the "Big Truth" as:

- Everything possible today was at one time impossible.
- Everything impossible today may at some time in the future be possible.
- The future is not something that just happens to us.
- The future is something we create.(May, 2005)

When I first started my career, I never thought the governor would call to seek my advice, or that I would be responsible for orchestrating a Kellogg grant for the entire state. The results of my efforts to adapt, to find solutions, have meant that for the first time in 20 years both the Oregon state legislature and the governor are in agreement that school health centers merit funding, because they provide comprehensive health care at sites where students spend the majority of their days.

Conflicts and tensions arise, funding disappears, social and economic changes occur, all of which sidetrack progress and call once again for committed time, energy, and desire to resolve the problems. The best analogy is Dora, a fish in the film *Finding Nemo*, when she responds to the question, "What do you do when things get rough?" with the answer as she flips her gills, "Keep on swimming. . . . Keep on swimming."

Inspiring and Leading Change: Courage, Confidence, Persistence, Positive Attitude

Success is the sum of small efforts, repeated day in and out.

—Robert Collier

As I have discussed, one success builds upon another. Sometimes the work is exciting, other times it is exhausting. The staff members have facilitated advisory councils composed of parents, staff, students, and community members, planned a parade at a city celebration that won the Best Costume entry, sponsored open houses to celebrate 20 years of existence for the health centers, and are leading a Teen Advisory Council, where high school students are learning to advocate for school health.

These activities have reenergized and motivated the staff to lead community support for school health. However, several people are now complaining that these projects are time consuming and may not have an impact on the community. This requires patience on my part to continue to convince everyone that advocacy is a part of our jobs if we want school health programs to exist and thrive. The words of Marabel Morgan are apt in this scenario, "Persistence is the twin sister of excellence. One is a matter of quality, the other is a matter of time."

I have spent many hours writing grant proposals, and then initiating new programs, and in the case of the Kellogg Foundation grant, essentially starting a new business. I have learned the importance of building and nurturing relationships, of articulating my vision in many different ways, of finding mentors to guide me, and of paying consultants for their expert advice on writing memorandums of agreement, setting up Web sites, planning public relations campaigns, and reviewing nonprofit applications.

I am learning to communicate with many and diverse people, which is especially challenging in state and nationwide endeavors. When I encounter difficult people, I luckily recall the words of Shirley Burke, former staff chair to Senator Robert Dole, "Lucky are the flexible as they don't get bent out of shape" (Burke, 2006).

Mary Wakefield also advises to maintain cordial relationships with others, and to, "Blow up a bridge only if you're sure you'll never need to cross there again" (Wakefield, 2006).

My strategies are always to address each issue positively and diplomatically; to not engage in disputes; to diffuse hard feelings by playing to the strengths of each individual.

Self-Knowledge and Renewal: Lifelong Learning, Self-Care

If you stop learning today, you stop leading tomorrow.
—Howard Hendricks

As a nurse leader I need to expand both the breadth and depth of my knowledge. I need to be well informed in health-related issues as well as current local, state, and federal happenings so that I can converse readily with politicians, and business and community leaders. I also need to avail myself of the expertise of others. Mentors are important as they guide me, listen to my thoughts, and offer advice. Consultants can lessen my workload, and bring objective and competent expertise to projects.

I share my knowledge, my experiences, my values, my heart, and my wisdom with my staff, with the parents, and above all with the children I serve. I continue to learn so that I can be open to change and new ideas. I read the *Harvard Business Review,* the *New York Times,* the current literature. I thrive on conversations with others around current events and am convinced that it is important to know what is really going on in this world of constant change to be able to make good decisions. I read, I think, I analyze, and then I speak for the cause.

Clarence Randall's thoughts summarize my thoughts about the importance of being a lifelong learner: "The leader must know that he knows, and must be able to make it abundantly clear to those about him that he knows." Knowledge brings confidence, and confidence invigorates one to dream and follow the dreams.

The final leadership lessons that I adhere to come from the following persons: Sue Hasmiller, Robert Wood Johnson Foundation:

> Work like a dog!
> Work like a dog!
> Work like a dog!

Tom Gordon, diversity consultant: "Fall 7 times/stand up 8. Learn. Be mindful/helpful. Prepare to soar."

Mary Ellen Withrow, past treasurer of the United States: "Follow what you say you will."

CONCLUSION AND IMPLICATIONS

Coming together is the beginning, keeping together is progress. Working together is success.
—Henry Ford

When a leader champions a worthwhile cause and collaborates with other leaders and agencies, while seeking support and advice from the consumers, many positive results occur. In the area of school health, nurse leaders must continue to rally for better nurse-to-student ratios, and for community support for school health programs like the health centers that provide comprehensive physical and mental health care to uninsured, low-income, homeless, migrant, and refugee children.

We have much to do. I will continue to use these competencies as I look for solutions to poverty and children's right to adequate health care. I learn and adjust as I go along; I am open to changes or risks; I work in teams; I seek opportunities.

As I continue on my journey, I think of Alfred Tennyson's words:

> Forward, forward let us range,
> Let the great world spin for ever down the ringing
> Groves of change.

If a child suffers, we suffer. If the bell rings, it rings for us to respond positively to change.

REFERENCES

Burke, S. (2006, April). Presentation at Robert Wood Johnson Executive Nurse Fellows workshop, Washington, DC.

Campaign for Children's Health Care. (2006, September 28). *No shelter from the storm: America's uninsured children.* Retrieved January 7, 2008, from http://www.childrens healthcampaign.org/tools/no-shelter-key-findings.html

Elders, J. (2006, November). Keynote presentation at the National Association of Education for Homeless Children and Youth, Little Rock, Arkansas.

Fuligni, A., & Hardway, C. (2004). Preparing diverse adolescents for the transition to adulthood. *The Future of Children: Children of Immigrant Families, 14*(2), 99–117.

Halton, N., DuPlessis, H., & Inkelas, M. (2007). Transforming the U.S. child health system. *Health Affairs: Designing Children's Health Care, 26*(2), 315–344.

Hernandez, D. (2004). Demographic change and the life circumstances of immigrant families. *The Future of Children: Children of Immigrant Families, 14*(2), 17–47.

May, T. (2005, October 19). *Health care: On the edge of something new.* Presentation at Robert Wood Johnson Executive Nurse Fellows workshop.

Minnesota Public Health Department, Henry Street Consortium. (2003, March and July). *Linking public health nursing practice and education to promote population health.* Retrieved January 7, 2008, from http://www.health.state.mn.us/divs/chs/phn/part nerships.html

National Assembly of School-Based Health Care. (2001). "Determining a Policy Agenda to Sustain School-Based Health Centers: NASBHC Assesses the Health Care Safety Net Environment."

National Center for Health Statistics. (2006, December 21). *National Health Interview Survey (NHIS)*. Retrieved January 7, 2008, from http://www.cdc.gov/nhcs/about/nhis/quest_data_related_doc.htm

National Association of School Nurses. (2001). *The role of the school nurse in providing health services*.

National Institute for Health Care Management (2005). *Children's mental health: An overview and key considerations for health system stakeholders*. Retrieved January 23, 2008, from http://www.nihcm.org/pdf/CMHReport-FINAL.pdf

Oregon Department of Human Services. (2007). *School-based health centers quality health care for kids. 2007 Status Report*.

Robert Wood Johnson Executive Nurse Fellows Program. (2003, July). Introductory Leadership Seminar, Santa Cruz, California.

Roberts, S. (2004). *Who we are now: The changing face of America in the 21st century*. New York: Times Books.

Rothstein, R. (2004, May). *Class and schools: Using social, economic and educational reform to close the black-white achievement gap*. Economic Policy Institute.

Schlih, J. (2007, June). Presentation at national school-based health care convention, Washington, D.C.

U.S. Department of Health and Human Services. (1999). *Mental health: A report of the surgeon general*. Retrieved December 30, 2007, from http://www.eurgeongeneral.gov

Wakefield, M. (2006, April). Presentation at Robert Wood Johnson Executive Nurse Fellows workshop, Washington, DC.

Zaslow, J. (2006, November 2). Is there a nurse in the house? Schools endure shortage as health needs rise. *Wall Street Journal*.

CHAPTER 4

People

Donna Thompson

THE IMPORTANCE OF EFFECTIVE TEAMS

There is nothing more gratifying and reassuring than a long-tenured CEO and a senior leadership team who have created a vibrant history of organizational success. It is an intoxicating experience to be part of a successful turnaround of a once struggling and failing organization. Governing board of director meetings that were once fraught with tension, disbelief, and mistrust while being further plagued by convoluted and depressing financial statements slowly are replaced by solid and straightforward financials, program expansion, and tangible operational results that codify and support the organization's strategic direction. The undeniable and compelling new success serves as a hypnotic veil that lingers and over time engulfs an organization, seducing the board of directors into feeling like this "Camelot" existence will last forever.

A savvy leader will intuitively build relationships based on trustworthiness and responsiveness to the intricacies and peculiarities of each board member as well as the opinions of leaders among their staff. Successful leaders have repeatedly demonstrated courage under fire as well as the tenacity to stay the course through the toughest times. They have earned their stripes, and hallway chatter among staff can easily validate their worthiness. They not only have the track record but in some instances have even laid down the tracks by successfully navigating the organization through complicated times and around unexpected hurdles. The organization is healthy, vibrant, and, in other words, their CEO does know how to get "blood out of a turnip."

Through the leadership of the CEO and while earning support by the governing board, there is an unwavering and exhaustive investment of gluing together an organization for which very few would have the courage to hang in for the long haul. The history of the why and how are paraphrased and strung together by catchy shorthand phrases that only the long-term historians around the table understand.

Thinking beyond the existing leadership feels almost like a betrayal to the current, dynamic, and trustworthy leader and senior team. It is like looking for a replacement of a cherished and well-regarded family member. The feelings run deep and the history of the organization is grounded by this CEO's leadership.

Why would anyone want to rock the boat when it is obvious that the magic of an impressive CEO and team are in place and consistently delivering positive results for the organization? However, it is because of the defined successes that the governing board should not take a laissez-faire stance but move into action to secure the organization's prominence and guarantee that future accomplishments will not be impeded because of lack of forward thinking by the governing board.

Surprises are for kiddie birthday parties and impromptu celebrations for families and friends. The exit of the CEO may or may not be planned; however, having a plan in place will assure that the organization will not be caught by surprise. Once the announcement has been made that the current CEO will no longer be at the helm of the organization, it is the governing board's responsibility to have had a plan in place that guarantees the smooth transition of one chief executive officer to the next.

The organization's strategic plan, the governing board's annual self-assessment, and the CEO's evaluation of competencies are just a few of the sources that the governing board of directors have at their disposal to use as a gauge for assessing the skill sets that the next CEO should easily demonstrate. The strategic planning process with the governing board and the senior leadership team is a great opportunity to focus on the strategic direction of the organization over the next 3–5 years. This brutal focus by the governing board should also create an opportunity to assess the executive leadership skills that are required to successfully move the organization in the new strategic direction.

The phase occupied by the interim CEO has some key areas of focus. The governing board and the interim CEO should agree on the parameters of decision making. Candid and frequent communication between the governing board and the interim CEO should strike a balance. This requires careful monitoring by the governing board of directors. The interim CEO should over-communicate to staff, external stakeholders, and the governing board of directors. Staff town hall meetings, employee newsletters, and structured meetings with key staff are just a few of the ways that the interim CEO can take the opportunity to assure that key and timely messages are delivered to staff.

LEADING THE TEAM DURING CHANGE

Key messages to staff and external stakeholders should have the purpose of moving the organization to stabilization. Strategically guided key messages can allow for healing and preparation for change while creating an opportunity to welcome the new future. The strategic plan should be used by the organization as a unifying guidepost. The interim CEO should not execute changes that require long-term follow-through. Rapid or unplanned change of the current culture can result in a complicated transition for the incoming CEO.

It is the end of June and our not-for-profit board will be meeting in a week to hopefully approve the imminent fiscal year budget. One of the best financial years in the history of the health center network is coming to a close. The economic success of the organization has been spearheaded by a long-term CEO and his executive team. Everyone is on a celebratory ride, feeling good about the accomplishments of the previous year and enjoying the serenity of a predictable organization.

We completed our second Joint Commission on Accreditation of Health Care Organizations (JCAHO) accreditation process 6 months earlier after absorbing 14 new health centers. The total number of health centers within our network is 46. It was quite a challenge to transition a new group of leaders into our health network with only 6 months to prepare them and their health centers for their first accreditation process. We did achieve an accreditation score of 94. The CEO walked out of the conference room and stood in front of 100 anxious managers, physicians, and staff and proudly announced that we received our second accreditation. He talked about the importance of quality for our patients and families, and in his true fashion let everyone know that as a team we were able to achieve this accreditation goal. We championed around our CEO. He had worked hard to secure the financial stability of the organization. This was achieved through a combination of health center acquisitions, expanded grant funding, and infrastructure realignment. Improvement in clinical quality was equally important and achieving Joint Commission accreditation was a major step in that direction.

The CEO and half of the senior management team will soon be leaving to attend a conference on "Best Practices" in community health centers. Following the conference, the senior management team will focus on the upcoming fiscal year goals and tactics during our quarterly retreat. The Best Practices conference has become an annual event that the entire senior management team looks forward to attending. It almost has become a ritual. In early spring we begin the budgeting process and finalize it by the end of May. We attend the Best Practices conference with 12 other community health center leaders from across the country in June. One week later, we bring a new fiscal year budget to our governing board of directors for their approval. The senior management team meets in the middle of July for the first of four quarterly retreats. It is at this July retreat that each senior manager will declare their department goals and strategies for the new fiscal year.

The Best Practices conference creates a lot of excitement and energy among the senior managers. There is usually a lot of bustle around the office for those preparing to present at the conference. Everyone gives suggestions in order to enrich the presentation. The medical director designed and implemented a new provider compensation system 1 year ago. This provider compensation system will be presented at one of the conference sessions. Our CEO is excited about sharing this new standard of compensation that rewards quality, customer service, good citizenship, and productivity. It is important for him to illustrate that this new method of compensation has improved overall clinical quality.

This is a different organization than the one I joined years ago. I'm approaching my tenth year as a senior leader of what is now the largest Federally Qualified Community Health Center network in the nation, recruited 1 year after the CEO's arrival as part of his "turnaround team."

Back then the organization was losing $7 to $8 million a year. Daily we were addressing overwhelming crises. Meetings were more like brainstorming sessions. Ideas flowed from everyone. Someone always had a solution to improve the broken systems. Ideas and suggestions came and went as did many of their inventors. It was a revolving door for those who didn't have the sustenance and patience for the long-haul commitment necessary for a sustainable change. If you had an idea or wanted something done, you delegated to yourself because that was the only way any issue was going to be addressed. Board meetings were unpredictable monthly events. The senior management team could not predict how dismal the monthly financials were going to be, nor the reaction by the governing board of directors. Everyone had their heart in the right place, advocating for the mission of the organization, as we were dripping red ink all over the place. The programs were just as scattered. Program infrastructure was nonexistent, and any grant funding that was awarded to support needed services was viewed by staff more as a detriment than a benefit. Program planning and execution were sporadic and haphazard.

An inner calmness has slowly grown over time as we have enjoyed more financial stability. I feel like the proud parent, seeing the child start to exert the potential that you knew was always there. I usually experience these sentimental feelings in very short spurts before reality kicks in and another work-related conflict or crisis is splashed in my face, reminding me that things are better but we still have quite a way to go.

But I'm really looking forward to this summer. It's a good time for me personally and professionally. My kids are 11 and 14. Nice ages for their expanding independence while I carve out additional morsels of my own limited free time. I learned early in my administrative career to grasp and savor those "throttle-down" times. No one is going to stand over you and tell you when to grab one of these precious moments. They come few and far between. When it is available, you have to be ready to reinvest in yourself so that you are prepared for whatever is waiting around the corner.

I chose not to attend the Best Practices seminar this year but rather take the time to regroup, catch up on paperwork, and enjoy the quiet environment that goes along with your boss being out of town with half of your peers. I knew that once everyone was back, the roller-coaster ride would start again. It was the cycle that I had grown accustomed to over the years. Every senior manager would be declaring their goals and objectives for the coming fiscal year as team assignments were made. Everyone had a can-do-anything attitude, especially at the beginning of the fiscal year when each of us would declare giant and ambitious goals that we were sure could easily be accomplished by the following June. Interesting enough, we usually landed most of those goals.

This year we will add two new positions to the senior team. This was part of our new team reorganization plan developed during our April quarterly retreat. We had tremendous growth with the addition of 14 health centers. Part of the reorganization meant a transition of some of my current responsibilities. I agreed and supported the transition, but I was also ambivalent about this change and had taken the last 2 months working through it with the affected staff. Other senior management roles were also being shifted. A previous senior manager would be returning after 3 years with another organization to resume her previous role, and another senior manager would be moving to a newly developed senior role. All of these changes would be effective in July and I assumed would take up much of our retreat agenda.

We are a Health Resources and Services Administration Bureau of Primary Health Care-supported health center. Federally Qualified Health Centers care for people regardless of their ability to pay and whether or not they have health insurance. They provide community-based primary and preventive health care, as well as enabling services such as transportation, language translation, case management, and outreach services. Many health centers also offer dental, mental health, and substance abuse care. Community Health Centers cared for 13.1 million people in 2004. The Health Resources and Services Administration (HRSA) funds over 1,000 health centers nationally. *Health center* is an all-encompassing term for a diverse range of public and nonprofit organizations and programs. Many receive federal funding under section 330 of the Public Health Service Act and may also be known as Federally Qualified Health Centers. The types of health centers funded under this act are community health centers (serving medically underserved and low-income people and including school-based sites), migrant health centers (serving migrant and seasonal agricultural workers and their families), homeless health centers (serving homeless adults, families, and children) and Public Housing Health Centers (serving residents of public housing). Others meet the requirements but do not receive funds and are designated Federally Qualified Health Center Look-Alikes by HRSA and the Centers for Medicare and Medicaid Services. Federally Qualified Health Centers (FQHCs) and Look-Alikes (FQHCLAs) are eligible to receive enhanced reimbursement from Medicare and Medicaid and to participate in the 340B Program that enables them to purchase drugs at reduced prices and pass that savings on to their uninsured patients. Federally Qualified Health Centers also have access to medical malpractice insurance through the Federal Tort Claims Act.

Health Center requirements are that they be located in a HRSA-designated (medically underserved) area or population; operate under a consumer majority board of directors governance structure; provide comprehensive primary health, oral, or mental/substance abuse services to persons in all stages of the life cycle, provide services without regard for a patient's ability to pay; charge for services on a board-approved sliding-fee scale that is based on patient's family size and income; and comply with all other program expectations and requirements and all applicable federal and state regulations.

Health centers focus on improving individual patient health and improving the health status of the entire community. As a Federally Qualified Health Center, we have been achieving a surplus following many years of annual operating losses. Over the last 10 years of consistent executive leadership, we have expanded from 90,000 patient visits in nine health center sites to over 500,000 patient visits in 46 health center sites. Our primary-care medical-only model morphed into expanded enabling services, colocated partnerships, and provision of specialty services. The complexities of the health center system expanded along with the growth in size. Grant revenue increased from 3% of the operating budget to 23%. We became a recognized leader among our health center peers, legislators, and community organizations as well as local and federal government entities. We were proud to be the turnaround story. After so many years of health care leaders politely nodding and asking us again, "Who are you?" We finally were getting recognized for living our mission while maximizing limited resources to the fullest. We wore our growth as a badge of honor for paving the way for low-income and uninsured people to have a true health care home. Our CEO was a recognizable and credible leader who championed the rights of the underserved. He also was expert in understanding key business strategies that led to the organization's turnaround. Most of all, he was caring and trusting of his employees. He was open and honest with his opinions and people quickly gravitated to his story-telling nature to explain any issue. Because of his early career in community organizing, it was mesmerizing to drive through poverty-stricken neighbor-hoods and listen as he told their neglected story. He could easily host and rub elbows with some of the most influential people in the nation and quickly switch gears and call a staff person and inquire about the health of their ailing child or parent that they had shared with him weeks before.

Within the last 2 years, we had completed our first capital campaign and exceeded our financial target by $1.25 million. Our second 3-year strategic plan was in full swing with goals that focused more on quality, growth, infra-structure, and partnerships rather than making budget, as had been our focus during the first six years. We were expanding our patient base beyond the city to include the suburbs.

It was comfortable and exciting. We were finally able to focus on the issues that would take us to the next level in our journey to improve the quality of care for the underserved in the city and suburbs. Four nights later, the phone rang at my house in the middle of the night and everything changed for me and the rest of the organization.

LEADERSHIP DURING A CRISIS

I had spent the majority of my health care career being awakened in the mid-dle of the night by some type of clinical or administrative crisis, which prob-ably explains why the phone was always on my bedside table rather than my husband's. That is why it is still surprising to me that I reacted to the ringing phone that night by leaping out of bed and running down a flight of stairs to answer the phone in the kitchen. All I remember is the complete calmness of his voice when my peer gave me the unwelcome news of the CEO's death a few hours before. I remember repeating the words but not registering the impact. My husband appeared and I watched his animated "Oh, my God" expression as he repeated the words that I heard myself saying but still was not registering. I asked about my other peers and the CEO's partner. He told me that everyone was still very numb. As he repeated the circumstances of the accident, I also heard that two of my peers were present during the accident and could have had the same demise. They were several thousand miles away and there was no way that we could easily reach them, nor could they return home promptly.

As the tragic event was recounted, I interrupted several times to ask my peer simple logistics such as the name of the hotel and city they were in as well as their phone numbers. It dawned on me that we had never discussed or set policy on travel, and that as daunting as it was about our CEO, it would have been far worse if the loss would had included our medical director and chief financial officer. Our strategies had been closely kept within the senior management team and randomly documented. We each had our special niches. Collectively it was a powerful team. Individually, we each held our own undisclosed methods to success. We were a team that learned over time to identify and avoid pitfalls as we captured and refined those strategies that lead to success. This knowledge was tucked away in each of our own memory banks, called upon when the need arrived.

After disconnecting from the long-distance call, I sat in the kitchen and felt totally numb and in disbelief. I could not cry. For some reason the tears would not flow. It would be weeks later before the tears of loss finally came. I still could not accept the news. The CEO's family in Chicago had been notified, so it was up to me to start the process beginning with the key stakeholders of the organization. It was 2 o'clock in the morning, and I decided that the best approach was to make a list and start the calls around 5 o'clock. There was no sense in waking anyone early. It was going to be a regrettably long day.

The board chairperson and the CEO of the health system that was our organization's affiliate were the individuals that I chose to call first. I knew neither very well, and except for cursory conversation at board meetings, I knew hardly anything about these two individuals and was sure it was mutual. Our CEO totally managed governing board and affiliate relationships. I felt awkward. What a message to give to people you hardly know.

I tapped into the nursing skills I had developed over the years from telling families tragic news and helping them process the unthinkable. Keep the message short and factual. Don't give too much information. Allow the receiver to grasp the tragic news. Carefully select your words—the simpler the better. Pace the message and prepare to repeat as many times as the receiver needs to process the information.

As I was going over these mental notes, I suddenly thought that I did not have their phone numbers. We had never thought to put an emergency notification tree of administrative numbers together in case of emergencies. I quickly grabbed my palm pilot and found out that I had a number for the governing board president but none for the health system CEO. In this day and age, everyone has unlisted numbers, so I thought checking the local phone directory assistance was a waste of time, but I tried anyway. The operator asked what city. I had no idea, and then I remembered several years ago hearing someone briefly mention the suburb where he lived. I said a quick prayer, told her the city, and thank goodness his number was listed.

It felt comforting to reach out to an experienced health care executive. I called him first and used the pacing of words. It was simple and deliberate with short factual messages to tell him the tragic news. His own retirement was to become effective within a few weeks. The implications of his retirement and the news of the loss of our CEO would have to be carefully managed to assure that panic and fear would not unsettle these closely affiliated organizations. I reviewed with him my immediate plans. He provided me with some additional advice. We agreed to meet at the office in 3 hours. I could tell he was shocked and saddened but his ability to rapidly regroup and go into strategy mode was also evident.

As I hung up the phone, my memory went back to April, 3 months prior to today's tragic news. We were sitting at a downtown hotel for our quarterly senior management team meeting. The news was hot off the press. The system chairman of our hospital affiliate was retiring. Everyone was shocked. What tenure! Twenty-eight years with the health system. These days that length of service is unheard of in health care. I remember our CEO talking about the almost fatal heart attack that the system CEO had suffered months before. The heart attack practically occurred at the doors of the emergency room. As our CEO sat in his chair, looking extremely healthy, he talked about how lucky the system CEO was to survive such a scary event and what an opportunity he now had to rethink his priorities and throttle down. "It's like being given a second chance," he said. Back in the present, we sat in that conference room and stared into space for a few moments. I glanced at the medical director, who had known the system CEO since his residency 28 years ago. I knew that he was the most touched by the news. I think the short silence allowed all of us to think about our own choices. That lasted for about 30 seconds and then we went back to the roller coaster frenzy of planning.

I notified the governing board chairperson and we agreed to meet in the office later that morning. We agreed which governing board members we each would notify. I and another manager were the only senior staff in town. Another senior manager was on the East Coast vacationing, and the remaining senior managers were at the conference. Prior to making staff calls, I thought about each person and the best possible way to deliver the news. After making the calls to the senior manager in town and our human resource manager, I made the trek to my office.

In retrospect, I can share that we came together as a team and then as an organization. We openly took support from our hospital affiliate crisis team.

They were present when we told the staff about the tragedy and provided on-going support over the next 6 months. Our clinics cover about 1,200 square miles. One of our managers suggested using our recently installed bioterror alert system of communication to arrange a telephone tree so that all staff could hear the news at the same time. Later, we would hear from many of our staff that it was hard news but comforting that the administrative team made sure that everyone heard the tragic news together.

The meeting with the governing board chairperson included me, the board president emeritus, and the system CEO of our hospital affiliate. It was a diffi-cult meeting. I made the mistake of gathering us in the CEO's office. Sitting in his office I visualized him at his computer checking his e-mail or gathering all of us around his round table for strategy meetings. I imagined that everyone in this meeting was half thinking of what our next steps should be and half thinking about the last time they were with the CEO.

I updated the governing board chairperson on the status of the staff meet-ings and media announcements that were being planned. I strongly encour-aged the governing board chairperson that an interim CEO would need to be appointed immediately by the board. I told him that the CEO had the talent to put together a very strong team, but that was also a weakness and unless an interim were named, it would be challenging to keep the organization on the right track. Ironically, today was the scheduled governing board of directors meeting. The CEO of the health system recommended that two issues would need to be completed by the board, the appointment of an interim CEO and the review and passing of the new fiscal year (starting in one week) budget. Both were accomplished that evening.

The next several days were consumed with notifying critical government agencies and key leadership partners as the news of the death hit the media. We were bombarded with calls. I had never spoken to the media before, but being named interim CEO quickly forced me into the role of organization spokes-person. I was reluctant in talking to the media. I knew of too many health care executives who complained of their words being taken out of context. I shared my concerns with our director of communications. She quickly ar-ranged for me to get some preparation and coaching by our media consultant. I learned that being vocal about my concerns allowed other experts to assist me; otherwise it would be assumed that I knew what to do or did not want as-sistance. All week it was a combination of newspaper reporters and television reporters. By the end of the week, I was out of steam and needed the weekend to recover and regroup. However, I got a call on Sunday about another televi-sion interview. I was asked to offer a location and suggested one of our health centers that had been built with the proceeds of our first and very successful capital campaign. We met and reviewed the contents of the interview. While

I was waiting for the start of the interview, I remembered the groundbreaking ceremony that we had the previous year prior to the beginning of construction of the new health center. Our CEO insisted that the cornerstone of the health center be a Shona sculpture. This special life-size African sculpture stands in the middle of the patient waiting area so all patients can enjoy it. The sculpture depicts a family nestled around a mother and her baby. The CEO enjoyed picking out the sculpture as his gift to the health center.

When the live interview started, I responded to the questions that the reporter had told me she was going to ask. Then, during the final seconds of the interview, she asked me how I have been personally affected by the death. Suddenly, I felt tears welling in my eyes and my mind going blank. It was at that moment, live in front of thousands of people, that I felt his loss. I heard my voice cracking as I responded. When the interview was over, I found myself raising my voice at the reporter and asking her why she asked me that last question. I knew at that moment that I was not allowing myself to get in touch with my own feelings. I soon sought out the crisis support that our hospital affiliate offered and continued that support over the next 3 months for myself.

The time preceding his wake and funeral service consisted of marathon meetings with staff. I encouraged their expression of loss. This process was draining but also cathartic. I used this time to speak of the future. We talked about the legacy of a leader. It was important for the staff to know that our future was contingent on our ability to continue the services that we provide to our communities.

LEADERSHIP LESSONS FOR TRANSITIONS

We used the meetings to celebrate the special ways that the CEO had touched many of the staff members' lives. We prepared printed communication bulletins for our staff that provided real time and factual information. Any change or rumor was addressed immediately. We worked with our media consultant to prepare ongoing communication for other community stakeholders, business partners, and government agencies.

We needed to assure everyone that the loss of the CEO did not mean the loss of the organization.

Fast forward 3 years. It is the end of May. The Joint Commission has just completed our first unannounced survey. The organization did well. Our nonprofit governing board will soon be meeting to hopefully approve our 2008 fiscal budget. We have stretched to 48 health centers serving close to 200,000 people annually. Our new 3-year strategic plan was completed in January.

Our previous plan ended in December. We were able to achieve all of our target goals. That plan had been our roadmap over the last 3 years, keeping us focused as an organization through our hardest tragedy.

Our organization-wide implementation team will be meeting soon to celebrate 3 years of success. We have invested in these leaders through education, mentoring and consistent face time with the senior leadership. Our tight and exclusive circle of senior leaders intentionally became inclusive, inviting leaders throughout the organization to learn the inner workings of how we achieved success. It is great to have empowered leaders beyond the senior team who understand the business strategies and can clearly articulate these strategies and the rationale. We celebrate those teams that are cross departmental in their approach to achieving goals. The value of senior leaders championing these teams while actively mentoring our emerging leaders has resulted in a strong cohesive network of leaders throughout the organization. We are a stronger organization because we are consciously investing in those leaders who can one day step into a senior role within our organization.

CHAPTER 5

Process

Gwendolyn A. Franklin

ISSUES IN PUBLIC HEALTH: THE PROCESS OF LEADERSHIP

This chapter provides insight into the process of public health leadership as it has been applied in southeast Michigan. The leadership process has been demonstrated by bringing to fruition a new collaborative multiagency institute, known as the Community Health Nursing Institute.

Leadership in public health is pivotal to protecting, promoting, and improving the public's health. "Healthcare is a major public health concern, and rapid changes are occurring in an attempt to reduce costs and improve the health and wellness of the nation" (Yoder-Wise, 2003). Many people delay routine, preventive, and even urgent medical care and eventually present at nearby emergency rooms as their last resort. To compound the access to care issues in vulnerable communities, hospitals become so overwhelmed with indigent care that many of them are forced to close. As millions of Americans live without health insurance, public health leaders develop processes to address the health of the population in their jurisdiction. Leaders must emerge at all levels of public health practice to find innovative methods to assure that individuals and the community have every opportunity to obtain quality health care in the face of hard economic challenges.

Public health practitioners often argue that their work is invisible. However, there are processes that take place in public health that need to be brought to the forefront and highlighted to demonstrate the extensive effort and successes that public health specialists have contributed. These contributions are evident in the virtual elimination of vaccine-preventable diseases such as smallpox and polio (Department of Health and Human Services, 2004). Some reduction in infant mortality is evident as well, for example, but much more work needs to be done in reducing health disparities.

Health Disparities

The U.S. Department of Health and Human Services (USDHHS) Office of Civil Rights (OCR) defines health disparities as differences in rates of diseases, and differences in health outcomes that affect the health status of certain racial or ethnic groups (Department of Health and Human Services, 2004). The USDHHS leadership has invested effort to "close the health care gap," and eliminate racial and ethnic health disparities as a Healthy People 2010 goal. A *USA Today* report on persistent racial disparities quoted Representative Jesse Jackson Jr. of Illinois as stating, "Racial and ethnic disparities in health care are a major problem throughout America. If we're to make progress in this high-priority area we must have a road map that the Institute of Medicine (IOM) has the credibility to provide" (Sternberg, 2002).

The Institute of Medicine publication titled, "Unequal Treatment: Confronting Racial and Ethnic Disparities in Health Care," released on March 20, 2002, was staggering. That report found consistent research indicating differences in the rates of medical procedures by race, even when insurance status, income, age, and severity of conditions were taken into account. The IOM continued to report that racial and ethnic minority populations are less likely to have routine health maintenance and to experience health care that meets standards lower than those adhered to for other members of the population. For example, minorities were less likely to receive proper heart disease medication, bypass surgery, dialysis, kidney transplants, maternal and child health service, mental health care, and intensive care. Minorities also received limb amputations for diabetes and other conditions more often. That report concluded that some factors that contributed to racial disparities were low income, reluctance to seek treatment, lifestyle choices, inadequate insurance, heredity, insufficient education, environment, and occupation (U.S. Institute of Medicine, 2002).

Health disparities in Michigan have been extensively described and documented. The Michigan Department of Community Health (MDCH) Health Disparities Workgroup produced a report demonstrating that Michigan has factors similar to the national parameters that contribute to disparities in health care. These also include poverty, education level, cultural norms, mistrust of the health care system, language barriers, provider cultural competency, and access to health care (Williams et al, 2005). The Health Disparities Workgroup contributors included representation from a cross section of divisions at the Michigan Department of Community Health such as the Bureau of Epidemiology, Bureau of Family, Maternal, and Child Health, Division of Chronic Disease and Injury Control, and the Division of Health, Wellness and Disease Control. The purpose of the Health Disparities workgroup was to make recommendations about six health categories. Those categories were adult immunizations, cardiovascular care, cancer care, diabetes, HIV/AIDS, and infant mortality. The findings from that workgroup were reviewed to understand the impact of health disparities in Michigan. That report described cancer incidence data derived from the Michigan Department of Community Health Vital Records Section. A summary of those vital records has revealed that the incidence of breast cancer is higher for white women than black women (123 versus 113 per 100,000 women), but the mortality rate is higher for black women compared to white women (nearly 33 versus 23.7 per 100,000 women) (Michigan Department of Community Health, Vital Records and Data Development Section, 2007). For males, the incidence of prostate cancer was distinctly higher for blacks than whites (274 versus 159 per 100,00 men); the rate of death from prostate cancer for black males is 45 versus 24 per 100,000 for white males. In 2003, differences in the incidence of lung cancer in Michigan were 95 for blacks versus 73 for whites, per 100,000 people; mortality rates were nearly 45 for blacks, versus nearly 24 for whites, per 100,000 (Michigan Department of Community Health, Vital Record, 2007). If, health disparities impact racial and ethnic populations in Michigan, then major metropolitan communities in Michigan must have a disproportionate share of people who are in need of quality and accessible health care. For example, in 2005, Detroit's population numbered 836,056. Of these, 69% were 18 years and older, and 10% were 65 years and over. Of the total population, 82% were African American, compared to 12% nationally, 11% were white, and 5.6%, Hispanic. Of the population 5 years and older, 21% are on disability status, compared to 14% nationally. Economically, 57% of the over-16-year-olds are in the labor force, compared to 66% nationally. Median household income is $28,069, compared to $46,242 nationally (U.S. Census Bureau, 2005). These data facts about Detroit residents indicate risk factors for health disparities potentially for 82% of the population.

The Michigan Department of Community Health, Bureau of Epidemiology, and the Chronic Disease and Epidemiology Section have published the Health Indicators and Risk Estimates Surveillance Report by Community Health Assessment for Geographic Areas and Local Health Departments. This report is called the Michigan Behavioral Risk Factor Survey (MBRFS) for 2005. In that study, the health status of Detroit's population was surveyed by a random-digit dialed telephone survey of adult residents age 18 years and older compared to Livingston, Macomb, Monroe, Oakland, St. Clair, Washtenaw, and Wayne Counties excluding Detroit which is described as Region One. Results of that report indicated that 25% of the respondents living in Detroit were more likely to report fair or poor physical health compared to 18% in St. Clair and 15% in Wayne Counties. Detroit residents ranked third (13%) compared to St. Clair County (14%), which was second highest, and Monroe County (17%), which was the highest in the percentage of residents who reported poor mental health. Further, 22% of the respondents aged 18–64 living in Detroit had no health insurance coverage compared to 17% of those living in St. Clair and 12% in Macomb Counties. Twenty-two percent (22%) of Detroit residents reported no health care access during the past 12 months due to the cost compared to 17% in St. Clair, and 10% in Wayne County. Access to care has long been a barrier for Detroit residents, and as a result Detroit residents ranked last in reporting that they had a routine checkup in the past year. In that survey, 24% of Detroit's population were more likely to report a disability than any other county in that region. These findings are consistent with the U.S. Census that reported 21% of Detroiters are on disability status.

The results of the Michigan Behavioral Risk Factor Survey also reported on the weight status of Michigan residents. By comparison, Detroit residents have the highest percentage of obese adults at 38%, compared to Monroe County at 27%, and Wayne County excluding Detroit at 26% reporting obesity as a risk factor. All of these risk factors, compared to other counties in the region, indicate a need for preventative strategies for the people living in Detroit who are at great risk for health disparities (Michigan Department of Community Health, 2005).

THE INITIATIVE

We needed to think creatively about how to address complex public health issues in Detroit, Michigan. There are many agencies and organizations in existence that deal with both broad and specific health issues in the city and surrounding region. However, it was evident that there were gaps, overlaps, and incomplete communication pathways among these agencies. More importantly, nursing leadership may have been absent from early efforts at collaboration.

To step up to the challenge of transforming nursing leadership in public health, two visionary leaders in southeast Michigan, Dr. Phyllis Meadows, director and health officer of the Detroit Department of Health and Wellness Promotion, and Dr. Linda Thompson-Adams, dean of Oakland University (OU) School of Nursing, established a partnership to create the Community Health Nursing Institute (CHNI). My role as the RWJ executive nurse leader for public health was to promote and manage the process so that communication was ongoing and so that its development continued at a steady pace.

Successful use of process skills was essential in initiating the CHNI. O'Neil stated that certain competencies are at the core of successful leadership. He has referred to these competencies as part of a "Leadership Compass" (O'Neil, 2007). The select technical process skills applied to the creation of the institute included (a) making a business case for a new project, (b) designing an operational plan to enact strategies, (c) using project management structures for planning, control, and evaluation, and (d) working with and through systems to demonstrate how complex public issues can be addressed through well-organized processes. Process is defined in this context as the ongoing activities and behaviors of health providers engaged in conducting care for clients (Stanhope & Lancaster, 2000). Leadership is defined as influencing others to achieve a goal (Yoder-Wise, 2003). The process of public health leadership begins with a work plan. The plan should be clearly written with objectives that are specific, measurable, achievable, relevant, and have time frames (Blancett & Flarey, 1995). This plan will guide the process to influence followers toward the achievement of mutually established goals. The work plan process has benefits for leadership development, because the leader has a myriad of activities that can be inefficient or ineffective if there is no defined outcome or purpose. This plan for the Community Health Nursing Institute would keep everyone focused on the new vision.

Several programs offered through the RWJ Fellowship provided me with the knowledge and foundation to prepare for the establishment of the institute. One of the RWJ seminars was lead by Rashi Glazer, professor of marketing at the University of California at Berkeley. He is well-respected for his innovative business plans and interactive marketing strategies (Glazer, 2005). Glazer's approach was used in the preparation of the business plan and his feedback was key to the relevance and success of the plan.

Establishing a partnership among a university, a public health department, and a community nonprofit agency under the auspices of an institute has a strong and successful precedent. Taylor and colleagues (1998) reported that since the late 1980s, state health departments in New York, California, and Massachusetts have had agreements to conduct research, education, and service activities through collaborative nonprofits established as institutes. Taylor also reported that other states including Michigan and Louisiana, and the U.S. Centers for Disease Control and Prevention as well, have established similar nonprofit institutes; the Michigan Public Health Institute is one example. To further tap Jeffrey Taylor's expertise, I met with him for a discussion of the Michigan Public Health Institute (MPHI) model. I also sought input from individuals involved with the Michigan chapter of the Hispanic Nurses Association, the Arab-American and Chaldean Council, the Michigan Public Health

Training Center, and the Greater Detroit Area Health Council. Marla Oros, independent consultant with the Mosaic Group, served as the consultant to record, organize, and advise as these partnerships evolved.

The public health nurse executive leader continued to articulate the strategic vision to create a Community Health Nursing Institute designed to address health indicators of Detroit residents. Over a 12-month period, this plan was discussed on several occasions among the executive leadership of the Department of Health and Wellness Promotion, the dean of the School of Nursing at Oakland University, and the consultant. This core planning team decided that the institute would be designed and well-served by residing within the university academic system. The institute would have strong community partnerships that focus on solutions. This vision is consistent with publications from the U.S. Institute of Medicine (IOM) report released in 2002, "The Future of the Public's Health." That IOM report supports the need for innovative strategies with key partnerships that include the official health agencies in the public health system, community organizations, academia, health care organizations, the media, and private industry. Representatives from these partnerships were invited to form the advisory committee for the institute.

As a result of those meetings, the Memoranda of Understanding between Oakland University School of Nursing and the Detroit Department of Health and Wellness Promotion were drafted. Once final approval is granted, the CHNI has formally become a part of the university. Once the memoranda were in place, the operational plan was designed. That carefully written plan included the vision, mission, key activities, core values, and program services. These are detailed as follows:

> **Vision:** The Community Health Nursing Institute will be nationally recognized for its dedication to health status improvement and reduction of health disparities through development, implementation and facilitation of community-based research, education, practice and dissemination activities that promote public health nursing and other evidence-based health science.
>
> **Mission:** the Community Health Nursing Institute is a unique collaboration between the Detroit Department of Health and Wellness Promotion and the Oakland University School of Nursing. The Institute will stimulate the creation of innovative programs and health policies that are based on public health nursing principles and engage community stakeholders with interdisciplinary health professionals to promote long-term improvements in health outcomes for Detroit residents. Committed to the reduction of health disparities in Detroit, the

Institute will target the development of evidence-based health promotion and disease prevention on health issues that negatively impact under-represented minority and vulnerable populations.

Key Activities:

1. Develop and collaborate with community health partnerships to identify priority health needs and concerns in the Detroit community.
2. Conduct neighborhood-based community assessments in partnership with residents and other key stakeholders to identify neighborhood-specific health issues and characteristics.
3. Establish a centralized database of neighborhood-level health and social indicators, community resources and other data for ongoing evaluation of needs and to serve as a resource for community organizations working to improve community health.
4. Design community-based health promotion, disease prevention and disease management programs targeting high priority needs and grounded in public health nursing practice.
5. Assist community groups in using health information to effect change and develop action programs.
6. Conduct community-based participatory research that links the University and other academic partners with community partners to test new models of health promotion, disease prevention and disease management.
7. Provide community education and training by offering community-based, accessible learning opportunities to advance public health practice for nurses and other health professionals, students, and community members.
8. Evaluate the efficacy of programs and policy to build sustainable models of community health practice.
9. Disseminate results of program evaluations and research to community members and local/national audiences to guide program and policy development.

Core Values: The core values that support the work of the Institute are

1. All communities are unique and therefore programs and services must be designed to respond to these factors;
2. Understanding and respecting diverse populations and cultures is essential to the work of the Institute;
3. Supporting and building lasting partnerships is a critical building block to enduring health improvement;

4. Research is critical to advancing science and will only be undertaken in partnership with communities that agree on the values, benefits and future application of the research endeavors;
5. Educating the future generation of public health nurse and health professionals is key to the future of community health improvement.

RESULTS

The first major outcome of the planning process was a retreat. After the plans for the institute were designed and the project management structure was written and discussed among the core planning team (health officer, OU School of Nursing dean, OU director of the doctoral program, and the consultant), the public health/RWJ nurse executive planned a retreat to launch the institute. Key partners were identified by the core planning team. Invitations were mailed to the following: the chief executive officer (CEO) and president of Children's Hospital of Michigan; the vice presidents of community health departments from two private medical systems, St. John's Medical system and Karmanos Cancer Institute; community-based organizations serving children and youth, represented by Metro Girls Scouts of America; administrative leadership from the Detroit Department of Health and Wellness Promotion, and a consultant from the Mosaic Group.

The invitation provided a brief statement about the partnership between the Detroit Department of Health and Wellness Promotion and the Oakland University School of Nursing, and the purpose of the institute. I, as the public health nurse administrator and the RWJ nurse executive fellow, followed the invitations with personal telephone calls to confirm attendance and answer any questions about the purpose of the retreat. The retreat was attended by almost all of the invited guests. The retreat was held at Oakland University, and 3 hours were devoted to the discussion, followed by a working lunch for the 13 attendees. The agenda included ample time for introductions, an overview of health disparities for obesity, cancer, and emergency preparedness, presentation of the concept of the institute, the role of community members and their reaction, next steps, and a proposed meeting schedule.

The group discussion and feedback on the overview of the institute was invaluable. For example, the group decided that more data would be needed to define the specific health disparities to be addressed, to clearly define a baseline of health indicators. This baseline data is necessary to understand if the interventions have made a difference in the research design. Multiple databases will be obtained from local, state, and federal data sources. Also, epidemiological data of specific diseases, diagnosis, treatments, and outcomes will be useful in program planning. Other members made offers to seek funding for support to conduct comprehensive needs assessment at the neighborhood level. The name of the institute was discussed at length. The attendees expressed that the name should reflect how future nurse leaders are trained, and the mission statement should be stronger. Sustainability was also discussed. While the focus initially will be on reducing health disparities in the city of Detroit, the group decided that at a future point, the institute should focus on health disparities in other high-risk population regions outside of the city. The participants were engaged in the discussion and networking and created a synergy that launched the institute into operation.

Institute Programs

Agencies within the institute have agreed on five programmatic areas. Programs and services that cluster in each of these areas will demonstrate our commitment to promoting healthier lives for Detroit residents. The institute will

1. strengthen the public health and community health infrastructure in Detroit
2. evaluate program effectiveness and promotion of best practices in public health
3. identify community health concerns
4. increase access to health care services and reduce health disparities
5. promote healthy behaviors
6. develop informed public policy that highlights and engages nurses

One specific initiative falls under the umbrella of program item 6. Tilson & Gebbie (2004) noted that many challenges face the public health workforce in the areas of professional entry-level education, recruitment, retention of competent staff, and the importance of continuing education. The institute will provide Web-based continuing education to maintain and improve the competencies that support the standards of practice for public health nursing. This will include state-of-the-art curricula on emergency preparedness specifically for nurses.

PERSONAL EXPERIENCE

This project provided me the opportunity to take risks and become creative. Envisioning and articulating this potential change for the future was a significant risk for me and a momentous accomplishment for the Department of

Public Health. Cocreating the institute project transformed the health department as it expanded its nontraditional processes of accomplishing sustainable goals. Articulating the strategic vision in the form of a business plan to the executive leadership at the health department generated receptiveness and fostered the opportunity for this leadership project to become reality. Creating this new institute became a shared vision. This gave me the opportunity to connect broad social, economic, and political changes to further infuse participating institutions with a sense of reinvigoration to make changes in the health of the community and build the groundwork for policy development.

LESSONS ENCOUNTERED/LEARNED

As health care moves into the twenty-first century, I can choose to let things happen or choose to guide and direct the processes of change within the discipline of public health nursing. The process of leadership is just as valuable as the outcome. This project afforded this RWJ fellow an opportunity to work with others to develop a clearer vision of the preferred future and to make that vision happen. To make the institute a reality, I embraced the journey and invested time and energy into applying administrative knowledge and program management experience to manage complex processes in the public health arena.

The first major lesson learned was how to write the business plan, taught by Rashi Glazer in one of the early RWJ seminars. The business plan was a 20-page document that was developed over a 6-month period of time, and the level of detail necessary to write that plan could not be condensed into a few paragraphs in this chapter. Yet preparing that business plan was the initial process of committing the vision to paper and to sharing the vision as a well-thought-out design that gave attention to the realities of market trends, competitors, customers, benefits, and costs.

Dynamic executive leadership, within the health department and at the university, was required to transform this initiative into reality. This executive-level leadership had enough influence over the stakeholders in the process to ensure a high likelihood of success. Support at this level was essential, because the process of establishing an institute crosses many organizational, political, and long-established boundaries. Also, top-level leadership was accountable for the judicious allocation of resources that were necessary for the institute to succeed.

Working with and through systems is a process and leadership skill whereby the leader must know and understand the strengths and challenges of each system and their potential for affecting the outcome. Collaboration is an essential standard of professional performance as outlined in the American

Nurses Association's "Scope and Standards of Public Health Nursing Practice" (1999). Achieving effective collaboration for this project challenged the leader to make time to listen to the planning team members' input and for trust to build within the relationship. The shared decision making that emerged from this process ultimately led to a consensus on the major issues and operations of the institute. This was far preferable, and much more likely to foster success, than if the leader had made decisions in isolation and attempted to move the project forward unilaterally.

Another profound lesson learned was recognizing that the responsibilities of working with and through systems would require the assistance of a consultant. The consultant provided insight, expertise, and another dimension of time to pull all of the information together about the design, the structure, and the interactions of systems processes that may have otherwise stalled due to over-analysis. The consistent dialogue with the Mosaic Group consultant, Marla Oros, was invaluable to this accomplishment.

CONCLUSIONS AND IMPLICATIONS

The RWJ Fellowship made it possible to initiate a change in the health systems of southeast Michigan. By providing the structure, enhancing the knowledge, and guiding me through the fellowship program, I was able to move forward with ideas, overcome the barriers of over-analysis and idealism, and bring to fruition the creation of a CHNI. This institute is now actively addressing health disparities in southeast Michigan and positioning itself to design, implement, and evaluate Web-based curricula for emergency preparedness for RNs.

This institute will facilitate a systematic, broad-based approach to collaboration and communication among private industry, community-based organizations, and governmental entities to improve health disparities in southeast Michigan. This could be a model for leveraging sustainability resources.

REFERENCES

American Nurses Association. (1999). *Scope and standards of public health nursing practice.* Washington, DC: Quad Council of Public Health Nursing Organizations Nurses Publishing.

Blancett, S. S., & Flarey, D. L. (1995). *Reengineering nursing and health care: The handbook for organizational transformation.* Gaithersburg, MD: Aspen Publishers.

Department of Health and Human Services, Centers for Disease Control and Prevention. (2004, January). *Epidemiology and prevention of vaccine preventable diseases* (8th ed.). Washington, DC: Public Health Foundation.

Glazer, R. (2005, October). *The business plan.* RWJ Executive Nurse Fellows Program, Leadership Seminar, San Jose, CA.

Michigan Department of Community Health, Chronic Disease Epidemiology Section, Bureau of Epidemiology. (2005). *Health indicators and risk estimates by community health assessment geographic area and local health departments, Michigan Behavioral Risk Factor Survey (2005).* Retrieved June 20, 2007, from http://www.michigan.gov/brfs

Michigan Department of Community Health Vital Records and Data Development Section. (2007). Retrieved June 20, 2007, from www.michigan.gov/mdch

O'Neil, E. H. (2007). *The leadership compass: Competencies for health care.* Unpublished manuscript, The Center for the Health Professions, University of California, San Francisco.

Stanhope, M., & Lancaster, J. (2000). *Community and public health nursing* (5th ed.). St. Louis, MO: Mosby.

Sternberg, S. (2002, March 21). Study: Racial disparities persist in medicine. *USA Today,* D06.

Taylor, J. R., Beane, G. E., & Genee, C. L. (1998). The Michigan Public Health Institute: A model for university, government and community research and practice partnerships. *SRA Journal/Case Studies* (summer), 17–24.

Tilson, H., & Gebbie, K. M. (2004). The public health workforce. *Annual Review of Public Health, 25,* 341–356.

U.S. Department of Health and Human Services, Office of Civil Rights. (2006). *Racial and Ethnic Health Disparities Power Point Presentation.* Retrieved June 10, 2007, from www.hhs.gov/ocr/healthdisparities.ppt

U.S. Institute of Medicine. (2002, March). *Committee on Understanding and Eliminating Racial and Ethnic Disparities in Health Care. Universal Treatment: What healthcare providers need to know about racial and ethnic disparities in health care.* Washington, DC: The National Academies Press. Retrieved June 15, 2007, from www.nap.edu

U.S. Institute of Medicine. (2002). *Committee on Assuring the Health of the Public in the 21st Century Board on Health Promotion and Disease Prevention. The future of the public's health in the 21st century.* Washington, DC: The National Academies Press. Retrieved June 18, 2007, from www.nap.edu

Williams, J., Chabut, J., Harris-Ellis, B., Edwards, K., Hines, S., Ahmed, F., et al. (2005). *Michigan Department of Community Health: Health disparities impacting racial and ethnic minorities in Michigan.* Retrieved June 15, 2007, from www.michigan.gov/mdch/healthdisparitiesinmichigan

Yoder-Wise, P. S. (2003). *Leading and managing in nursing* (3rd ed.). St. Louis, MO: Mosby.

CHAPTER 6

Personal

Jeannie K. Hanna

A retired leader in his or her rocking chair thinks not about wealth or positions held or titles earned, but about memories of people successfully mentored and developed.

—Michael Feiner

OVERVIEW

Occupational health nursing began as industrial nursing in nineteenth-century Great Britain and paralleled the rapid growth of industry (Salazar, 2006). The foundation of occupational health nursing is based on the concepts and principles of public health practice. Public health nurses were actually the first nurses who worked in manufacturing, department stores, and mines. They provided community health for employees and their families. Their focus was on preventing and treating communicable diseases (Salazar, 2006). In the last few decades, the occupational health nursing practice has expanded and evolved into a highly specialized field with major emphasis on health promotion and prevention of illness and injuries in worker populations and on role expansion in clinical education, entrepreneurial management and research areas (Rogers, 1994).

Comprehensive health and safety programs include programs that impact health and productivity of employees, such as injury/illness prevention programs, wellness interventions, and disease management programs. Also included in comprehensive programs are medical surveillance programs mandated by Occupational Safety and Health Administration (OSHA) standards such as hearing and respiratory protection. These programs are designed to protect and improve work-related and non–work-related health for employees, retirees, and their families (Salazar, 2006). These programs are designed to assist employees in promoting health, preventing illness, detecting disease at its earliest stages and rehabilitation (Wachs & Parker-Conrad, 1990).

The occupational health nurse plays a primary role in helping employees attain their maximum level of health and improving overall employee productivity. Many occupational health nurses provide health care at the work site—whether at a manufacturing site, an office setting, or a health care institution. The occupational health nurse must understand the different types of work sites, the expectations and needs of the employer, and the company philosophy and culture, along with the regulatory requirements that govern occupational health and safety (Salazar, 2006). It is also critical to understand business trends and how these may impact the work environment.

Occupational health nurses must provide leadership to set strategy, implement programs, and evaluate the outcomes as they relate to employee health and safety. As businesses seek new solutions to the continued increase in health care costs, leadership skills are critical for occupational health nurses in order to maintain, promote, and restore employee health and to positively affect the corporate bottom line.

Management's goal for developing or maintaining occupational health and safety programs is often to contain costs. According to the American Association of Occupational Health Nurses (2007), as health care benefit costs are increasing at an unprecedented rate, businesses must focus on long-term strategies instead of short-term fixes for immediate health care needs. A long-term strategy for corporate success must include provisions for keeping healthy employees healthy, improving the health status of all employees, and creating a company culture that supports, promotes and actively engages employees in achieving optimal health (AAOHN, 2007).

Average employer health care costs rise at an annual rate of 15%. U.S. employers typically pay 8%–11% of payroll on unscheduled absences. This includes both direct costs (salary continuation, insurance premiums, and disability benefits) and indirect costs (overtime work, temporary help, and lost productivity).

> Obesity and overweight conditions contribute as much as $93 billion to the nation's yearly medical bill, according to studies reviewed by the National Business Group on Health, a Washington, D.C.-based non-profit organization that represents large companies. Of that amount, the total cost of

obesity to U.S. companies is estimated at more than $13 billion per year—a price tag that includes $8 billion for added health insurance costs, $2.3 billion for paid sick leave, $1.8 billion for life insurance and $1 billion for disability insurance. According to recent studies on the economic cost of workplace obesity, that translates into 39 million lost work days, 239 million days where work activity is restricted, 90 million sick days or days in bed and 63 million visits to physicians. (Efforts are Growing, 2006)

Health conditions caused by lifestyle choices and health and safety problems have a significant impact on a company's bottom line. Each company must identify these conditions by analyzing their own data from health care, pharmacy, disability, workers' compensation, and absenteeism and then design benefits and wellness programs that are targeted to address these conditions. The health of employees is critical to overall business success. Protecting employee health and safety from adverse effects from the work environment, and helping employees to make healthy lifestyle behavioral changes will drive company profits. Companies that focus on the value of human capital understand improved health yields greater productivity. Companies that focus on systematic population health management can improve workers' health and performance. Over time, wellness programs can positively impact absenteeism, presenteeism (people who are present at work), and lifestyle-related health claims.

The best-performing companies utilize data and metrics to drive programs and have senior management support of integration of all programs that support employee health, including benefits, disability, workers' compensation, human resource policies, operations, legal issues, information technology, health services, wellness, and safety. These companies utilize health outcomes and lost workdays more frequently than return on investment calculations as a basis for their purchasing decisions and design of programs that support health and productivity.

The occupational health nurse leader has a unique opportunity to provide tremendous value within the complex business environment that companies face today. The nurse leader can assist the employer today with integration of critical data and metrics, development of standards, protocols, and methodologies to effectively measure and evaluate program cost effectiveness and quality outcomes. Ultimately, the goal is to validate the relationship between health, productivity, and health status by documenting a return on human capital investment. According to findings of The Executive Survey of Workplace Safety (AAOHN, 2007), close to 95% of business executives report that workplace safety has a positive impact on the company's financial performance. Of these executives, 61% report their companies receive a return on investment (ROI) of $3 or more for each $1 they invest in improving workplace safety. Figure 6.1 helps to illustrate the concepts of investment in prevention along with integration of processes and actions, which leads to improved performance for employees and the company's bottom line.

A CASE STUDY

I began my occupational health nursing career after several years in more traditional health care settings including the hospital and physician clinics. During the first 8 years of my career as a nurse, I worked in the clinical areas of psychiatry, alcohol and drug abuse, medical-surgical, and ophthalmology. I took my first position in occupational health nursing as the nurse at a large manufacturing plant as I was completing my masters program in nursing administration. My development as an occupational health nursing leader began in that first plant setting. I learned about health and safety, production schedules, organizational culture, and how critical it is to help employees become and stay healthy.

For the past 13 years, I have held various corporate roles with several different employers. I have led the development and implementation of global occupational health programs that were focused on regulatory compliance and company requirements. I have led teams in designing occupational health programs for employee populations in manufacturing, the airline industry, sales organizations, and for migrant workers in agricultural settings. The teams I have been responsible for have developed and implemented a corporate risk management program and worked on integration of disability programs. All of these experiences have prepared me for my current role. I am now the Director of Integrated Health and Productivity for The Hershey Company and am a part of a very progressive and innovative benefit organization.

I moved into this new position and was charged with leading the organization in development and implementation of a comprehensive health and productivity initiative. Efforts to build a foundation for a health and productivity culture had been undertaken in the past. There was some skepticism that the current initiatives would not be any more successful than those tried in the past. My challenge was to motivate the team so this time the initiative would be successful. I began this project by first assessing the current environment and then making recommendations to move forward.

Based on my prior leadership experiences, I believed the best approach to take was to utilize a strategic planning model. Time was spent first in reviewing the work that had been undertaken in the past. I interviewed staff who had been involved in the earlier efforts, analyzed prior documents and presentations on recommendations for a health and productivity program,

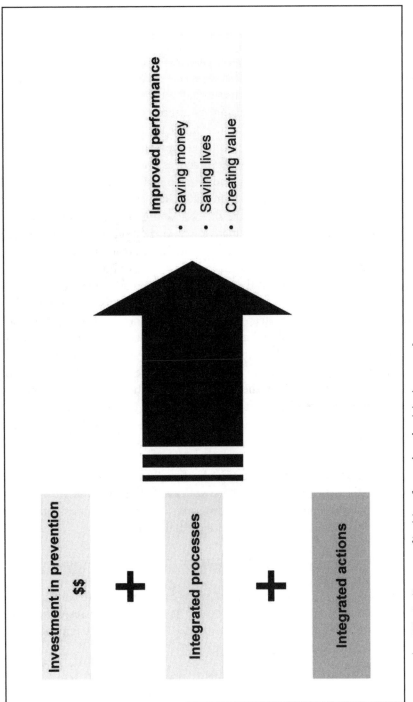

FIGURE 6.1 Why is alignment of health, safety, and productivity important?

benchmarked externally with colleagues and organizations that had been successful with building health and productivity programs, and solicited the help of an outside benefits consultant.

After reviewing the U.S. historical data, we assessed the status of the current disability, risk management, benefits, and occupational health and safety programs at our company locations throughout the United States by utilizing a survey that was sent to key customers at each location. We reviewed the corporate vision so we could make sure our health and productivity programs would be aligned to support the overall business strategies. After benchmarking our own data against industry best practices, we were able to begin formulating recommendations for design and implementation of strategies to build a health, safety, and productivity team within The Hershey Company.

Our next step was to define the purpose and expected outcomes for our health, safety, and productivity initiative. The current organizational structure for health and safety is decentralized. Through the creation of an integrated, cross-functional team we could focus all our strategies on improving health, safety, and productivity across the organization. A broad, integrated approach would provide synergies of managing programs across disciplines and effective use of resources. The team approach would help create a process for streamlining decision making around initiatives that involve multiple disciplines. It would represent a team versus a discipline-specific approach.

The next important step involved engagement of senior management to support moving forward with this new strategy for health, safety, and productivity. Several discussions and presentations were held with the key stakeholders, the Chief People Officer, and the Senior Vice President of Global Operations, who both report directly to the CEO. Senior management support is critical to the success of such a broad undertaking. The support was obtained and the Health, Safety and Productivity team was officially launched.

Prior to the first team meeting, I met with each of the proposed team members to review the mission of the team and the overall composition of the team. The mission of the team includes the following:

- Enhance the health and safety of the work environment for our employees.
- Advance proactive health and safety as a Hershey core value.
- Streamline and strengthen health and safety processes, letting the process improvements drive needed resource levels and organizational structure.
- Improve performance through consistency, best practices, and a common preventive strategic plan for health, safety, benefits, and risk management, which will result in:

- better compliance
- more effective risk control
- competitive advantage
- lower costs
- improved health and productivity

Figure 6.2 depicts the membership of the Health, Safety and Productivity team and outlines the areas of responsibility of each team member. The cross-functional team members represent:

- Environmental Affairs and Safety
- Benefits
- Health Services
- Information Services
- Human Resources and Employee Relations
- Risk Management

As the Director of Integrated Health and Productivity, I have responsibility as the team leader. The senior leadership for the team includes the vice president for Total Compensation and Benefits, the vice president for Quality and Regulatory Compliance, the vice president and global Chief Customer Officer, and the Vice President for Manufacturing in North America—all appointed officers of the company. The executive champions for the team include the Chief People Officer and Senior Vice President for Global Operations. Additional team resources that are consulted on an as-needed basis include Human Resources Policy, Communications, Legal, and Security. The time spent getting to know the key stakeholders was time well spent. By achieving their buy-in up front, it will help when there are tough issues that need to be addressed. It also helps to establish credibility and trust.

To build consensus within the team, the first two meetings were led by Human Resource professionals skilled in organizational development and team building. During these sessions, the team established a set of ground rules to govern how we would treat each other and how we would work together as a team. Because our individual goals were already established for the year, we reviewed each team member's individual goals to ensure we were aligned within the team mission, team objectives, and strategies to achieve each objective of the team. The objectives and strategies for the team are outlined in Table 6.1.

Once the team was aligned with the mission, purpose, objectives, and strategies we began work on developing a set of goals for 2007 and metrics

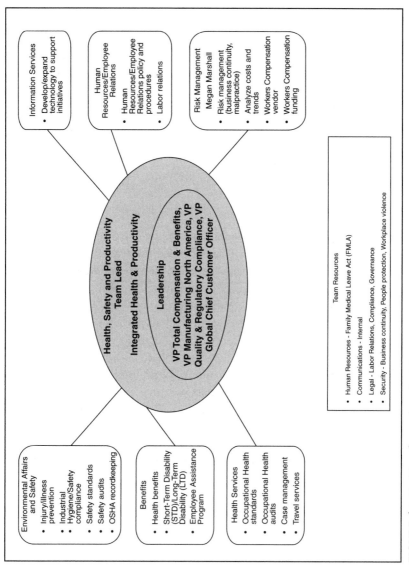

FIGURE 6.2 Health, safety, and productivity team.

TABLE 6.1 Objectives and Strategies

Focus strategies on prevention and improving health and productivity.	Develop global strategic plan for health & safety. Identify resources and skills required across the organization. Focus benefits and health promotion on prevention, education, and well-being.
Drive accountability across organization.	Establish a core value related to health & safety. Create a mechanism to drive accountability through performance management process and incentives at all levels. Embrace international and industry standards for global health & safety excellence beyond compliance. Build a benefits platform that rewards participation and healthy lifestyle choices.
Ensure consistency and compliance globally.	Develop and implement global health & safety standards. Create procedures, guidelines and tools that are region specific. Execute a global audit program across disciplines Foster networks of health & safety professionals across the company to support regional projects and promote sharing of best practices.
Drive efficient, effective management across organization.	Conduct risk/hazard assessment of all job tasks. Identify priority gaps to be addressed. Build a centralized absence management program to track all types of absences for salaried and hourly employees. Develop and implement Information Services systems that: enable common core business processes while supporting regional requirements; produce enterprise-wide performance metrics; facilitate communication between health & safety professionals and line and senior management; deliver cost-effective and targeted health & safety programs; Drive performance through health & safety scorecard

for measuring our progress. We are working on global standardization of all policies, procedures, and processes to

- ensure consistency across all Hershey locations
- ensure compliance with local regulatory and company requirements
- ensure systematic management of health and safety.

Our 2007 initiatives include:

- minimizing the effects of our company's reorganization on health, safety, and productivity by developing a checklist to help locations manage dramatic changes such as downsizing and closing of plants
- leading development of a company core value on health and safety
- development of a corporate scorecard for health, safety, and productivity that is consolidated across all parts of the business, is global, and shows historical trends
- lead development and implementation of a global tobacco-free workplace policy
- lead development and implementation of programs that support reducing the number of occupational incidents and workers' compensation costs

We are leading the strategies to build a company culture where health and safety will not be compromised and where our programs are sustainable. We are benchmarking with the "best in class" companies. Experience from other companies that have undertaken a health, safety, and productivity approach demonstrates that we are embarking on a 3–5 year journey to ingrain the culture, change processes, and see significant improvement in our results.

At our first quarterly meeting with senior management and our executive champions, we reviewed the process that we went through to focus our collective energy on projects and programs that will drive improvements in health and safety. We discussed that today with the senior management commitment and the shared vision of this cross-functional team, we now have the focus that our company needs on health, safety, and productivity. Our manufacturing and sales organizations are applying the correct diagnostics, such as proactive training, auditing, and supervisor and plant manager focus, along with needed corrective actions such as holding individuals accountable for health and safety through discipline for violations of policy and actively engaging employees so they better understand unsafe and unhealthy behaviors. This team is very passionate and committed to making a difference. As a team we will drive the results for the company by developing programs, procedures, and tools to help our locations deliver sustainable results. The focus of all our efforts during this first year is building a company culture that is the foundation for our long-term results in health, safety, and productivity.

LESSON LEARNED

So what have I learned from my occupational health nursing journey? I've learned becoming a true leader takes a lifetime of learning and growing. The process begins with developing self-knowledge and awareness about who you are, what you value, what drives you, and what you are passionate about. Once you understand self, then you can begin to effectively lead others.

An effective leader provides direction to the team by identifying where we have been, what are the challenges for today, and what does the future looks like. The leader of a high-performance team must be able to translate the purpose and vision of a project into a picture that appeals to the heart and mind of each team member so there is consensus among the team players about a shared vision for the organization. This was accomplished through the initial one-on-one meetings that I had with the team members and key stakeholders.

Leadership involves supporting, motivating, and mentoring others so they can develop their own self-awareness. Great leaders believe in the abilities of others and leverage the strengths of others to help the team accomplish their collective goals. A quote from Ken Blanchard holds true—"none of us is as smart as all of us" (Blanchard, 1999).

Leaders must be able to set a strategy and build the case from a business perspective. Timing is everything to the success of a project or program. An effective leader can "read" the organizational climate and knows when the environment can and will be supportive of a new project. The ability to know when to move forward and when to be patient and wait is a critical success factor of a true leader. Keeping the team motivated during the waiting period is also a key skill. Knowing how difficult it had been in the past trying to move this initiative forward, I knew that this project would not be successful if I did not pay attention to the organization's readiness for change and at the same time keep the team connected and believing that this time we would be successful.

CONCLUSIONS AND IMPLICATIONS

Throughout my professional career I have been fortunate to be able to utilize my nursing knowledge in a variety of nursing roles—both traditional and nontraditional. My early clinical experiences led me to the specialty of occupational health, where I've spent the majority of my nursing career. My roles in occupational health have all been diverse. My first position was as a traditional occupational health nurse delivering direct care and health education, and ensuring regulatory compliance for health and safety in a manufacturing plant. I then led the development and implementation of a start-up occupational health program within a large hospital system. This new program delivered clinical occupational health services for local employers and provided contract nurses at the work site for employers. From managing and marketing these services, I next moved into a corporate role where I was the lead health care professional responsible for setting corporate policy and ensuring compliance for occupational health globally for 60,000 employees. From this role with a manufacturer of medical products to an entrepreneurial company setting up clinics for an airline to other corporate roles in the chemical, pharmaceutical, agricultural, automotive, and food industries, my nursing skills have been the foundation for my leadership development. I've learned how to think and act strategically, make high-level decisions, implement complex projects, influence others, communicate effectively, problem solve, and deliver health care through benefit design. My personal journey has taught me the value of enhancing and understanding my leadership skills so I can help influence the health of people—the core of public health nursing.

Being an avid reader and constant learner on leadership, I recently stumbled upon a book that captured the heart and soul of what I believe is key to being a leader. The book is called *The Velveteen Principles—A Guide to Becoming Real*. The book is based upon the journey for the Velveteen Rabbit in Margery William's enduring fable. The book really hit home for me as the legacy that I hope to leave behind.

> If you become more *Real* in your own life and bring that to your relationships, you are practically guaranteed to leave behind an inspiring example for others. Your life's message will encourage everyone you touch to live with a sense of wonder, curiosity and openness, rather than cynicism and fear. It will say, "I was *Real*. And you can be *Real*, too." (Raiten-D'Antonio, 2004)

When asked what I do for a living, I often hear the response "so you're not a real nurse now." I proudly respond "yes, *I am still a nurse!*" I am a nurse who combines my training, experiences, knowledge, skills, and leadership to improve people's health. Occupational health nursing requires a leader that can translate the language of health into the language of business. I've been blessed with both nursing and business leaders and with parents who have seen the potential in me that I could not often see myself and have given me opportunities and direction that have stretched me beyond my comfort zone. They've believed in me and challenged me to develop and understand my own personal leadership skills, to take risks, to be adaptable, to trust my instincts, to believe in others, to be courageous, to find my voice, and to believe in my dreams! My passion is nursing and yes, I'll always be a NURSE!

REFERENCES

AAOHN publishes business case for OHNs—Report highlights profession's value to employers. (2007, June). *AAOHN News, 28*(6). p. 1.

Blanchard, K. (1999). *The heart of a leader.* Tulsa, OK: Honor Books.

Efforts are growing to trim the fat from employees—And employers' health care costs. (2006, November 1). Retrieved January 4, 2008, from http://knowledge.wharton.upenn.edu

Feiner, M. (2004). *The Feiner points of leadership: The fifty basic laws that will make people want to perform better for you.* New York: Warner Business Books.

Raiten-D'Antonio, T. (2004). *The velveteen principles—A guide to becoming real.* Deerfield Beach, FL: Health Communications, Inc.

Rogers, B. (1994). *Occupational health nursing—Concepts and practice.* Philadelphia: W. B. Saunders Company.

Salazar, M. K. (Ed.). (2006). *AAOHN core curriculum for occupational and environmental health nursing* (3rd ed.). Philadelphia: W. B. Saunders Company.

Wachs, J. E., & Parker-Conrad, J. E. (1990). Occupational health nursing in 1990 and the coming decade. *Applied Occupational and Environmental Hygiene, 5*(4), 200–204.

PART III

Leadership in the Education Industry

Current Issues in the Education Industry

Linda Thompson Adams and Edward H. O'Neil

Nursing education, traditionally, has operated as an independent entity. Standards are set and accredited based on an academic platform rather than a practical one. Yes, clinical practice is a component and new nurses must show competency in their skills, but overall the way in which nurses are educated needs to be restructured in order to properly prepare nurses for the 21st century and satisfy the current and future needs of health care organizations.

Currently, there exists a disconnect between nursing education programs at the university and the needs of hospitals and health care organizations. It has become increasingly more apparent that leadership representatives from both the academic and health care arenas need to engage in discussions and commit to achieving cohesiveness of skills and knowledge to ensure that the required competencies for clinical practice are mastered in the educational setting. Working together with hospital personnel, nurse educators can develop coursework and simulation scenarios to mirror real-life issues and patient complications. Collaborating on the design and development of nursing education ensures that nurses will be better suited to fit into the hospital environment and increases the safety of both patient and health care workers.

Collaboration, as simple as it may appear, is anything but and requires respect and consideration of internal and external forces which tend to hamper its progress towards achieving set goals. As health care needs change, universities strive to provide programs to meet these demands and are faced with a continuously burdensome shortage of faculty. Universities compete with the very same health care organizations they aim to serve for qualified individuals to teach in their programs. However, due to funding restraints, they are unable to match salaries and there is little or no incentive for nurses to become full-time faculty. Furthermore, there are even fewer prepared nurses who possess the skills and techniques necessary to become teachers of their profession in an academic setting.

Hospital organizations have their own hurdles and complexities which impede progress towards accomplishing collaborative objectives. It is difficult for hospital leaders to assess future needs when they are already facing a shortage of nursing staff. Many nurses are required to work overtime, which puts both patient and nurse safety at risk. Attrition rates for nurses in their first year are alarming and as positions become vacant, current nursing staff is shuffled around to fill in the gaps, which in turn causes job dissatisfaction and adds to the initial problem to be solved.

Revamping nursing programs is crucial to the success of collaborative efforts and transitioning nursing students to nursing professionals. One of the key areas to examine when reorganizing nursing education programs is the way in which students are taught. Over the past three decades, extensive research has been conducted to identify which teaching methods are most effective and coincide with optimal student learning potentials. Studies on conventional didactic teaching methods have been shown to be less effective than alternative interactive approaches. Typical teaching styles that merely pass on information are not very effective because much of the knowledge is not retained long-term. It is more about rote memorization than reaching a level of true understanding for the material and then being able to apply the knowledge and put concepts into practice.

Alternative interactive approaches to teaching involve engaging students in hands-on activities or by utilizing simulation learning management systems which allow for a real-life application and an opportunity for students to experience a clinical setting and practice mastering specific skills. This, in turn, reduces the potential of putting patient safety and well-being at risk when students enter the workforce. Simply reading about scenarios or being lectured to in a classroom does not provide students with the same knowledge and understanding as having participated in an engaging activity or hands-on situation.

Technology is driving the future of health care and nurses must be familiar with informatics and equipment. Introduction of such advanced technology begins at the university level and is becoming an integral part of how nurses are educated. Health care organizations benefit from divulging information to universities as to which direction their technological adaptations will flow.

Nurse educators in universities and administrators in health care organizations have a shared responsibility to work together to develop and implement a comprehensive nursing education curriculum. The disconnect between the two must be remedied and the barriers to a successful collaboration addressed if the current tide of faculty and nursing shortages is to be shifted. The problem has reached a pivotal point and each brings its own strengths and contributions necessary to balance the burden and begin to move in a more positive and productive direction.

CHAPTER 7

Purpose

Janis P. Bellack and Jeanette Ives Erickson

Without purpose we would not exist. It is purpose that defines . . . and purpose that binds us.

The Matrix Reloaded, 2003

A SENSE OF PURPOSE

Without purpose, nursing education would exist in a vacuum, unclear about why or to what end it exists. A sense of purpose is essential for creating a context of meaning and direction for nursing education, guiding intentionality, and serving as both beacon and benchmark.

In his recent book, *A Larger Sense of Purpose,* Shapiro opines that "universities, like other social institutions . . . ought to serve interests that include but move beyond narrow self-serving concerns. The . . . Latin phrase *non nobis solum,* 'not for ourselves alone,' echoes this thought" (2007, p. 13). Both higher education and health care systems espouse a commitment to serving the broader interests of community and society, but as Shapiro but notes, "this is one of those ideas that, while applauded in principle, is easily lost in the challenge of meeting one's day-to-day responsibilities. This makes it even more important to pause once in a while to adjust our sails and correct our course."

Being clear about purpose and staying true to and on course with it requires continual mindfulness about why individuals and organizations engage in a given endeavor. For nursing education, clarity about and commitment to the purposes of both higher education and health care are essential. In fact, the purpose of nursing education must connect with the purposes of both higher education and health care, each reinforcing the other. For example, if one of the purposes of nursing education is to prepare a well-qualified nursing workforce to meet the public's need for high-quality nursing care, then the impact of meeting the public's need for that care reaffirms and sustains one of nursing education's core purposes.

The Dual Context of Higher Education and Health Care

As a higher education enterprise with an overarching duty to serve a public purpose, nursing education has specific aims to prepare new graduates to enter the profession, to contribute to the body of nursing knowledge through research, and to serve the community through application of knowledge through nursing practice for the ultimate purpose of improving health and health care of the public. As such, nursing education's purpose also is shaped by the overarching purpose of health care to improve the health of the public through effective systems of care delivery. Because nursing education operates within these dual systems of higher education and health care, academic nurse leaders and nurse educators must be familiar with and ever mindful of the respective purposes of each. To pay heed to only one or the other would compromise the purpose of nursing education, which must of necessity be responsive to the broad, sometimes overlapping, sometimes conflicting, purposes of higher education and health care.

Both higher education and health care, as well as nursing education, espouse a purpose of human betterment and share a vision of improving the quality of life and well-being for all. In particular, higher education advocates educational preparation for work and citizenship, the development and transfer of knowledge to enhance economic development and global competitiveness, and service outreach to improve the quality of life in the community and society. Its primary reasons for being are learning and the development and exploration of ideas. Although higher education's end goal is increasingly becoming more instrumental—preparing knowledgeable, skilled workers and contributing to economic and social development—colleges and universities continue to preserve as well—at least in the core arts and sciences disciplines—their historical commitment to learning and knowledge development for their own sake, absent a need for application to solving real world problems.

Health care, on the other hand, has as its espoused primary purpose the delivery of high-quality, accessible, and affordable care to improve the health of communities and reduce the economic burden of illness. In the case of for-profit sectors of both higher education and health care, a further purpose is continuous economic growth and payoff for investors, with the "purer" goal of learning or knowledge for its own sake as secondary or nonexistent. Nursing education, as a practice discipline, is most closely aligned with the applied purpose of higher education, and the service purpose of health care.

Higher education today is bombarded by multiple forces, the vast majority of which also affect nursing education. These forces impinge on and can divert attention from nursing education's core purposes. Specifically, nursing education is faced continually with expectations for adding more and more to the curriculum, including such areas as genetics, quality improvement, disaster preparedness, geriatrics, alternative and complementary therapies, and public policy, among others, on top of an already burdened curriculum. The impact of technology on program delivery through e-learning, simulation, and clinical information and management systems has been profound, and the emergence of for-profit and corporate universities is addressing consumer demand for education that is accessible, timely, convenient, and in a growing number of instances, customized. Nursing education also faces a myriad of student issues, including often inadequate precollegiate preparation for a nursing curriculum that is increasingly complex and rigorous, generational differences between students and faculty and between students and employers, the need to recruit and retain a more diverse faculty and student body, student resistance to a growing emphasis on learning "how to learn" in place of acquiring content-specific knowledge for immediate application, and often litigious responses to unwelcome academic decisions.

Nurse educators themselves are faced with an array of ever-increasing expectations and stressors, including changing teaching methodologies ("guide on the side" versus "sage on the stage"), use of new technologies for teaching and learning, a push for research and scholarship supported by external funding, the need to remain current with the profession and education in general while developing a specialized program of scholarship, salary inequities compared with the practice sector, and a serious faculty shortage created by aging of the nursing professoriate and more attractive opportunities outside of academia for nurses with advanced degrees.

Further, the historic commitment of higher education to certain core values, including shared governance; critical, and often lengthy, inquiry; and collaborative decision making often conflicts with the needs and expectations of health care to meet its own purpose of care delivery through the rapid production and development of a skilled workforce. Nursing education finds itself having to balance these conflicting contexts, and its purpose must reflect a commitment to both.

Fundamentally, the overarching purpose of nursing education is to prepare cadres of learners to enter the profession as competent beginning practitioners of nursing and educated citizens of a global world, and to do so for the ultimate benefit of the public. However, this purpose will vary among and be guided by the nature of particular institutions in which nursing education takes place. Such differences as public versus private; secular versus religious; not-for-profit versus profit-driven; type of institution—liberal arts, comprehensive, research-intensive, or specialized; as well as local and regional contexts, will shape the purpose of both the nursing education organizational entity and the individuals who work within it. Goodness of fit, or lack of it, between the organization's purpose and the individual's commitment to it will determine to a greater or lesser degree the success of the organization in achieving its purpose. To be successful, the majority of nurse educators who are part of the nursing education unit must agree with its purpose and operate in ways consistent with that purpose.

Further, while all nursing education entities—programs, departments, schools—share a common purpose to prepare the next generation of nurses and to serve both their institutions and their communities, differences exist with respect to the degree of emphasis placed on the traditional three-fold mission of colleges and universities, namely, teaching, research, and service. Teaching, even in research-driven institutions, is still the primary purpose of colleges and universities, especially in the eyes of the public and taxpayers. Increasingly, the teaching mission is undergoing change, shifting from an instructional model to a learning model, with new modes of delivery emerging at a rapid pace. At the same time, traditional notions of research as discovery are giving way to broadened definitions of scholarship that embrace integration, application, engagement, and teaching forms of scholarship (Boyer, 1990).

The service purpose of nursing education is shaped by the broader institutional mission. Invariably, service includes service to the institution, typically shared governance, and committee work, but may also involve outreach service to the community, service to the nursing profession at the association or organizational level, and increasingly, service in the form of clinical practice, including the delivery of nursing services by the nursing education unit itself, often in nurse-managed centers or affiliated community-based settings.

In sum, purpose is the *why* of nursing education, its *raison d'etre*. When faced with new opportunities, a clear sense of purpose enables the academic nurse leader to decide whether to proceed, and often, how to proceed. For example, if an institution's purpose is to prepare nurses and other health professionals at the graduate level, while the local health care delivery sector is demanding more entry level RNs, the response to a request to establish an accelerated BSN program for post-baccalaureate applicants must be made with consideration of the overall purpose of the institution and its existing commitments that were made to reflect that purpose. The institution may decide to reaffirm its purpose of preparing nurses and other health professionals solely at the graduate level and decide against offering undergraduate preparation, or conversely, may revisit and redefine or modify its purpose to incorporate the preparation of nurses at the post-baccalaureate level. Failure to revisit and reaffirm or modify the institution's purpose prior to deciding what types of programs to offer decouples purpose from process and renders meaningless the institution's espoused reason for being.

The Effective Academic Leader: Grounded in Purpose

The effective academic nurse leader understands the need for a clear purpose in building on what has come before, facing the challenges of today, projecting where to go in the future, and inspiring and motivating others to join. The effective academic leader helps others to continually link their work to the broader vision and purpose of that work—for example, not simply teaching classes and supervising students, or engaging in research and publication, or serving the institution, profession, or community—but being continually mindful of the reasons, or purposes, that give both direction and meaning to these aspects of the educator's role. Thus, teaching is linked to the preparation of the next generation of practicing nurses to meet the public's need for high-quality nursing care, research is guided by the institutional goals of expanding nursing knowledge to improve the public's health while also advancing the worth and reputation of the institution and the individual researcher, and service focuses on serving the internal governance and development needs of the institution as well as giving back to the local community to improve their health and health care, while also advancing the contributions of the nursing profession to benefit society. Thus, preparing new graduates, expanding nursing knowledge, meeting the institution's operating needs, engaging in community service, and advancing the nursing profession all share in common the larger purpose of improving the health of individuals, families, communities, and society.

The role of the nursing education leader is to clearly and compellingly articulate the nursing education unit's as well as the broader institution's purpose along with the core values that give meaning and direction to that purpose. The effective leader is able to create a clear sense of where the institution or program has been and where it is going, and in so doing, motivate the faculty and staff to willingly and enthusiastically join the leader in helping the institution fulfill its purpose in a continually evolving way.

The effective academic nurse leader must have a broad understanding of both higher education and health care, as well as nursing education, and be well versed in the current state of their contexts and knowledgeable about the trends that are likely to affect their shared and independent purposes, in both foreseeable and distant futures. In today's rapidly shifting environments, this is not an easy task. A clear sense of purpose, however, provides a guidepost for sustaining both focus and commitment, which in turn assists the academic leader in making decisions consistent with that purpose.

Purpose, however, is a necessary but insufficient guidepost for operating within today's resource-constrained environment of nursing education. Purpose answers the why but not the what or how for the academic nurse leader. Unfortunately, nursing education today continues to be governed by traditional paradigms, typically pursuing solutions that require more resources rather than engaging in efforts to imagine new possibilities, redefine what must be learned and how it must be learned, reallocate existing resources, and develop new tools and techniques to maximize both capacity and desired outcomes. Nursing education programs look suspiciously upon each other as competition for scarce resources rather than focusing their efforts on creating a synergistic scenario of sufficiency for all, in which their common purpose along with a commitment to sharing resources—with each other and to and from their clinical partners—allow for new forms of nursing education and student learning to be designed, tested, modified, and continually improved.

The context in which nursing education currently finds itself—one of growing nursing workforce shortages and an even more critical nursing faculty shortage—calls for redefining purpose from the narrow perspective of individual institutions to the broader one of responding to societal needs. It also calls for engaging in strategic thinking and action to create new scenarios of nursing education and practice, and new—and different—partnerships to achieve the profession's shared purpose of a well-qualified nursing workforce to meet the public's health care needs.

Even if nursing education programs double or triple their current enrollments, projected demands for nurses in the current health care system will not be met. Such projections assume the continued delivery of nursing care and the continued education of nursing students as they are, instead of as they might be. Relying on a status quo forecasting model will not get the profession where it needs to go to respond effectively to societal needs. Rather, effective academic and practice leaders must envision—and try out—new models of both education and practice in ways that are complementary and synergistic.

While clarity of purpose is necessary to guide effective academic and practice leaders, corresponding innovations in strategy and action also are necessary; without them, neither education nor practice will advance. In the education arena, this calls for rethinking current assumptions about what is needed, that is, more faculty, more clinical sites, and more resources to meet the demand for more graduates. Such assumptions mask the fact that a clear purpose guides not only what to do—produce an adequately prepared nursing workforce to care for the public's health needs—but how to do it, and specifically, how to do it in more effective and efficient ways. A clear sense of purpose enables focus on more than producing the greatest number of nurses in the shortest time possible. Rather, purpose ensures that the knowledge, skills, and values needed for the delivery of safe, competent, and high-quality nursing care to individuals and groups guide not only the why, but the what and how of nursing education. A clear sense of purpose pushes the thinking about scarcity of faculty, clinical sites, and fiscal resources in a new—and entirely different—direction.

Barriers to Transformation

Certainly there are barriers that work against such strategic thinking and transformational change. Perhaps the greatest barrier is the institutional inertia and snail's-pace decision making that characterize higher education, made worse by a labyrinth of rules and regulations for enacting change. Regulatory barriers, especially the regulations that govern the approval of nursing education programs at the state level, are especially onerous.

The historic chasm between nursing education and nursing practice that began with the shift of nursing education to colleges and universities—a necessary move to advance the profession but one with unanticipated and unintended costs to the critical link between educators and practitioners—has created an unwieldy system of nursing education in which nurse educators by and large are visitors to the clinical setting rather than an integral part of it, often to the detriment of student learning.

Revisioning the Future

Despite these barriers, opportunities exist for rethinking—and retrying—the way nursing education is organized, structured, and delivered. In 1997, Norris offered a visionary look into the future for higher education, positing revolutionary strategies for the knowledge age of the twenty-first century. A full decade later, most of mainstream higher education and nursing education remain at what Norris (1997) calls the misleading leading edge (a "quality era"), an era in which the focus is on information, characterized by technology that is not seamless or coherent, curriculum and learning structures and processes that offer only modest alterations of traditional ones, and purpose that is driven by competition rather than collaboration. At the misleading leading edge, there is overemphasis on analysis rather than vision, incrementalism instead of transformation, and strategic planning instead of strategic thinking and action.

Instead, the effective and purpose-driven leader must create a vision of the future by thinking in future tense: imagining what might be, engaging in continual strategic thinking and action, projecting a range of simultaneous possible scenarios, thinking of success as a variety of possible futures rather than a single preferred future, and positioning for next steps instead of attaining specified goals (Norris, 1997). As Norris notes, "The only way a learning enterprise can establish a sense of relative assurance is to develop competencies that allow it to take advantage of emerging opportunities before others do" (p. 13). He goes on to say that "no single path or . . . strategy will do" (p. 13).

The effective nurse leader, whether in education or practice, must be able to engage multiple others in creating alternatives to current educational structures and practices. Such strategic alliances will be essential in the future for addressing both workforce and faculty shortages and will require strong leadership to convince nurse educators to let go of the notion that nursing education must be the controlling partner and that nurse educators know best what students need to learn to become competent beginning practitioners.

Effective academic nurse leaders engage themselves and their constituents in continuous strategic thinking, not once-a-year or once-every-five-years strategic planning. They encourage faculty, staff, students, clinical partners, advisory boards, and other strategic partners to "continually question the assumptions about the future that emerge" from ongoing strategic thinking (Norris, 1997, p. 10). Using Norris's paradigm, effective nurse leaders find ways to consider, create, and test a range of possible futures through such avenues as:

- convening the program's best thinkers to engage in imaginative thinking about alternative futures for nursing education, and challenging them to think beyond existing structures and processes
- constructing possible scenarios of what the future might look like
- engaging a broad range of stakeholders in dialogue about the possible scenarios and involving them in "participatory strategy setting"
- building capacity by developing needed competencies and overcoming barriers to change
- deciding on and launching new initiatives, capitalizing on those aspects most amenable to experimentation and change (instead of attempting to change the entire program or academic culture)
- redesigning or redirecting existing processes to support the new initiatives
- reallocating existing resources to support the new initiatives while also securing the investment of new resources, especially from strategic alliances

A CASE STUDY

Given the opportunity to establish a new baccalaureate degree program, consistent with the vision and purpose of the educational institution's mission to prepare leaders for sustainable careers in health care, Massachusetts College of Pharmacy and Health Sciences (MCPHS) initially reached out to chief nurse executives in several of the Boston health care systems to ascertain their interest in partnering with the college to design a program and curriculum that would prepare new graduates for both contemporary and future nursing practice. With concerns expressed by other area nursing programs about a shortage of faculty and capacity constraints in clinical settings, MCPHS wanted to ensure there was both interest and capacity on the part of potential clinical partners. The reception was enthusiastic, accompanied by expressions of surprise at being invited to cocreate the program, gratitude for being included from the start of the planning process, and enthusiasm to work with MCPHS to design and implement a new model of BSN education.

The planning process began with and was grounded in the respective missions of the two institutions (see Exhibit 7.1). Further, the particular missions of Massachusetts General Hospital (MGH) Patient Care Services and the School of Nursing at MCPHS provided specific purposes to serve as guides as the program and its operational facets were developed (see Exhibit 7.2). Continual reference to the overall purpose of each partner institution as well as its nursing-specific purposes was critical to the development of a program that

---

EXHIBIT 7.1 INSTITUTIONAL MISSIONS

Massachusetts College of Pharmacy and Health Sciences provides a unique academic environment to guide and support students toward successful, sustainable careers and leadership in health care. As a private independent institution with a long and distinguished history of specializing in health sciences education, the College offers traditional and non-traditional programs that embody teaching excellence, active scholarship and research, professional service, and community outreach. The College embraces a set of core values that reflect commitment to preparing competent, caring, ethical health professionals and scientists to meet the public's need for high quality health care and cutting-edge knowledge development.

The **Massachusetts General Hospital** exists to provide the highest quality care to individuals and to the local and distant communities we serve, to advance care through excellence in biomedical research, and to educate future academic and practice leaders of the health care professions.

EXHIBIT 7.2 NURSING VISION AND VALUES

MGH Patient Care Services Vision and Values

Vision—As nurses, health professionals, and Patient Care Services support staff, our every action is guided by knowledge, enabled by skill, and motivated by compassion. Patients are our primary focus, and the way we deliver care reflects that focus every day. We believe in creating a practice environment that has no barriers, is built on a spirit of inquiry, and reflects a culturally-competent workforce supportive of the patient-focused values of this institution.

Values—It is through our professional practice model that we make our vision a demonstrable truth everyday by letting our thoughts, decisions, and actions be guided by our values. As clinicians, we ensure that our practice is caring, innovative, scientific, and empowering, and is based on a foundation of leadership and entrepreneurial teamwork.

MCPHS School of Nursing Vision and Values

The nursing program's **vision** is to create an environment of partnership whereby nursing education, practice, and scholarship connect for the education of nurses, the advancement of health care, and the profession of nursing.

The future of nursing rests with those entering the profession. The beliefs and **values** that sustain our program are expressed at every level of the educational experience. Our curriculum, built on the core values of respect, literacy, practice, and integration, will sustain and enhance resiliency as well as personal and professional growth. We are dedicated to the advancement of all engaged in this endeavor, and we foresee significant personal and professional growth outcomes for students, faculty, and clinical partners.

---

is responsive to the multiple drivers and constraints of the nursing education environment and to the continually evolving health care system.

Commitment from the top in each institution was essential to establishing and sustaining the partnership. The senior nurse leaders—sponsors—in both institutions, through a round of strategic negotiations, agreed on a set of guiding principles that would foster collaborative association between the two entities in which resources, knowledge, and expertise were both shared and reciprocal. Initially, we explored our shared goals for the MCPHS–MGH clinical partnership and developed five key principles. They included a commitment to:

1. Engage collaboratively to inform nursing education through clinical practice and influence clinical practice through nursing education,

2. Provide a solid, functional and rigorous foundation for evidence-based nursing practice,

3. Create a teaching-learning partnership that enables students to develop and integrate the core competencies of critical thinking, communication, assessment, and technical skills,

4. Promote individual and collective development of faculty and clinical partners through collaborative teaching, practice, service, and scholarship, and

5. Mentor students in the transition from student to entry-level practitioner of nursing.

These principles then served to guide the next stages of our developing partnership model.

Convening the Best Thinkers

Convening the best thinkers among the faculty and clinical staff was an important initial step in validating the collective vision as well as providing an opportunity for all stakeholders to share in developing the curriculum and learning structure. The initial task force consisted of clinical educators and clinical nurse specialists from MGH and nurse educators from MCPHS. As the work was being shaped, input was sought from clinical staff nurses and preceptors. The sponsors guided the initial process by outlining the broad purpose and guiding principles, as noted earlier, and then delegating the crucial work of developing the curriculum structure, process, desired outcomes, teaching–learning methods, and implementation strategies to an appointed group of clinicians and educators. The sponsors also outlined a commitment to a new model that would provide student immersion in daily practice through intensive rotations of 4–6 weeks, following didactic immersion and then integration in each clinical nursing course, rather than confining immersion to an end-of-program capstone experience. Further, the model was designed to also enhance the professional development and satisfaction of clinical staff serving as educators by engaging them actively in the design and execution of the nursing curriculum. The group was then given its charge along with parameters and limitations (e.g., resource constraints, commitment to not displacing existing clinical placements of other schools, etc.) for developing the program.

Together, both education and practice partners developed the curriculum, using the American Association of Colleges and Universities of Nursing (AACN) *Essentials of Baccalaureate Education for Professional Nursing Practice* (1998) as a guiding document. In addition, the group committed to design a program to assure that students would be prepared for the new graduate role in today's complex health care environment. This commitment had the dual purpose—and benefit—of grounding nursing education in real world practice, with the expectation that new graduate orientation time, costs, and turnover would be reduced and satisfaction, competence, and confidence increased in the new graduate role.

To assist the strategic thinking group early in the collaborative process, two consultants were retained, one a former national association leader now based in Boston who was already consulting regularly with the clinical partner on the use of clinical narrative to enhance meaningful, purpose-driven clinical practice and staff satisfaction. She was able to identify key individuals from the clinical environment to include in the group and assisted in helping both academic and clinical members bridge the gap between education and practice in terms of language, norms, role expectations, and other structural and process differences that often contribute to miscommunication and misunderstanding between the two environments.

In addition, Dr. Patricia Benner was employed to conduct a workshop with the strategic thinking group, which included the leader and core faculty group from MCPHS, leaders and potential clinical faculty from MGH, and the other consultant. The decision to innovate a new model of nursing education stemmed in part from Benner's (1984) belief that "nurses graduate with little understanding of the strategies for clinical skill acquisition" (p. 185). Benner further notes that clinical educators "need to be expert at making visible the explicit guidelines and principles that will get the novice into the clinical situation in a safe and efficient manner. As . . . students advance . . . they need teachers who can themselves demonstrate advanced clinical judgment" (p. 185). Thus, the commitment to engage masters-prepared clinicians as clinical faculty was founded on the belief that students would have opportunities to witness firsthand how a highly competent, actively practicing clinician assesses for patient responses that deviate from the norm, and how clinical judgment provides the foundation for developing and implementing the plan of care, and continually evaluating and modifying it based on the patient's response.

Constructing Possible Scenarios of the Future

Purpose-driven leaders are able to think systemically about the future and imagine a future that is malleable rather than fixed. Johnston, Rogers, Cross and Sochan (2005) note that futures may be *possible* (what may happen), *plausible* (what could happen), *probable* (what likely will happen), or *preferable* (what we want to happen). Norris (1997) suggests there are multiple versions in any of these categories.

Our commitment was to imagine a plausible future within existing resources and constraints, and then to create a preferable future by developing an innovative approach to clinical nursing education beyond the traditional model of one instructor for 8 to 10 students, with the instructor a guest in the setting rather than an integral part of it. Time on learning is compromised under such an arrangement, as students often need to wait for the instructor to be available to supervise any nursing skill interventions. In our shared partnership model, whose purpose is to maximize learning, improve learning efficiency, and create a pathway to future employment while reducing time and costs of the transition from student to practicing RN, clinical instruction is provided by master clinicians in the nursing settings where they actually practice. Thus, they have familiarity with, and credibility and ownership for patient care being provided by the students for whom they serve as the responsible clinical instructor.

During the Benner workshop, the group worked collaboratively under Benner's guidance to review the proposed curriculum and further explore the proposed teaching–learning structure and methodology for the clinical learning experiences at all levels of the nursing curriculum, which were developed using the *Essentials* competencies of critical thinking, communication, assessment, and technical skills, as well as Benner's *novice to expert* framework. A goal was set to graduate students at the advanced beginner level, prepared to move to the competent level within 18 months to 2 years.

Engaging Stakeholders

Throughout the process of program development and curriculum design, a wide array of stakeholders was engaged in the process, some more directly and intensively than others, to assist with "participatory strategy setting." The primary stakeholder group included, as noted earlier, core faculty from MCPHS, master clinicians from MGH who would serve as clinical faculty, and key operations personnel from both institutions. This group had frequent and ongoing contact with the sponsors.

Other stakeholders invited to learn about and provide input to the developing model included staff from the state board of nursing, other potential clinical partners from the community, and senior leaders at the two partner institutions (presidents, chief operating and finance officers). Going forward, the intent is to also involve students, and eventually alumni, to provide feedback for ongoing improvement and redesign in response to changing needs.

Building Capacity

Capacity building focused on not only developing the curriculum and teaching–learning strategies, it included the development of a sound affiliation agreement that encompassed our shared principles and commitments, the selection of clinical faculty and their development in clinical teaching and evaluation principles and methodologies, reorienting traditional core faculty, and developing logistics for communication and support of faculty and students.

In addition to commitment to a new model of BSN education, the sponsors worked to develop an affiliation agreement that supported the goals and desired outcomes of the partnership and assured the necessary support and infrastructure for doing so. A major hurdle was to determine how to support the costs associated with release time for clinical faculty, which was viewed as mutually beneficial. By expanding and enhancing the master clinician's knowledge and skill set to include the educator role, the MGH sponsor viewed the change in role focus as an opportunity for the clinician's renewal as well as further professional development. The MCPHS sponsor saw the partnership as an opportunity to reduce the high number of clinical teaching contact hours to enable core faculty to focus additional effort on scholarship, and in some cases, practice, while also reducing the total number of core faculty needed to support clinical education, especially critical in this era of faculty shortage.

Master clinicians were recruited by MGH to serve as clinical faculty, using a set of mutually established criteria. These well-qualified MGH clinicians hold clinical faculty appointments at MCPHS, and share clinical teaching, mentoring, and student evaluation responsibilities. They also have opportunities to provide input on curriculum evaluation and improvement and teaching–learning strategies, and participate in classroom and seminar instruction. The latter often occurs through the sharing of clinical narratives but also involves sharing didactic teaching responsibilities. Thus, the partners share in the investment in the overarching purpose of nursing education as well as in student success.

Development of the clinical faculty in teaching and evaluation principles and methodologies occurs in several ways. MCPHS core faculty conduct workshops specific to the nursing program around such topics as developing clinical learning objectives, teaching and evaluating student performance, and handling difficult student situations. Clinical faculty are invited to MCPHS faculty development seminars, and MCPHS has made a commitment to support the cost of clinical faculty enrollment in online continuing education coursework related to educational methodologies for both classroom and clinical learning, from the program's professional development budget. In turn, MGH has committed to provide release time for clinical faculty to enroll in such coursework. Further, each clinical faculty member works closely with a seasoned MCPHS nurse educator, with the educator mentoring the clinician in clinical teaching while the clinician mentors the educator in the latest clinical practice developments.

Reorienting traditional core faculty for their new roles as partners in the shared curriculum and teaching–learning process has been part of capacity building. Nurse educators have had to acclimate to a shared voice model, rather than reserving for themselves the traditional dominant voice in determining the most effective clinical teaching and evaluation strategies. However, the benefit has been to provide greater flexibility, and thus satisfaction, in the core faculty role by increasing time available for scholarship and other commitments. Going forward, we envision that the clinical–core faculty partnership will also provide collaborative opportunities to engage in clinical research, and greater interface between education and practice in responding to the changing environments of both education and practice.

Infrastructure capacity has also been an important part of our partnership model, in two key ways—the integration of clinical simulation and the use of Blackboard™ courseware. A state-of-the-art eight-bed clinical simulation unit, along with a 10-station health assessment lab on the college campus has enabled students to learn assessment as well as basic and advanced technical skills in a safe learning environment. MGH clinical faculty assisted in identifying the critical technical competencies students needed to be equipped with prior to beginning their actual clinical rotations. As a result, lab and simulation experiences help students prepare for exactly those skills the clinicians expect them to have, and in turn, ensure students are ready to apply their knowledge and skills in the real world of practice.

The use of Blackboard™ courseware, supported by MCPHS, allows all faculty, including clinical associates, access to curriculum materials and teaching–learning resources while serving as a vital communication link between the two institutions. Further, clinical faculty have electronic as well as on-site access to the MCPHS library and its division of learning resources, while in turn, MCPHS faculty and students have access to the rich array of professional development resources available through MGH.

Launching the New Initiative

Sponsorship from key leaders in both education and practice arenas becomes especially critical during the launch phase, as barriers, conflicts, and rough terrain are encountered—"the devil is in the details." The program admitted its first class in fall 2005 as freshmen, and the collaborative clinical learning model was launched in summer of 2006, with the introduction of clinical narratives and simulation learning. The first clinical immersion experience occurred in summer 2007, and will continue through spring 2008, upon completion of which the first class will graduate.

The program method was developed by a triad model of MCPHS core faculty, MGH clinical faculty, and MGH clinical associates. As noted earlier, clinical faculty from the MGH nursing staff are masters-prepared clinicians from a range of clinical areas within the institution. Clinical associates are baccalaureate-prepared experienced staff nurses in the various clinical practice areas.

The model provides for each clinical faculty member to supervise five to seven BSN students, with the ratio dependant on unit and patient acuity, and assisted by two clinical associates who provide individual instruction, guidance, and support to students during their clinical learning time. Core faculty make regular visits to the clinical sites to confer with clinical faculty and clinical associates and engage with students about their learning. Thus, students benefit from this shared involvement and commitment from both education and practice.

As the initiative was launched, key leaders from both institutions communicated regularly, sharing progress, potential roadblocks, and unanticipated issues, as well as ideas for ongoing improvement. For example, it became apparent during the students' first clinical immersion experience in summer 2007 that they were unfamiliar with the meaning of Magnet status, earned by MGH several years ago. In response, information and a web resource for nursing students on Magnet status were provided and will be included in orientation of future classes, emphasizing how the purpose of Magnet status is to recognize excellence and innovations in professional nursing that promote high-quality patient care, including the benefit to student learning and socialization. Going forward, our aim is continual reinvention of the shared partnership model. As we learn what works and what needs to be changed, we will respond accordingly.

Redesigning and Redirecting Existing Processes

In addition to the commitment to a new model of BSN education, the sponsors worked to develop an affiliation agreement that supported the goals and desired outcomes of the partnership and assured the necessary support and infrastructure for doing so. A major hurdle was to determine how to support the costs associated with release time for clinical faculty, which was viewed as beneficial to both clinical and education partners. By expanding and enhancing the master clinician's knowledge and skill set to include the educator role, the MGH sponsor viewed the change in role focus as an opportunity for the clinician's renewal as well as development. The MCPHS sponsor saw the partnership as an opportunity to reduce the high number of clinical teaching contact hours to enable faculty to focus more on scholarship, and also reduce the total number of core faculty needed to support clinical education, especially critical in this era of faculty shortage. Because we are early in the unfolding of the process, we will continue to evaluate its effectiveness in achieving our shared vision and purpose.

Reallocating Existing Resources and Investing New Resources

Nursing education is an expensive undertaking. As programs moved out of hospital settings and into colleges and universities, the cost of nursing education for individuals rose and continues to rise dramatically. Traditionally, nursing education programs have expected hospitals and community-based settings to provide opportunities, space, and resources to support student learning experiences in the clinical environment, still the predominant model in use today. The cost of this teaching–learning paradigm to the care delivery system is born solely by the system, with the only expectation of return on the investment being students as potential future employees. In locales with multiple nursing programs, the burden on the care delivery system can become onerous.

Our partnership was designed to address resource issues, reduce the burden on the clinical learning environment, and improve student learning processes and outcomes in two ways: (a) reallocation of a selected number of budgeted nursing faculty lines at MCPHS to pay institutional stipends to MGH to compensate MGH clinical faculty time spent teaching and supervising students, and (b) investment of new MCPHS resources in simulation technology to assist and support students in mastering an array of basic and more advanced nursing skills prior to actual patient care assignments in the clinical arena.

The payment of institutional stipends involved several iterations of negotiation between the sponsors, considering cost and expense realities for the school and the health system, while being ever-mindful of our shared purpose of educating a cadre of well-qualified, ready-to-work new graduates. Dollar-for-dollar payment to MGH for actual clinical faculty release time was not feasible, especially given disparities in compensation between education and practice sectors and the need to limit the number of students with clinical faculty in the various clinical placements; this despite nurse educator salaries at the 75th percentile for the North Atlantic region, among the most competitive in the Boston market. Nevertheless, both sponsors believed fervently that the new model would ultimately reduce costs for both institutions, especially in retention and satisfaction of clinical staff and faculty as well as orientation of new graduates. On several occasions, we committed out loud to each other—"We are going to do what it takes to make this work."

In turn, MCPHS agreed to pay a "per student, per rotation" fee from existing faculty lines; orient MGH clinicians to the curriculum, teaching-learning expectations, student evaluation, and clinical teaching-learning strategies through online or instructor-led programs to assist their development as clinical educators; support participation of clinician faculty in professional development opportunities related to clinical teaching and evaluation; and provide ongoing assistance and support to clinician faculty by the MCPHS core faculty. Such a partnership between education and practice is essential in fulfilling nursing education's ultimate purpose.

Our agreement called for MGH to provide qualified clinicians to serve as clinical faculty for groups of five to seven students, teaching and supervising the students' clinical immersion experiences for 30 to 36 hours per week, plus time for preparation and evaluation. This model of clinical education is used for all inpatient and ambulatory clinical learning experiences throughout the BSN program, and not only during the final clinical rotation as is the case in most nursing programs. MGH agreed to accommodate up to 75% of the students from any given class, based on the system's ability to provide clinical faculty and learning experiences appropriate to student learning objectives. Clinical experiences may occur on day, evening, and weekend shifts (during the clinical immersion experiences, students attend classes on campus only 1 day per week, thus allowing flexibility in scheduling their clinical hours). While this has challenged classroom utilization on campus as it does not fit the traditional academic scheduling model, we found ways to work around the model and capture available space to meet program needs. Also, MGH has offered to provide some classroom space on-site during the clinical immersion weeks, thus easing the difficulty of travel between MGH and MCPHS in a congested Boston transportation system.

To achieve the purpose of adequate student clinical skills preparation prior to the clinical immersion experiences, the vision and purpose of the clinical partnership model was presented to MCPHS administrators, and the MCPHS sponsor advocated successfully for investment in a state-of-the-art clinical simulation laboratory and a full-time lab manager/instructor. In this simulated environment, students learn through constructed patient care scenarios the skills agreed on by the core and clinician faculty, and in so doing, are well-prepared to begin the intensive, immersive clinical learning experiences. Feedback from both students and clinical staff indicate that our shared purpose of better student preparation for the actual clinical environment is achieving our desired outcomes, thus reinforcing the investment of these new resources in maximizing student learning and, ultimately, readiness for beginning nursing practice.

CONCLUSIONS

Use of the Norris (1997) model has been helpful in guiding our process, and keeping the process connected to our shared vision and purpose. Going forward, the sponsors will continue to provide leadership and monitoring of the partnership and its benefits and progress. The sponsors, as academic and practice leaders, will continue to articulate and advocate for sustaining our "supercharged alliance," which will assure we remain true to our shared purpose of educating the next generation of professional nurses in this new model of teaching–learning. We also will continue to engage key stakeholders, including students, in ongoing dialogue, evaluation, adjusting our sails, and correcting our course as needed. Keeping sight of our ultimate shared purpose—the delivery of safe, competent, high-quality nursing care for the public through continuous preparation of a qualified new graduate nursing workforce—also assures that our respective institutions are able to achieve their related yet distinct purposes.

Continual connection of strategic thinking and action with our vision and purpose ultimately is aimed at achieving an innovative, efficient, and sustainable model of nursing education. As Norris (1997) advocates, as purpose-driven leaders, we will continue to think forward to imagine what might be, engage in perpetual strategic thinking, try out multiple scenarios "all at the same time," and position (and reposition) for next steps, in a continuous loop of learning and adjustment. Although our model has not yet achieved full implementation, and we do not yet know whether ultimately it will be successful, we fully expect that both education and practice partners will continue to lead through our shared "purpose in action."

REFERENCES

American Association of Colleges and Universities of Nursing. (1998). *Essentials of baccalaureate education for professional nursing practice.* Washington, DC: Author.

Benner, P. (1984). *From novice to expert excellence and power in clinical nursing practice.* Menlo Park, CA: Addison Welsey.

Boyer, E. (1990). *Scholarship reconsidered: Priorities of the professoriate.* Stanford, CA: Carnegie Foundation for the Advancement of Teaching.

Johnston, M., Rogers, M., Cross, N., & Sochan, A. (2005). Global and planetary health: Teaching as if the future matters. *Nursing Education Perspectives, 26*(3), 152–156.

Norris, D. M. (1997). *Revolutionary strategy for the knowledge age.* Ann Arbor, MI: Society for College and University Planning.

Shapiro, H. T. (2007). *A larger sense of purpose: Higher education and society.* Princeton, NJ: Princeton University Press.

CHAPTER 8

People

Sara Barger

The supply of nursing faculty is a limiting reality as schools and programs struggle to respond to the overall nursing workforce crisis facing the nation. The responses on the part of leaders will of course be highly varied, but this case study demonstrates the core relationship between those leadership strategies in the general domain of people and the development needs of faculty.

BACKGROUND

Ask anyone in a leadership position in nursing education what is their number one concern and the most likely answer will be finding qualified faculty. But what if that issue were reframed from "finding qualified faculty" to "growing qualified faculty"? This case study describes the current state of the faculty shortage in the nation, the southern region, and one southern state. It describes one college's efforts to address the problem, and how accomplishing work through others can result in viable solutions to the thorniest of issues.

The problem of the faculty shortage becomes clear when data from the latest national sample survey of registered nurses are examined. The average age of faculty in BSN or higher programs is 50.4 years. Thirty-eight percent of nursing faculty is 55 years or older (U.S. Department of Health and Health Services, 2004).

The 2006 survey on vacant faculty positions conducted by the American Association of Colleges of Nursing (AACN) found that, of the 329 AACN members responding (55.3%), 66.6% had vacancies and another 16.7% had no vacancies but needed additional faculty. Moreover, an earned doctorate in nursing or a related field was a requirement for a faculty position in 53.7% of the nursing programs. When administrators were asked to rank the major reasons precluding schools of nursing from hiring additional full-time faculty, inability to recruit qualified faculty because of competition for jobs with other marketplaces ranked number three, and unavailability of qualified applicants for faculty positions the geographic area ranked number four (Fang, 2006).

A 2006 survey of schools in the southern region conducted by the Southern Regional Education Board's Council on Collegiate Education for Nursing yielded similar results. With a response rate of 55%, from the 532 institutions that offer undergraduate and graduate nursing programs, administrators indicated that they had 384 unfilled positions. There were 283 retirements during that same year. The respondents anticipated that 596 faculty would retire by 2009.

Within Alabama, the picture is much the same; an aging faculty workforce and too few doctorally prepared faculty members to replace them. In December 2006, a survey of nursing education programs within the state of Alabama was conducted by the Alabama Center for Nursing (Alabama Board of Nursing Center for Nursing, 2006). Nursing program administrators were asked to respond to questions regarding the number of qualified students turned away due to a lack of sufficient numbers of faculty. The results were staggering. In 2006 alone, 4,046 qualified applicants to Alabama nursing programs were turned away because of a lack of sufficient numbers of faculty to accommodate the number of students. Program administrators estimated that a total of 391 graduate-prepared faculty will be needed within 5 years. This includes 228 faculty needed to accept all qualified applicants who had been turned away. In addition, 163 faculty members are needed to fill faculty positions that are vacant now as well as faculty positions that will be vacant due to retirements. While there is much agreement on the scope of the problem, there has been less movement to implement viable solutions. To address the problem, I built my strategy around the four interrelated core leadership dimensions, particularly the people dimension. This is not surprising, given that my personal definition of leadership is getting things done through others.

The story at the University of Alabama's Capstone College of Nursing is not unique. Enrollment in the college soared over the last 5 years from about 500 students to more than 1,200. At the upper division, the college went from promoting 80 students annually to promoting 176 into the upper-division nursing courses. During that time some positions were added and others turned over, resulting in a continuous state of faculty recruitment. Since nursing programs throughout the United States were facing similar issues, we were all competing for the same small pool of doctorally prepared faculty, and there simply were not enough to go around.

However, we were very successful in recruiting bright, young, and clinically competent masters-prepared nurses from the local area into instructor positions. While they did not have teaching experience, they had a wealth of clinical experience, were eager to learn, and were excited about the faculty role. I met with each new instructor individually and explained that she would remain at the instructor level and would only be eligible for a one-year renewable contract without a doctorate. My belief was that after a year of teaching, these instructors would be so enamored with the faculty role that they would rush to enter doctoral programs. While they did love the faculty role and had looked at doctoral programs, they did not rush to apply. Three to four years later, not a single new instructor had entered a doctoral program.

A review of the data for our own college was rather alarming. Within just 5 years, our percentage of doctorally prepared faculty had gone from 82%–60%. In addition, a review of the profiles of our doctorally prepared faculty indicated approximately two-thirds could retire within 5 years. Finally, we continued to have limited success in recruiting doctorally prepared faculty from outside the area. Clearly, a new strategy was needed.

STRATEGY

Several exploratory sessions were held with the leaders in the college; both those in formal administrative positions and those at the senior ranks of the professoriate. All were concerned about the future of the college if we were unable to increase our numbers of doctorally prepared faculty. We explored reasons why the younger faculty members, unlike their senior counterparts, had not rushed to enter doctoral programs soon after entering academe. Several themes emerged. These instructors were young women with young children. They were motivated by different values than their senior counterparts. Also, since the college has had several unsuccessful years in recruiting doctorally prepared faculty, the masters-prepared instructors felt no sense of urgency that they were likely to lose their position to someone with a doctorate. They were also concerned with the cost of doctoral education, particularly because we were encouraging them to get degrees from diverse institutions. With these themes in mind, the groups explored strategies and identified several with a high potential for success. First, at the time of the instructors' annual evaluations, when goals were being set for the next year, they would be encouraged to include doctoral education in their goals. If they were enrolled in a doctoral program, they would be able to have two contracts of 3 years each. Thus, with adequate progress, they could be assured of 6 years of employment. A percentage of the merit raise for all instructors would be tied to enrollment and progress in doctoral study. Thus, those instructors not enrolled would receive smaller raises than those who were. It was also determined that the college would be able to give a lighter teaching load during one semester of each academic year to instructors enrolled in doctoral study.

These plans were shared with instructors during meetings of the undergraduate faculty. Interest in doctoral study grew as instructors requested individual meetings with the dean to discuss their plans and began requesting references for the institutions to which they were applying.

At the same time, the Alabama State Nurses' Association's (ASNA) strategic planning committee appointed a special task force to look at the faculty shortage throughout the state of Alabama. Heading the task force was a well-respected nursing leader from the public health sector who had retired. It was critical for me to be a part of this important initiative. The task force's first action was to collect data. I and a faculty member from the college designed a survey instrument to be administered to all nursing programs throughout Alabama. The survey was administered and tabulated by ASNA. The findings were consistent with the situation within my own college; large numbers of retirements, with more expected within five years, and current vacant positions.

The task force reviewed the current law that provided scholarships for "graduate education of nurses." A bill revising the existing legislation was drafted. Important components of the revision included preference given to students pursuing a career in nursing education. The amount of the scholarship was increased from $3,000 to an amount not to exceed $20,000. Moreover, the amount to be appropriated for these scholarships was increased from $57,000 to $900,000. I and a senior faculty member from the college met with a member of the Alabama House of Representatives from our district. A physician himself, he was very supportive of the need for this funding and offered to file the bill himself. The bill was passed by the House but never came to a vote in the Senate. Despite the fact that this bill did not pass, $500,000 was included in the state's education budget to fund scholarships for students pursuing graduate degrees to become nursing faculty. These funds will provide scholarships for faculty from my own college and for faculty at other nursing schools throughout Alabama.

WORKING THROUGH OTHERS AS A KEY LEADERSHIP STRATEGY

The leadership compass developed by the Center for the Health Professions at the University of California, San Francisco (UCSF) was built around four interrelated core leadership dimensions. "The essential difference between doing a good job and doing a good leadership job is the ability to accomplish work through others" (O'Neil, 2006). A number of elements of the "people" leadership domain were an important part of the program to enlarge the number of doctorally prepared faculty at Alabama.

One of the most important dimensions of people leadership is motivating others by connecting them to the work, developing their skills, and informing them of their progress, and this was clearly a central part of what went on within the college. In this context it was important for all faculties to internalize the challenge and need for advanced education. Senior faculties were connected to their work as they reviewed the current status of the college, existing trends, and future probabilities. They engaged in the process of not only looking at what existed, but also at what strategies led to a high probability for success. Junior faculty were connected to the work through providing realistic opportunities for them to get additional education and then informing and rewarding them for that progress through the annual goal-setting and merit raise process.

This first step in the process makes it possible to develop others in the organization for their own improvement and to achieve institutional goals. Clearly the college needed to increase the number of doctorally prepared faculty. However, instructors had not seen this as a personal goal for themselves. By tying this goal for the organization to the goal-setting process for instructors, institutional goals are met and junior faculties improve their status in the organization. In other words, the strategic direction and needs of the college became the strategic goal of individual faculty members. Their success was made to contribute directly to the success of the college.

The process used in this case study also built effective teams to address a pressing problem and sustain institutional action. Senior faculty and administrators were engaged in a process of determining the state of the college regarding adequate numbers of doctorally prepared faculty and then identifying strategies to assure the desired result. As recognized leaders in the college, they rose to the challenge of developing plans with a high probability of success. Moreover, after the meetings, they talked with instructors individually and encouraged them to apply for admission to a doctoral program. This allowed everyone to contribute to the situation and prevented scapegoating on the problem of one group by the other.

At the state level, it was important to understand how to legitimately gain and use personal and institution power to advance the work of the organization. In this case, the goals of ASNA were consistent with the goals for my college. By being a part of the ASNA task force, I was able to help set the direction for the work of the task force and the resulting legislation. My expertise in developing the survey instrument enabled me to use that power to obtain important data and influence strategy, while advancing the goals of my own college. It should also be noted that having interacted with my member of the Alabama Legislature on many previous occasions gave me access and credibility to this legislator that otherwise would have been impossible. Such alignments of interest allowed us to generate some new power around the issue.

The outcomes of this effort are already evident. Moreover, the experience has demonstrated an important leadership lesson. The challenges in all of health care are enormous; the nursing faculty shortage is just one small part of the overall health care crisis the nation now faces, but it offers some insight to how leaders might respond to other challenges. We often believe that if we could only get more money, the issue could be addressed. While I am always for new resources, much of what we were able to do at Alabama was to address the situation using our existing resources more creatively. By deploying a set of "people strategies," we were able to get others in the college to see the challenge as theirs. The core elements of this were broadening ownership for the problem, building intergenerational teams to address the issue, connecting the problem to existing activity such as annual review, and aligning the problem with the change agenda of others outside of the Capstone College of Nursing. However, our work with people is not over. We will need to continue the process of encouraging the nine faculty members who have started down the path of obtaining a doctoral degree to continue that journey. At the same time, we will need to work with other schools of nursing and other legislators to not only increase the funding for nursing faculty scholarships next year, but also to support the policy changes needed to gain ongoing support. These initial successes have made us optimistic about the future. More faculty members mean more students. More students mean more nurses. And more nurses means better health care for all of us.

REFERENCES

Alabama Board of Nursing Center for Nursing. (2006, December). *Analysis of faculty needs survey.* Montgomery, AL.: Author.

Fang, D. (2006). *2006 survey on faculty vacancies.* Washington, DC: American Association of Colleges of Nursing.

O'Neil, E. (2006). *The leadership compass: Competencies for health care.* San Francisco: San Francisco Center for the Health Professions, UCSF.

U.S. Department of Health and Health Services, Health Resources and Services Administration. (2004). *National sample survey of registered nurses.* Washington, D.C.: U.S. Department of Health and Human Services.

CHAPTER 9

Process

Michelle Taylor-Smith and Linda Thompson Adams

By the year 2020, while significantly less than previously projected, the national shortage of qualified nursing professionals is still expected to be nearly triple that of today (Auerbach, Buerhaus, & Staiger, 2007). The concern is one of the most pressing problems facing nursing executives and health care industry leaders nationwide—an entrenched challenge that requires creative solutions and strategies. Nurses can take the lead in reversing this workforce trend by advocating for new human resource practices, bridging the transition from student learner to practicing nurse, and creating organizational vehicles at hospitals and other nurse employer settings in which institutional and cross-sector transformations can take place. Such changes have the potential to increase the numbers of well-trained entrants into the nursing employment pool as well as present opportunities to improve the overall quality of health care in the United States.

According to Buerhaus et al. (2007), a survey-based report that was co-funded by the Johnson and Johnson Campaign for Nursing's Future and continuing education provider Nursing Spectrum, prolonged nursing shortages could have harmful consequences, including reduced "quantity of patient care, increase(d) operating and labor costs, and decrease(d) efficiency and effectiveness" (p. 854). Confronting these challenges head-on requires nursing leaders to commit to ever-evolving processes while leveraging lessons learned by other organizations already addressing the issue. In this chapter, the Nursing Workforce Transformation initiative at southeastern Michigan-based St. John Health System, and their partnership with Oakland University's School of Nursing, will be used as a model and case study for what can and already has been accomplished in this arena.

OVERVIEW OF THE PROBLEM

Nationally in 2006, hospitals in the United States needed approximately 118,000 registered nurses to fill vacant positions, reflecting a national 8.5% vacancy rate (American Hospital Association, 2006). Long-term, government analysts are projecting that more than 1.2 million new and replacement nurses will be needed in coming years nationally as a result of growth in the sector and anticipated position turnover (U.S. Department of Health and Human Services, 2002). As identified in the Buerhaus and colleagues 2007 article cited previously, Harris Interactive surveyed nationwide perspectives of physicians, registered nurses, and hospital CNOs/CEOs between 2005 and 2006 to ask them about the nursing shortage. The polls' results, Buerhaus et al. asserted, showed direct correlations between those shortages that began in 1998 and present-day viewpoints held industry-wide about the effect they are having on quality of care received by patients. What is causing this nursing shortage? Several key contributing factors have emerged as having the greatest impact:

Market Supply and Demand—The aging Baby Boom generation has created an increased demand for nursing professionals as they simultaneously leave the workplace in retirement as well as require additional health care as they live longer. According to the Watson Wyatt Study cited by Crain's Business Detroit (Begin, 2006) and commissioned by the six major health systems and hospitals in southeast Michigan, there is a projected shortage of 18,000 registered nursed by 2012 in the area. The supply pipeline for educating nurses is also inadequate, with a shortage of faculty and an excess of qualified candidates compared to available training opportunities. Last year, according to the Michigan Center for Nursing (2006), there were a combined 4,298 more qualified applicants than available education slots for practical nursing, associate degrees in nursing, and in bachelor of science in nursing programs in the state.

Issues of Job Satisfaction—In a survey by the American Nurses Association (American Association of Nurses, 2007), 53% of registered nurses indicated they "enjoy" their work, while 63% reported satisfaction with their jobs. Through ANA's National Database of Nursing Quality Indicators (NDNQI), registered nurses (RNs) report the highest levels of satisfaction in their interactions with peers (67%) and lowest level in regards to their compensation (40%). As presented by the Nursing Workforce Transformation Steering Committee of St. John Health System's internal study, "2006 Top Box Work Environment Survey Scores," levels of satisfaction among organization leadership expressed in work environment studies ran high (above the 60% mark), while nursing professionals showed much lower satisfaction levels (30% to 35%;

St. John Health System, 2007a). Factors considered included satisfaction with leadership (accessibility, availability, and recognition gained), scheduling (including staffing and workload), teamwork (conflict resolution and physician relations) and equipment/supplies (access to and conditions of items).

New Graduate RN Turnover—Nationally, the new RN turnover rate is estimated to be 35% to 65% in the first year post-graduation, a critical factor in the nursing shortage at all levels. In a health system like St. John Health, which hires upward of 750 new and replacement nurses annually, the financial toll on human resource expenditures as well as patient care is enormous. Projecting that the voluntary turnover rate of registered nurses is around 10% and coupled with a new RN turnover rate of 30%, the estimated cost of RN turnover approaches $20 million at St. John Health per year.

Gaps Between Academia and Practice—The absence of adequate knowledge, skill, and support levels is directly related to high rates of turnover among new hires and recent graduates. There is often a great disconnect between what is taught at nursing school, and what graduates find in real-life patient care settings—this leads to such problems as job dissatisfaction and potential patient endangerment. New strategies must be employed to better equip nursing personnel to deliver high-quality patient care post-graduation, and to recruit and retain students looking for accessible learning options that can be integrated into their work, family, and social lives. This will better prepare nurses to avoid job burnout and dissatisfaction and is why it is so crucial to incorporate schools of nursing in initiatives to address issues of nursing recruitment and retention.

Quantifying the problem through numbers can help to illustrate the extent and scope of the looming scarcity of nurses. The U.S. Department of Health and Human Services (2002) reports the following statistical information as it pertains to the current context and future outlook for the national nursing shortages and the impact on the health care industry as a whole:

275,000—Anticipated shortage, represented in number of nurses, by 2010

83.2%—Percentage of licensed RNs who are actively employed in nursing

56.2%—Percentage of nurses who worked in hospital settings in the year 2004

45 to 75%—Percent of nurse work time spent on non-direct patient care activities

43—Age, calculated in years, of the average RN

31%—Percentage of hospitals using internal agencies to meet staffing needs

20%—Percentage more paid for agency rather than regular staff assistance

17%—Present day, average RN turnover rates nationwide

12%—Percent of RNs who are less than 30 years of age

ISSUES ADDRESSED IN CASE STUDY

In April 2006, St. John Health Services (SJHS) of Southeast Michigan hosted an internal Nursing Summit. This institutional retreat resulted in the formation of a steering committee and nurse-led teams tasked with prioritizing the organization's nursing staff needs, devising a 3-year strategic plan to meet them, and rolling out three core charters aimed at addressing the following related issues that affect health care organizations nationwide: recruitment, retention, and transformation of care at the bedside. SJHS's stated goals were, as expeditiously as possible, to reduce the number of nursing vacancies and lower position turnover, establish the system as an employer of choice for prospective nursing school students and graduates, and leave lasting impressions on patient populations by providing them with the highest quality health care experience possible.

Nursing Retention—SJHS's aim was to eliminate issues that motivate nurses to leave the organization after their first year of employment. Demonstrating concern for nurse safety, providing for their contentment in the workplace, and giving higher levels of support were identified as three critical ways to reduce the hospital system's 18% turnover rate and save $46,000 to $64,000 per nurse in annual replacement costs. Centralizing recruitment staffing models, adopting entrepreneurially driven and results-oriented team approaches, and introducing flexible scheduling options to meet new and existing RN needs for work–life balance, were targeted as ways to avert issues that typically lead to turnover. Education loan forgiveness and other incentive programs were also discussed as potential parts of the solution.

Nursing Recruitment—In the fall of 2006, SJHS experienced a nurse vacancy rate of 9.7%, which was equivalent to 337 positions. Additionally, the organization was spending $500,000 per month contracting nursing staff members through temporary agencies. A recruitment component of the SJHS initiative was established to increase recruit satisfaction rates (which directly impacts retention), curtail spending related to temporary staffing, and increase satisfaction levels among patients, physicians, and other impacted staff members. Standardizing orientation and on-boarding processes and developing early detection and intervention plans were also identified as ways to help transition new nurse recruits into long-term employees.

Transforming Nursing Care at the Bedside (TCAB)—In addition, SJHS focused on increasing the levels of efficiency and effectiveness with which bedside care is delivered. The approach encourages collaboration among all service aims to better meet patient needs and aims to reduce the amount of time spent on noncaregiving related activities. SJHS included in its plans a need to address the effects that WHPPD, or Worked Hours per Patient Day, would have on its ability to make measurable progress in the targeted areas. WHPPD averages are nationally recognized and endorsed by the National Quality Forum and measure the number of hours of direct care a patient can expect to receive from an RN, along with LPNs and nursing assistants, within a 24-hour period (HealthSouth Rehabilitation Hospitals of Western Massachusetts, 2007).

Nursing School Partnership—In what evolved into a second phase of St. John Health System's initiative, the hospital strategically partnered with Oakland University School of Nursing to supplement their internal interventions. Traditional professional nursing training programs often leave graduates not fully ready to work in fast-paced, demanding patient care settings. This is in part because the typical pedagogical approach is focused on theoretical learning with an over-reliance on lecture and classroom modalities, usually at an educational institution campus. New nurses often are not exposed to multidisciplinary team environments, have not gained enough field experience, and do not receive adequate transitional support to move successfully from student to employee. In response, the School of Nursing at Oakland University proposed an enhanced nursing training model that could meet the following needs: (a) better prepare nurses so they remain working in the field after graduation, lowering human resources costs of St. John Health System; (b) improve patient quality of care and safety by producing nurses satisfied with their jobs, oriented to customer service, and with real-life patient care field experience; (c) expand the faculty pool by integrating the classroom into field training opportunities; and (d) standardize curriculum using technology and student progression based on competency, and through other development and incentive initiatives. The university and hospital began partnering in a range of ways to bring these ideas to life and to supplement SJHS's internal activities.

DESCRIPTION OF CASE STUDY

The Nursing Workforce Transformation project was officially launched in July of 2006 (to coincide with the organization's fiscal-year calendar), involving six St. John Health System-run facilities in southeast Michigan. The initiative helped St. John Health System (SJHS) begin to internally alleviate the shortage, now of critical proportions, of qualified nursing professionals, which continues to plague the health care industry nationwide. Other institutions and systems that employ nurses can learn from SJHS's experiences, and leaders in those settings can adapt the lessons learned through the Nursing Workforce Transformation (NWT) initiative. By breaking the process into four distinct stages, which are outlined below, SJHS was able to get the NWT project off the ground:

Step One: Vision and Related Calls for Action—Nursing, work-life services, and strategic planning leaders participating in the Nursing Summit at SJHS identified critical issues and areas to achieve based on the following organizational vision: "To be the place professional nurses want to work because our culture supports providing the highest quality care." They used brainstorming techniques to identify issues needing resolution and uncover opportunities for improvement. Grouping and prioritizing issues into appropriate action steps allowed for the scheduling and assignment of tasks to corresponding teams: Recruitment, Retention, or Transformation of Care.

Step Two: Data Collection—Data gathered from internal and external sources helped SJHS to clearly identify the issue at hand, define the extent of its impact within the organization, give weight and heft to the proposed project and its related initiatives, and provide direction at all points along the process from problem recognition to implementation steps and eventual, positive resolution of the issue:

- *SJHS Work Environment Survey*—SJHS employs more than 20,000 in the Detroit metro area, offering comprehensive prevention, primary care and treatment programs with approximately 3,200 physicians, 125 medical offices, and 10 hospitals placed in six counties. Surveying the day-to-day operations and functioning of its work environments was crucial to its NWT program.
- *Nursing Time and Motion Studies*—The Robert Wood Johnson Foundation (in partnership with Ascension Health and Kaiser Permanente) conducted a multi-site, phase I study on behalf of St. John Hospital and Medical Center in Detroit, Michigan, which focused on documenting how medical surgical nurses spent their time. The results were incorporated into SJHS's plans to increase time spent providing bedside care while reducing time devoted to the completion of non-caregiving tasks (Robert Wood Johnson Foundation (n.d.).
- *Ascension Health Nursing Shortage Data*—SJHS is a member of Ascension Health, a national, faith-based health ministry sponsored by the Sisters of St. Joseph of Nazareth, the Daughters of Charity, and the Sisters of St. Joseph of Carondelet. Ascension Health, one of the largest

not-for-profit Catholic health ministries in the United States, maintains acute care facilities in 20 states and the District of Columbia; national data provided another benchmarking perspective for setting the project's scale and quantifiable outcomes.

Adopting a rationale and forming assumptions that are culled from these varied data sources, the SJHS steering committee could view the issue of nursing retention from a broader viewpoint and devise methodologies for approaching the issue that were well-informed and action-oriented. Identifying who, what, when, where, and why leads to the construction of initiatives that have a greater chance of delivering desired outcomes and moving an organization forward to reach its goals.

Step Three: Prioritization and Planning—Building a structure that supports the carrying out of required processes is imperative if true success is to be attained. SJHS employed the following processes to do just that:

- *Prioritize Issues Using a Model of Hierarchy*—Employing a ranked needs model brings order to the program planning and implementation process and ensures that the strategies developed to carry out initiatives are in concert with the desired end goals and contribute to the attainment of the organization's overall vision.
- *Establish Three-Year Operational Plans for Each Critical Area*—The establishment of a longer term day-to-day blueprint for implementation which addressed each critical area of change helped to set goals to track progress and encourage reflection, reorganization and realignment at regular intervals.
- *Develop Critical Area Charters With These Characteristics:*
  - *Description*—State the issue, outline ways it impacts the organization, and provide an overview of desired and/or anticipated outcomes.
  - *Deliverables*—Identify all programs and policies that will be put in place to effect change in each area of concern. Under its "Retention" plan, SJHS identified the rolling out of system-wide programs that address, among others, workplace violence and safety. In "Recruitment," SJHS set goals to standardize nursing residency programs and nursing orientation. With "TCAB," SJHS targeted the development of models of care that were holistic and relationship based.
  - *Time Schedule*—Set target dates for initiation, follow-up, and completion of all steps involved in the improvement process.

- *Success Metrics*—Metrics are defined measurements that help guide and gauge progress. Their role is to incite success and clarify or refine the organization's vision for each area of improvement and are generally quantifiable. Metrics set for retention by SJHS included "Improvement in FY07 Culture of Safety Survey from FY06" and a "10% improvement in Work Environment Scores (WES) scores for nursing."
- *Reporting Frequency*—Establish guidelines that encourage an accountability culture with regard to project management. Encourage collection and sharing of information at regular intervals, be it through in-person meetings and/or written communication. Set monthly deadlines for project manager reporting to executive sponsors and chief nursing officers.
- *Resources*—Set expectations for time commitments from each committee member that are reality-based. Executive sponsors, as in the case of SJHS, will likely spend 5% of their time addressing the issues of each charter, program managers 20%, and finance personnel, team leaders, and other team members 10% each.
- *Factor in Oversight*—Avoid operating in a vacuum. Like communication, oversight mechanisms encourage a checks and balances approach that, if leveraged correctly, will lead to an increase in the success of any program. In this day and age of heightened regulations, the increased risk for legal ramifications that can be brought when there are missteps, and an increased sensitivity to and encouragement of diversity in the workplace, objective oversight plays an even more significant role in the modern patient setting.

Step Four: Implementation—Carrying out project-related initiatives, or implementing the process, required that attention be paid to all of the following, as illustrated in the case of the Nursing Workforce Transformation (NWT) project at St. John Health System (SJHS):

- *Organization*—The sum of its parts, the Operations Strategy Council was responsible for carrying out initiatives and meeting stated goals and was headed by the Steering Committee executive sponsor, who oversaw the activities of initiative leaders and project manager(s). They, in turn, worked closely with the Steering Committee and various team members to execute the plan.
- *Team Composition*—To ensure success, all areas and departments within the organization that are affected by stated initiatives must be represented and take part in the program development process. At

the team level, that includes nurse educators, RNs, finance representatives, project managers, team leaders, and executive sponsors.

- *Management Structure*—Project managers were empowered with developing action plans and setting related milestones and outcomes measures with input from their teams, providing support for their execution, communicating with the appropriate executive sponsor (to include tracking and reporting action plans and metrics), planning and facilitating meetings, and coaching team leaders in the use of project management principles.
- *Project Budgeting*—In the SJHS model, finance resource personnel partnered with project managers and executive sponsors to: (a) identify financial needs, (b) recommend specific financial resources, (c) calculate the costs and benefits associated with the recommended changes in process, (d) ensure that the financial impacts of the undertaking are understood, and (e) monitor expenditures and develop related financial reports.
- *Communications*—Regular communication and reporting lead to a higher level of achievement and accountability. Keeping operations strategy councils and governing boards abreast of progress fortified buy-in, averted misunderstandings, and minimized resistance when project modifications were needed.
- *Process Improvement*—Initiatives, by design, cause improvements in processes that help streamline day-to-day operations and achieve desired outcomes. An example, in this case, included the initiation of programs like "No Nurse Left Behind," a revamping of system-wide recruitment strategies and the establishment of care models that are aligned with the goals of the larger NWT project.

Second Phase: Bringing in an Educational Partner—Early on, the St. John Health System realized it could not address issues related to the nursing shortage without involving the primary trainers of nurses, particularly local universities and colleges. Dedicated to professionalism through caring, commitment and service, the Oakland University School of Nursing (OU-SON) in Rochester, Michigan, offers undergraduate, degree-completion, and master's degree programs in nursing that are accredited by the American Association of Colleges of Nursing, including distance learning and on-the-job training opportunities. OU-SON became an important collaborator with SJHS in support of the NWT project, in part by providing input that helped guide and influence the program's overall design. It is not hard to see how bridging the gap between nursing education and practice, reducing first-year RN turnover, and increasing related retention levels are tied to the success of the educational programs that feed the pool of prospective employees for health care organizations.

By adopting a shared vision of success, OU-SON and SJHS joined to make strides toward achieving those goals together. In soliciting feedback from and working closely with representatives of the university, SJHS successfully introduced on-board programs to reduce new graduate RN turnover rates. Onboarding initiatives provide specialized and targeted support for new nursing student graduates as they enter the workforce. Making institutions of nursing education an essential and intrinsic part of such processes by, for example, setting shared goals and co-implementing activities, exponentially increases the likelihood that such projects will make a meaningful impact and contribute to successfully addressing the shrinking pool of new nurses into the workplace, expanding rates of attrition and the increasing strain both put on health care organizations' ability to consistently provide quality patient care. The partners' joint efforts at reaching shared NWT goals commenced in 2006 during year one but was fully launched in the spring of 2007 through the implementation of several pilot project components. Activities included targeted nurse training cohorts at specific SJHS facilities, implementation of a new nurse on-boarding program to help transition graduates from school to employment, and workplace mentoring opportunities to provide additional on-the-job support through one-to-one professional role model relationships with experienced nurses.

Oakland University designed and developed an enhanced nursing curriculum and training delivery model to meet the workforce and human resource needs of St. John Health System, generating lessons germane for employers across the county. The goal was to create a larger pool of nurses better-equipped to work in patient care settings post-graduation, significantly increase degree-track openings through Web-based instruction and distance learning opportunities, offer flexible training options for a continuum of student types (e.g., accelerated to extended nursing programs), expand the faculty pool through a range of strategies, and improve nursing pedagogy through virtual clinics, supervised field experiences, and other innovations. Specifically, the pilot project augmented the existing nursing curriculum at Oakland University's School of Nursing through changes designed for working nurses at St. John Health System, so access was convenient and students were supported both academically and professionally.

This phase of the project provided additional learning experiences to reflect the team environment in which nurses participate, exposed students to the multiple perspectives found in a cross-disciplinary setting such as a hospital, and prepared new nurses to handle the stressful, fast-paced, complex environment that differs so greatly from the classroom. The initiative with the School of Nursing at Oakland University created proprietary cohorts of students who completed a more extensive clinical experience within a single unit such as St. John Health System. Existing nurses at the hospital were compensated and supported to serve in preceptor roles. These clinical precept roles were linked to development programs to encourage nurses to become educators. The purpose was to ease the role transition from student to professional nurse, to balance nursing theory with clinical competency, and to improve student confidence and student ability to perform the skills that encompass nursing (assessment, teaching, and other theoretical and technical skills) while facilitating the progression of the student nurse to assume increasing responsibilities and manage larger numbers of patients.

ANALYZING THE RESULTS

In less than 1 year through the Nursing Workplace Transformation initiative, St. John Health achieved reductions in nurse turnover rates across the board; increased its workplace safety and climate score by 18% while exceeding its target score by 300%; and adopted nine key dimensions or "Pillars of Success," which support the holistic and relationship-based care philosophies that are being employed to bring about change at the bedside. Two pilot units at an eastside Detroit site rolled out holistic nursing programs. Two acuity-adjustable units each at three locations were selected to participate in leadership transformation pilot programs. An equipment management program was implemented at two sites, which is expected to allow nurses to spend a higher percentage of their time on patient care.

By and large, goals set in all targeted areas of improvement have seen some or significant improvement. External agency hours were reduced from 35,000 plus in the third quarter of fiscal year 2006 to just over 25,000 by the same time in 2007 and came in at an additional 7,563 hours under target for more than a 25% decrease in outsourced hours. Responses to questions of satisfaction levels among RNs in top-box Work Environment Survey scores improved by 28% to surpass the NWT steering committee's goals for an improvement rate of 10%. Top-box refers to the upper-most category of the rating scale of the survey administered, while the data was evaluated based on frequency distribution rather than average values. Assessing and analyzing the outcomes stemming from this initiative can help nurse leaders at any stage of their career fine-tune the focus of their own current and future efforts in addressing these issues. In the case of St. John Health System, results from the NTW Initiative were compiled through a system of reporting, tracking, and survey mechanisms. In its third quarter report for 2006, the organization documented these achievements:

- *Enhanced on-boarding:* Aimed at addressing the needs of new nurses, first-year nurses, and those seeking new assignments, processes were launched to standardize hiring and on-site education provision, improve preceptor roles and increase opportunities for mentorship, forge stronger alliances with institutions of nursing education, and pave the way for more equitable, performance-based development programs.
- *Adequate staffing:* The goal of the FlexChoice program, rolled out in November 2006, was to establish a new, internal nursing resource pool. By January 2007, 46 nurses had enrolled in the program—ensuring experienced staff coverage. Other programs have also been launched to stabilize midnight and afternoon shifts.
- *Better recruitment and retention:* SJHS established a pilot program, in partnership with a local community college, which led to the hiring of 20 students as patient care technicians, which helped to lighten RN workloads. It also rolled out a first-of-its-kind (in the Detroit area), system-wide ER Nurse Orientation Program to attract larger numbers of nurses to its emergency care arm. In addition, the organization sponsored a November 2006 continuing education program that attracted 500 nurses—300 (60%) of whom were non-SJHS staff members. Six new nurses were hired from that pool of potential candidates, with offers pending for five others and 23 being actively recruited to fill staff positions as of the date of the report.
- *Improvements in physician-nurse communications:* SJHS's Providence facility began pilot testing of PerfectServe software, which, if successful, will be implemented system-wide as a time-saving alternative to traditional nurse-to-physician paging and communication methods.
- *More sensitive nursing assignment and scheduling:* SJHS established a "No Nurse Left Behind" program to address the needs of nurses who cannot withstand the rigors of floor nursing by providing more flexible staffing options that are intended to help nursing staff members strike a better home–work life balance.
- *Increased quantity and quality of bedside care:* Tracking down supplies, transporting patients, and tending to other nonnursing tasks takes staff members away from valuable caregiving activities; SJHS recognized and implemented several strategies to lighten their noncaregiving load. (Joseph & Naber, 2007; St. John Health System, 2007c)

REFLECTIONS ON LESSONS LEARNED

Turning attention to the valuable lessons learned from this case study makes it obvious the impact such initiatives can have. What follows is a list of key realizations and lessons learned during the initial stages of SJHS's Nursing Workforce Transformation program:

- *Gathering Relevant Information:* Utilizing internal data and surveys to drive program design and customize improvement efforts is crucial. Gathering and culling information received from staff members and others during planning and execution should be made a top priority.
- *Achieving Across-the-Board Buy-In:* Ensuring stakeholder ownership, from associate to executive levels, is imperative and must be a system-wide effort—one that is incorporated across multiple facilities and that crosses disciplinary lines.
- *Ensuring Return on Investment:* Deliverables must be clearly defined and plans to execute them must be efficient, easily understood, and achievable. In that way, facilities will achieve higher levels of return on their investment and benefit from an overall reduction in costs.
- *Allocating Adequate Resources:* Underestimating figures related to timelines, staff hours, and monies required to achieve meaningful results is a recipe for failure. Use a Return on Investment (ROI) matrix to adequately estimate resource commitments that are based on real numbers and will yield tangible results. Such a matrix provides an internal measuring stick to track achievement of project milestones.
- *Anticipating Change:* The improvement process is an ever-evolving one. Anticipate and be willing to morph and/or adapt plans—the continuums along which organizations make significant strides, thrive, grow, and achieve success—at every stage in the cycle.
- *Building Infrastructure:* Take issues of infrastructure (including software, technology, training, and equipment) into due account. Major capital outlays and funding must be in place to provide a framework upon which to build a better work environment.

CONCLUSION

Retention. Recruitment. Transformation. By providing a safe and supportive environment for nurses to perform their jobs, meeting the needs of nurses by creating a desired work climate, and increasing the amount of time nurses spend at the bedside providing patient care, organizations can tailor solutions to these issues to fit their own system and reverse the contributing factors to nurse dissatisfaction that has fueled the national shortage.

Launched in June 2006, the St. John Health System's Nursing Workforce Transformation program offers important lessons for hospitals and other nurse employers on how to alleviate nurse human resources dilemmas that continue to challenge the health care industry as a whole (St. John Health System, 2007b). Utilizing strategic planning techniques, encouraging institutional investment, and soliciting stakeholder buy-in can help hospitals transform practices so that they are able to improve recruitment processes, retain valuable and qualified nursing professionals, and improve the overall quality of care that is delivered to patient populations. A long-term replicable innovation of the initiatives described in this chapter was the creation of a model partnership between St. John Health System and Oakland University's School of Nursing. This collaboration is demonstrating novel and effective educational approaches to dramatically increase the supply of new registered nurses, improving career outcomes of nursing graduates and increasing human resource investments for hospitals.

Nurse leaders are crucial to such strategies, as differences in perception at various levels (from frontline staff to executive and leadership positions) are partly culpable for the escalation of the nursing shortage and create barriers that prevent organizations from making significant strides forward. Identifying appropriate solutions in this or any situation that calls for great change demands staunch dedication and commitment to process-based evolution and a willingness to learn from mistakes made along the way. The rewards have potential to benefit many people—employees and patients alike. Outcomes in this project included a reduction in nurse-to-patient ratios, improvements in managerial spans of control, and an enhancement of Worked Hours per Patient Day (WHPPD).

The consensus in the national nursing community is that immediate action is required to counter what has now become a shortage, of critical proportions, of qualified nursing professionals in the workplace. The Nursing Workforce Transformation Initiative offers a blueprint for others to emulate across the country. In moving forward at St. John Health System, in areas where outcomes did not meet expectations, new goals are now being set that take into account deficiencies in the original plan, and fresh perspectives can be gained from the experience. Perceived setbacks are being leveraged against gains achieved and are invigorating those who have both a direct and indirect influence in the implementation of the project, and those who are part of years two and three of the initiative from

2007 to 2009, during which Oakland University's School of Nursing will assume a larger role.

The task at hand for nursing leaders today is a meaningful improvement in the quality, quantity and satisfaction level of existing and new nursing professionals who are available and willing to provide health care nationwide tomorrow and beyond. Standing firm to commitment to process-based change and utilizing field-tested best practices can bring such a vision as this into reality. Reducing vacancies and lowering turnover among nurses is a challenge that all leaders in the nursing field will continue to face for years to come, yet a challenge that can be met through clear planning, strategic partnerships, and results-focused implementation.

REFERENCES

American Association of Nurses. (2007). Retrieved July 14, 2007, from www.nursing world.org

American Hospital Association. (2006, April). *The state of America's hospitals—Taking the pulse.* Retrieved January 23, 2008, from http://www.aha.org/aha/content/2005/pdf/TakingthePulse.pdf

Auerbach, D. I., Buerhaus, P. I., & Staiger, D. O. (2007). Better late than never: Workforce supply implications of later entry into nursing. *Health Affairs, 26*(1), 178–185.

Begin, S. (2006). St. John program eases its nursing shortage. *Crain's Business Detroit,* September 24, 2007. Retrieved December 20, 2007, from http://www.crains detroit.com/apps/pbcs.dll/article?AID=/20070924/SUB/709240329/1033/toc

Buerhaus, P. I., Donelan, K., Ulrich, B. T., Norman, L., DesRoches, C., & Dittus, R. (2007). Impact of the nurse shortage on hospital patient care: Comparative perspectives. *Health Affairs, 26*(3), 853–862.

HealthSouth Rehabilitation Hospitals of Western Massachusetts. (2007). *What are worked hours per patient day (WHPPD)?* Retrieved July 14, 2007, from http://www.healthsouthrehab.org/whatsnew_patients_first.asp

Joseph, E., & Naber, M. (2007). *Internal memorandum: St. John health system third quarter report.* Warren, MI: St. John Health System.

Michigan Center for Nursing. (2006). *Survey of nursing education programs: 2005–2006 school year.* Retrieved December 20, 2007, from http://www.mhc.org/mhc_images/edprogramsurvey06.pdf

Robert Wood Johnson Foundation (in partnership with Ascension Health and Kaiser Permanente). (n.d.). *Phase I study unit summary created for St. John Hospital and Medical Center.* Robert Wood Johnson Time and Motion Study.

St. John Health System. (2007a). *2006 top box work environment survey scores.* Warren, MI: Nursing Workforce Transformation Steering Committee Power Point Presentations: St. John Health System.

St. John Health System. (2007b). *Healthcare nursing workforce issues.* Warren, MI: Nursing Workforce Transformation Steering Committee Power Point Presentation: St. John Health System.

St. John Health System. (2007c). *FY07 nursing transformation scorecard: SJHS 3rd quarter report.* Warren, MI: St. John Health System.

U.S. Department of Health and Human Services. (2002). *Projected supply, demand and shortages of registered nurses: 2000 to 2020.* Retrieved July 14, 2007, from http://www.ahca.org/research/rnsupply_demand.pdf

CHAPTER 10

Personal

Margaret Grey

The purpose of this chapter is to describe and discuss the use of self as an instrument in educational leadership in nursing. The personal domain in the leadership compass focuses on the leader and his or her personal attributes. In this chapter, I address the use of self in leading a culture change in a school of nursing known primarily for its clinical expertise toward research.

THE CONTEXT

In 1993, I was recruited from the University of Pennsylvania to the Yale School of Nursing to serve as the first associate dean for Research and Doctoral Studies. At the time, the school had been through a serious university review and had emerged with the goal of enhancing faculty research, beginning a doctoral program, and managing the budget. I was the first of a series of senior faculty recruited toward these ends. The task was clear, to continue my own research, to work with faculty to increase research funding especially at the federal level, to develop the scientific base to support the doctoral program and enhance our scientific reputation on campus, and to secure funding to open the doctoral program.

The Yale School of Nursing was founded in 1923 and was the first university-based school of nursing in the United States. With a grant from the Rockefeller Foundation, Dean Annie Goodrich founded the school as an experiment in a focus on academic learning for nursing education rather than hospital service (Goodrich, 1932). For many years, the school admitted women who had been educated at the best women's colleges and provided basic nursing education resulting in the master of nursing degree. In the 1930s, the basic program was phased out in favor of focusing exclusively on graduate preparation for advanced practice, commensurate with the university's Corporation bylaws that all professional education at Yale should be focused on graduate preparation (Burst, 1998). The history of the school is replete with many firsts, including what is acknowledged as the first clinical research project in nursing, conducted by then faculty member Rhetaugh Dumas. The school was also known for the development of a theoretical approach to the integration of practice, education, and scholarship that paid homage to the knowledge that arises from clinical practice.

By 1993, the school had focused exclusively on the education of advanced practice nurses in multiple specialties including adult and family nurse practitioner, adult clinical specialist, pediatric nurse practitioner, and psychiatric clinical specialists. There were approximately 200 students and 50 faculty. The great majority of the faculty held master's degrees and was jointly appointed to a clinical agency. Of the 50 faculty, only 15 held doctoral degrees and several others were nearing completion. Several of the doctorally prepared faculty had held moderately sized grant awards ($50,000–$100,000).

Thus, the vision was to reclaim Yale's leadership position in clinical nursing research, build a base of research that would support a strong doctoral program, and enhance our reputation on Yale's campus. The challenges were substantial. Nursing was not seen as a research "player" on campus; material support for research (e.g., statistical, data management) was nonexistent; and faculty were wary of a shift away from the emphasis on clinical practice and clinical scholarship. Nonetheless, the dean and the senior faculty knew that success was critical and were supportive.

While many personal competencies were necessary to effect this change, those that were most important in achieving this vision were: developing self-knowledge and awareness; interpersonal and public communication skills; and for me, achieving work–life balance.

CASE STUDY

It has been said that the essence of leadership is not to manage change, but to lead effectively in the face of change (Johnson, 1998). Clearly, change had to happen at the School of Nursing, but in addition to the purpose, people, and process skills inherent in building such change, this journey and its success was predicated on my ability to grow and change in my own leadership skills to make it happen.

To understand this, a bit of personal background is in order. I was raised in a middle-class family where "doing your best in everything" was paramount. Self-reliance was a valued trait. As my career in nursing developed, my academic and research career was built around trying to do it all. I spent most of my early academic career striving for excellence (read: perfection) in everything. I worked hard, seven days per week almost every week, and rarely took time off. I rarely took vacation without calling into work regularly or bringing work along. While I eventually learned that some things did not need to be proofread three times (letters), I still believed that I needed to touch everything to assure that things were done "right." I brought these biases and traits to my new position at Yale.

I knew I had to write grants to support my own work and a training grant for the doctoral program. I knew that I had to help the faculty move their research funding from whatever it was—small grant to medium, medium to large, foundation to National Institutes of Health (NIH). I knew that I had to build a support system for the work of grant production and implementation. I knew that I had to be able to articulate to the faculty how one managed to be a good teacher and clinician while building and maintaining a program of research.

So the work began along two lines. First was to meet with faculty to understand their programs of research, needs, and plans. Second was to assure that my own research continued while the vision and strategy were developed. There were not discretionary monies to buy help at the time, so part of the strategy had to be how we would garner funds to develop the support systems we needed while we developed the faculty. This reality also meant that much of the work fell to me.

So in the first several years, we set out to engage more faculty members in larger research projects and to use the funds generated to develop an office to support research. The rhythm of the work involved the following. I met with faculty about their work, engaged them in discussions about where they saw their research going, and helped them develop new proposals. I read multiple drafts of proposals, provided ongoing feedback, and served as the preliminary statistician by helping develop analysis plans and running power analyses. Over the course of these few years, we doubled our research income, and the dean reassigned a staff member to work on grant activity. The Office of Research Affairs was born. My own grant was funded as were several others, and combining forces allowed us to hire a biostatistician to support our studies and to provide support for faculty without major grant support.

It was important also to be seen as a "player" on campus with regard to research and science. I was assigned to several key campus committees that were related to research, such as Human Subjects Review and Cooperative

Research. Having a nurse participate in these committees was designed to enhance our scientific reputation on campus. Communication about what nursing science is and how it contributes to the greater good was crucial to our success. Within the school, communication skills became even more important. Because the majority of the faculty was not doctorally prepared, it became clear that they felt threatened by this change of emphasis at the school. They were concerned that their positions would be in jeopardy if they did not change from a clinical focus to a more traditional academic research focus. Certain aspects of the curriculum, in particular the master's thesis, were potentially problematic, as each student was required to do an independent project. This requirement took an inordinate amount of faculty time that could be focused on faculty research development. I was asked to head a task force that would make recommendations about the future of the thesis. Clearly, I had become the symbol of a culture change that threatened the beliefs and values of the faculty.

I had always been a good public speaker but relied heavily on extraordinary preparation. Scientific presentations of 10-minute abstracts required the talk to be fully written out. Suddenly, I could not present myself with prepared remarks. I had to be ready to respond on short notice. I learned quickly to be able to do so in front of the faculty. It would be some time before I could do that in public.

Fortunately, I had the support of the dean, who was well-liked and respected by the faculty. Together, we worked to assure that the faculty understood that adding research to our capabilities did not jeopardize our embrace of our strong clinical values. Indeed, the message was that both were important values for the school and that different expertise would continue to be valued. The discussions about the thesis were prolonged and painful, but in the end, the changes that needed to be made were supported by the faculty and implemented. Throughout all this time, I continued to do most of the work described previously, in addition to teaching and running the doctoral program.

In 1997, the dean announced her intention to step out of the deanship, and a search was launched. A new dean brought new challenges and expectations. Another faculty member was recruited to run the doctoral program, and I was to focus exclusively on research development. This organizational change brought many challenges for me and the organization. It became clear that while I was respected by the faculty, many held the opinion that they didn't want to work so hard. Further, as the dean had come from outside Yale, she relied on me to explain the Yale culture and to help her articulate her vision to the faculty. By this time it became clear that my usual modus operandi of doing it all by myself was not going to work. I had to develop much more self-knowledge and awareness to be effective in my work and continue to expand my communication effectiveness.

Developing self-knowledge and awareness was not easy. I was successful, so it was scary to change how I did my work. I thought I was a leader who developed others, but I learned, painfully, that many saw me as interfering with their development because I didn't let work go to others. I also learned that others thought I was too businesslike. I rarely took time to ask personal questions of others and almost never talked about myself. This behavior created the impression that I didn't really care about the people behind the work, just the work. When I learned to be more open and to let work go to others and coach them to do it well, we began to see even more growth in our research dollars and our ranking. What happened was that people began to believe that they too could be successful, that we were all a part of making this new research-intensive environment live, and that our success was due to all of us working together rather than my efforts as the leader; there were new incentives for all to participate in the research enterprise.

I learned that my public speaking manner did not convey the passion that I had for my work. I was so focused on being right that I lost the audience in that perfection. I had to challenge myself to learn to speak in public without a script. This forced me to let the passion for the need for the work we were doing about managing chronic illness to come to the forefront and let the details fall to the background. The more I did so, the more invitations I received to give keynote and other key addresses, raising the profile of our school as a player in the research arena, an important step in an important goal of raising our reputation and ranking.

While doing all of this, I continued to rely primarily on myself to work with faculty. We had hired a statistician and a data manager, but the task of reviewing grants was mine. It wasn't that I thought others couldn't help, but that it was my job. I didn't seem to be able to extend the delegation of responsibility to the faculty as I had learned to do with the staff. Like a perfect storm, a number of events coalesced to make me change.

It became increasingly clear that to continue to do everything myself was not in service of the organization. I was working all the time and getting further behind. My ability to step back and look carefully at our effectiveness was compromised. Others were trying to help me change, but like my organization had, I was resisting. Then, my body decided to tell me. I had a massive gastrointestinal bleed and had to be hospitalized. Clearly, I could not continue to not care for myself or I would be less effective. I finally got the message that I needed to achieve a balance between my work and my life to enhance my effectiveness.

Giving up working every day was not easy, but the best advice was provided by a colleague who said, "If you continue to work every day, you will always work every day. The only way to stop is to just stop." I took 1 day per week and got out of the house, so that I wouldn't be drawn to the desk or e-mail. After a month or so, it became clear that when I took that day completely off, I had more energy for my work for the next week. I could use myself as an instrument of change in the organization in a more effective way. The faculty and staff noticed and were more likely to hear a discussion about workload now than before.

A few years later, the school was ranked in the top 10 in funding from the National Institutes of Health and in *US News & World Report*. We had increased our research funding from less than $1 million to over $7 million, and from less than 5% of our income to over 30% of our income. The university saw the important work that we were doing and was supportive, supporting the transition from a Doctor of Nursing Science (DNSc) program to a PhD. None of these would have been accomplished in the short 10 years without increasing my self-knowledge and awareness, improving my ability to communicate, and achieving work–life balance.

SUMMARY

It might be easy to think that the need for these skills in this situation of leading cultural change were a function of my own needs at the time. Indeed, that is the case, but to learn these skills at a critical time in the organization's development was the key to our success in changing this culture and achieving our vision of high rankings in research. As we face an increasing nurse faculty shortage, the need for our educational leadership to use such skills in developing the next generation of leaders is critical.

Communication is key. Leaders must articulate a vision and use self in bringing others to that vision. No matter what the role held by the leader is, the ability to clearly articulate a vision and to persuade others to embrace that vision is critical to success. In nursing in particular, with such a history of disagreement and strife, the ability to communicate effectively may yield important results in decreasing some of the controversies in how best to educate nurses for the future.

Leaders in nursing education must have self-knowledge and awareness of how they use themselves in the course of their work. I certainly could not have been as effective with leading staff and faculty without improving my self-knowledge and learning how to overcome certain perceptions. I never envisioned being a dean. But in the time I have been dean, I have used these skills, making sure that I take the time to know people and to stay in touch. I learn much more about what is on people's minds by wandering the halls and visiting than I could ever learn in a day of meetings. It's important that no one believes that I am out of touch.

As nursing has often been seen as a calling characterized by self-sacrifice, the achievement of work–life balance sends an important message to my colleagues and to the profession. I believe nursing is an intellectual pursuit, so self-sacrifice is not the model we are trying to put forward. Thus, the model of academic leaders sacrificing family life in order to effect change in nursing and health care simply is not what the system needs. Most importantly, the next generation who must take over do not view work as my generation has. They believe in and want to have a balance between work and their personal lives. If we persist in demonstrating that the only way to lead is to work all the time, then we will lose an entire generation of new leaders we are responsible for educating.

REFERENCES

Burst, H. V. (1998). *Yale school of nursing: 75 years of excellence.* New Haven, CT: Yale University Press.

Goodrich, A.W. (1932). *University schools of nursing. The social and ethical significance of nursing.* New York: McMillan.

Johnson, S. (1998). *Who moved my cheese?* New York: G. P. Putnam's Sons.

PART IV

Leadership in the Service Industry

Current Issues in the Service Industry

Linda Thompson Adams and Edward H. O'Neil

How could the U.S. health care system, which is largely a private system and characterized by arguably more competition than any other health care system in the world, be performing so poorly? Why are costs among the highest in the world even though many citizens do not have health coverage? How could costs, already so high, still be rising so rapidly? Why is quality so uneven? Why is there growing evidence of alarming quality problems in the system? These are just a few of the issues facing the health care system today.

Hospitals and health care organizations in the United States are on a collision course with patient needs and economic reality (Porter & Teisberg, 2007). Rising cost, mounting quality problems, and increasing numbers of citizens without health insurance are unacceptable and unsustainable in today's society. One strategy to reform health care in America is to invest in nursing leadership development. According to the Bureau of Health Professionals, nursing is the largest group of health care professionals, with a workforce of 2.9 million (U.S. Department of Health and Human Services, 2004). Nursing executives in health care service must lead change by redefining strategies, practices and structures to unleash stunning improvements in the value and quality of the care delivered to the general public. This section describes the major issues confronting hospitals today. It follows with examples of nurse leaders working to transform the system of care within their health care institutions.

Despite major advances in technology and treatment options, the U.S. health care industry remains mired in complex, deeply rooted challenges (Porter & Teisberg, 2007). A variety of market forces and systemic deficiencies are undermining the quest to deliver the best possible care in the most efficient and cost-effective manner. There are significant pressures on the system. Hospitals strive to fulfill their mission while maintaining their profit margin. They cope with workforce shortages and scarce resources amid rising competition and demand for services. They routinely grapple with issues related to capacity and access to care, patient safety, technology adoption, staff satisfaction, reimbursement, and retaining top talent. The industry's vital signs are raising red flags and nurses in leadership are needed to design sustainable solutions to the issues, equip teams with evidence-based practices and design processes to improve performance and management systems.

Is this an impossible mission? Can nurse leaders overturn a century of tradition in terms of workflow, culture, financial management and maintain quality and safe care? Can we speed up the process of change and effectively spread the gains across an entire service line, hospital or integrated delivery network? Perhaps the question should be: *can we afford not to?* The need for large scale change is not going away. Patients continue to utilize emergency rooms as their primary care center without follow up or leave overcrowded emergency rooms without being seen. Medical and technological advances continue to outpace the required adjustments in process and education.

An aging and informed populace places higher expectations and added strain on the system. An unacceptable percentage of revenue continues to slip through the cracks of a fractured charge capture system. In addition, although we have made strides in reducing medical errors, recent reports underscore lingering problems with the quality of patient care. To top it off, health care providers increasingly find themselves in the unfamiliar and often untenable positions of having to compete for physicians, staff, patients, resources, and dollars.

In this competitive and complex environment, average performance in terms of quality and financial indicators is no longer enough to ensure long-term viability. It is admittedly tough to manage through turbulent times. But if health care organizations cannot stay ahead of the game now, how can they compete with new complexities and expand into areas such as digitization and personalized medicine? The answers—like the issues—are multifaceted and are an opportunity for nursing leadership.

Nurse leaders must work with hospital organizations to redesign processes and address the human side of change. New technology, clinical breakthroughs and digitization will only carry us part of the way on a journey to transform care. *So what will it take to transform health care?*

Solving today's problems and ensuring a viable system for the future will require a fundamental shift in mind-set and management models. It will take the combined power of proven best practices, evidence-based process control, change management techniques, and leadership strategies. It will take a guide who has traversed the territory, knows the obstacles and can customize a road-map to reach the destination. For those ready to take the lead in shaping a stronger health system for the future, please learn how other leaders addressed some of the challenges, developed solutions and obtained real world examples of success. This section shares a few inspirational, real world stories of nursing leadership.

REFERENCES

Porter, M., & Teisberg, E. (2007). *Redefining health care: Creating value based competition on results.* Boston: Harvard Business School Press.

U.S. Department of Health and Human Services. (2004). *The registered nurse population: Findings from the March 2004 national sample survey of registered nurses.* Retrieved January 4, 2008, from http://bhpr.hrsa.gov/healthworkforce/rnsurvey04/default.htm

CHAPTER 11

Purpose

Jeanette Ives Erickson

To accomplish great things we must first dream, then visualize, then plan . . .
believe . . . act!

—Alfred A. Montapert

OVERVIEW

Leadership is a critical factor in today's busy and challenging health care environment in achieving a variety of outcomes including: excellence in patient- and family-centered care, professional development, the advancement of nursing as a clinical discipline, and staff satisfaction. All nurses, through formal and continuing education, have been introduced to the art and science of leadership and education and the application of these skills in the delivery of patient care. It is within the context in which we practice that determines how those skills are applied.

A leader analyzes situations and works to solve problems in creative ways, even if it means breaking the rules within moral boundaries. A leader anticipates problems and opportunities before they arise and takes risks in exploring new approaches. Nursing leaders possess a passion for nursing and the ability to inspire an optimistic vision for the future. In health care, the best leaders are committed to improving patient care. Best practices must be recognized, encouraged, and supported.

Nurses utilize critical thinking skills and effective communication strategies to react to and influence the future. The application of these skills is dependent upon the area of practice at any given time. For example, a staff nurse will use these skills in working with the interdisciplinary health care team. A chief nurse will use these skills in working with their nursing colleagues, other disciplines, administrators, the media, and politicians. Nurse leaders at any level in the organization understand the concepts of power and influence and incorporate that understanding into their interactions with patients, families, staff and others.

Nursing leadership in health care is necessary because nursing is the backbone of the health care system. Nurses know that the health care system in this country and in the world would not exist without them. Nursing leaders need to continually identify opportunities to improve care, implement new initiatives, and monitor existing programs and services. In health care today, quality and safety are our highest priorities. We need to commit to a culture of quality and safety while maintaining a competitive edge in the marketplace. No one knows better than nurses the enormous economic pressure on hospitals today. Nursing leaders need to identify strategies that meet the needs of patients and families, maintain and enhance clinical excellence, improve quality and safety, and meet our financial targets.

Leadership, an essential component of all nursing roles, is defined by Kouzes and Posner (2003) as "challenging the process, inspiring a shared vision, enabling others to act, modeling the way and encouraging the heart."

Three of the 10 leadership competencies cited by Kouzes and Posner speak directly to the articulation of a clear strategic direction and purpose. (See Exhibit 11.1). In their writings, they focus on the critical importance of nurse leaders mastering these competencies and describe components of an infrastructure that supports this work. This chapter will focus on how to translate these three competencies into reality.

BACKGROUND

Setting the strategic direction for a service, department, or institution is an integral part of a leader's work. No matter what term is used—whether purpose, mission, or calling—leaders want to do something significant, to accomplish something no one else has yet achieved. What that something is—the sense of meaning or purpose—comes from within. No one can impose a self-motivating vision on another person. It is important to clarify your own vision of the future before enlisting others in a shared vision. To create a climate of meaningful participation, you must first believe in something yourself. Before you can inspire others, you must first *be* inspired.

EXHIBIT 11.1 LEADERSHIP COMPETENCIES

Inspires a Shared Vision and Purpose: engages others in the dynamic process of integrating mission and values in the drive towards inventing the future.

Thinks Strategically: critically evaluates, synthesizes, and interrelates information from internal and external sources when solving problems and making decisions.

Transforms Vision to Reality: gets results by managing strategy to action in the context of continuous change; assumes responsibility for achieving outcomes; willingly offers to take on new responsibility.

Communicates Effectively: leads others in two-way communication both verbally and in writing; uses effective listening skills by demonstrating attention to and conveying an understanding of the ideas and opinions of others.

Enables and Empowers Others to Act: creates and sustains an environment that integrates the values of shared decision making into clinical and administrative practices; celebrates achievements of others.

Establishes Collaborative Relationships and Promotes Teamwork Within and Across Departments: creates strategic internal and external alliances to drive towards organizational goals.

Seizes Opportunities: takes decisive action on emerging opportunities in a rapidly changing environment; removes barriers to achieve outcomes and facilitate the work of others.

Recognizes, Develops, Implements and Shares Best Practices: demonstrates enthusiasm and openness to change based on new knowledge and utilization of internal and external expertise.

Acts with Integrity and Demonstrates Ethical Behaviors: demonstrates principled leadership; walks the talk.

Develops Oneself: demonstrates commitment to self-awareness, balance, lifelong learning and teamwork.

Adapted from Kouzes and Posner (2003)

One of the first steps in setting a direction is to discover and appeal to a common purpose. Why do people come to work or stay with an organization? They want to respond that they like the work they do and find it challenging, meaningful, and fulfilling. This is grounded in the mission. A well-defined mission statement succinctly describes the reason why the organization exists. It sets a direction for organizational planning, decision making, and allocation of resources. When nurse leaders listen with sensitivity to the aspirations of others, common values that link people together are identified. The best organizational leaders are able to communicate the meaning and significance of the organization's work so people understand the important role they play in creating it. When leaders clearly communicate a shared organizational vision, they empower those working to achieve it. And they enroll others in pursuit of the vision.

HOW DO WE BUILD A SHARED VISION?

Building a shared vision is only one piece of a larger undertaking—developing the governing ideas of an institution, its vision, purpose, and core values. Peter Senge, in his hallmark book, *The Fifth Discipline* (1990) notes that these governing ideas answer three critical questions: What? Why? and How? Taken together, all three governing ideas answer the question, "What do we believe in?" (Senge, 1990).

Core values are necessary to help people with day-to-day decision making. Purpose is abstract. Vision is long-term. People need "guiding stars" to help them navigate and make decisions on a daily basis. But core values must be translated into concrete behaviors. (Senge, 1990). An organization's value statements have implications for strategic planning, as organizational results are the sum of the decisions and behaviors of the individuals making up the organization. The decisions and behaviors of each person are directed by the person's own values and those of the organization. (See Exhibit 11.2).

STATISTICS

It is more important than ever that nurse leaders clearly articulate the important work of the profession and create a robust pipeline of future nurses. Some

---

EXHIBIT 11.2 THE FIFTH DISCIPLINE

Vision is the *"What?"*—the picture of the future we seek to create.

Purpose (or mission) is the *"Why?"*—the organization's answer to the question, "Why do we exist?" Superior organizations have a larger sense of purpose that transcends meeting the needs of shareholders and employees. They seek to contribute to the world in a meaningful way, to add a distinct value.

Core values are the *"How?"*—How do we want to act on the path toward achieving our vision? A company's values might include integrity, transparency, honesty, freedom, equal opportunity, leanness, merit, or loyalty. They describe how a company wants life to be on a day-to-day basis while pursuing its vision.

Reprinted from The Fifth Discipline (Senge, 1990)

of the most compelling numbers in health care today are the predictions related to the growing nursing shortage. According to Auerbach, Buerhaus, and Staiger (2007), the nursing profession will reach a shortfall of 340,000 nurses by 2020. Today, 1 in 10 nursing jobs is unfilled in the United States. It is predicted that this nursing shortage will be more severe and last longer than any other shortage previously experienced. (Bureau of Labor Statistics, 2003).

Nursing has an image problem. Surveys of high school students and adult career-switchers show that only 3% of adults would choose nursing as a career. Yet, year after year, the Gallup survey tells us nursing is the most trusted profession (Gallup News Service, 2006). How can we overcome the deep-rooted stereotypes and barriers that are keeping people from choosing nursing as a career? Key factors contributing to the shortage are: differences in the work environment compared to past shortages, an ongoing struggle with the image of nursing, recruitment of new nurses, retention of current nurses, and regulatory and policy changes that negatively impact recruitment or speed the attrition of nurses.

Making visible the contributions nurses make in the lives of patients and families is a critical step in reversing the nursing shortage. The American Nurses Association (from the ANA Nursing Social Policy Statement) defines nursing as "the protection, promotion, and optimization of health and abilities, prevention of illness and injury, alleviation of suffering through the diagnosis and treatment of human response, and advocacy in the care of individuals, families, communities and populations" (American Nursing Association, 2003).

According to the ANA (2003), essential features of professional nursing include:

- provision of a caring relationship that facilitates health and healing
- attention to the range of human experiences and responses to health and illness within the physical and social environments
- integration of objective data with knowledge gained from an appreciation of the patient's or group's subjective experience
- application of scientific knowledge to the processes of diagnosis and treatment through the use of judgment and critical thinking
- advancement of professional nursing knowledge through scholarly inquiry
- influence on social and public policy to promote social justice

There is no silver bullet to solve the nursing shortage. It is going to require a multifaceted approach. In addition to providing a strong, positive work environment and competitive salaries, having nurses speak about the profession in high school classrooms and getting nurses out in the community to talk to young people and potential career-switchers is an important step in recruitment of the next generation. "Shadow a nurse" programs are effective in attracting young people to the profession—participants have an opportunity to observe firsthand the important work nurses do with patients and families.

A CASE STUDY

When I assumed the position of senior vice president for patient care and chief nurse at the Massachusetts General Hospital in 1996, the organization had just undergone a "re-engineering" initiative that had created a sense of concern among staff. A new hospital president was hired a few months before my appointment. He valued nursing and the other health care disciplines and worked collaboratively with me to create an environment in which staff felt valued, powerful, and recognized.

In 1996, Patient Care Services was comprised of many disciplines functioning largely in silos. My immediate challenge was to identify strategies to bring down those silos and get the disciplines talking to one another, working with one another, and more importantly, heading in the same strategic direction. To bring about this transformation, I used a number of high-leverage strategies I like to think of as the seeds of change. It took years for these seeds to grow, and they required ongoing care and cultivation.

The processes I employed to create a new culture and strategic direction included:

- retreats, where we articulated a shared vision, guiding principles, and long-term strategic goals
- a description of a patient care delivery model
- articulation of the components of a professional practice environment
- the design and implementation of the Staff Perceptions of the Professional Practice Environment Survey to measure key characteristics of a healthy practice environment.

Let's examine each of these processes more deeply.

Development of a Strategic Plan

Aligning the 4,200-strong leadership and staff comprising Patient Care Services (PCS) around a common purpose and direction is accomplished through

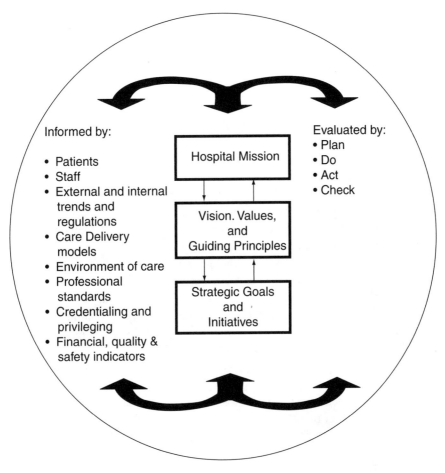

Informed by:

- Patients
- Staff
- External and internal trends and regulations
- Care Delivery models
- Environment of care
- Professional standards
- Credentialing and privileging
- Financial, quality & safety indicators

Hospital Mission

Vision. Values, and Guiding Principles

Strategic Goals and Initiatives

Evaluated by:
- Plan
- Do
- Act
- Check

FIGURE 11.1 MGH Patient Care Services strategic planning process.

the Patient Care Services strategic planning process. (See Figure 11.1.) Strategic goals are driven from the foundation of the hospital's mission and Patient Care Services' vision, values, and guiding principles. These governing ideas and statements guide our daily work.

The process is a dynamic one and is informed by a multitude of information sources, including patient and staff feedback through formal and informal channels; care delivery models; external and internal trends and regulation; professional standards; the environment of care; credentialing and privileging requirements; and financial, quality, and safety indicators. Patient Care Services' strategic goals are continually assessed and reassessed as new information from these sources becomes available.

In addition, the strategic goals, initiatives, and tactics are continually evaluated through the Plan-Do-Check-Act (PDCA) process of performance improvement. Likened to the steps in the nursing process with which we are all familiar, the steps in the PDCA process guide refinement of the strategic plan.

Description of the Patient Care Delivery Model

The Patient Care Delivery Model is interdisciplinary and patient- and family-centered. It articulates a care-delivery system that is supported by a philosophy of care and an environment that enhances patient outcomes. These elements include staffing patterns, strategies for aggregating patient populations, reimbursement methods, and effective communication systems that report and document outcomes of patients' hospitalizations.

Patient care is expected to be of the highest quality, comprehensive, accessible, supportive, and personalized. An important aspect of the vision statement for Patient Care Services says, "Patients are our primary focus, and the way we deliver care reflects that focus every day." Patient- and family-centered care optimizes this relationship. It creates a care-delivery system that is centered on the patient.

The diagram (Figure 11.2) depicts the patient and family at the center of our work. Involvement with the patient and family is central to professional practice at Massachusetts General Hospital (MGH). Value is placed on the dynamic and therapeutic interactions that occur between the nurse, the patient, and the family.

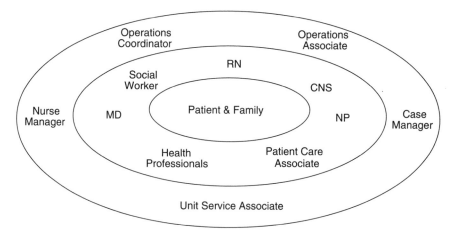

FIGURE 11.2 Patient and family centeredness.

Decisions about care and the environment of care are made at the practice level by clinical staff and unit leadership through the patient care delivery model (Figure 11.3). Published previously by Nevidjon and Ives Erickson (2001), this model places the authority, responsibility, and accountability for the nursing care of patients and families with registered nurses. Nursing care is prescribed by a registered nurse and delivered by a registered nurse (or delegated to competent nursing assistants, when appropriate). Accountability for nursing care and outcomes of nursing interventions is always assumed by the registered nurse assigned to the patient. Patient care is influenced by the patient's overall health status and a variety of contributing biophysical, psychosocial, and cultural influences. Within the nurse-patient relationship, the nurse creates a therapeutic environment that ensures mutual trust, safety, privacy, and respect.

As a nurse comes to know a patient and the patient's unique response to certain situations, the nurse designs a care plan based on that knowledge and best practices. The nurse's practice has two components: *doing for* and *being with*. *Doing for* includes assessment, diagnosis, planning, intervention, and evaluation of outcomes; *being with* refers to behaviors that create an environment where patients can heal. The diagram in Figure 11.3 illustrates this aspect of nursing practice. Nursing care requires nurses to be present to patients and families—to listen, to know, to advocate for throughout the health care experience. Our culture encourages professional autonomy and clinical decision making and supports interventions that promote optimal patient care across a variety of health care settings. Nurses are creative in their approach to care and use knowledge to improve outcomes. They optimize patient strengths and provide support for limitations. Nurses at MGH are afforded an environment that optimizes professional practice and enhances patient care.

The nurse–patient relationship, central to the work of nursing, is based on mutual trust and respect and is therapeutic in nature. The partnership forged between a nurse and patient (family and community) is essential to promoting health, managing illness, and negotiating changes in lifestyle patterns. Nurses identify concerns related to the human experience (i.e., birth, health, illness, and death) and engage in clinical reasoning processes to identify problems, define outcomes, and generate interventions based on goals shared by the nurse, the patient, and the family.

Articulation of the Components of a Professional Practice Model

The MGH Professional Practice Model (PPM) was developed to provide a comprehensive view of professional practice and the discipline-specific contributions of providers engaged in patient care. It is developed around nine

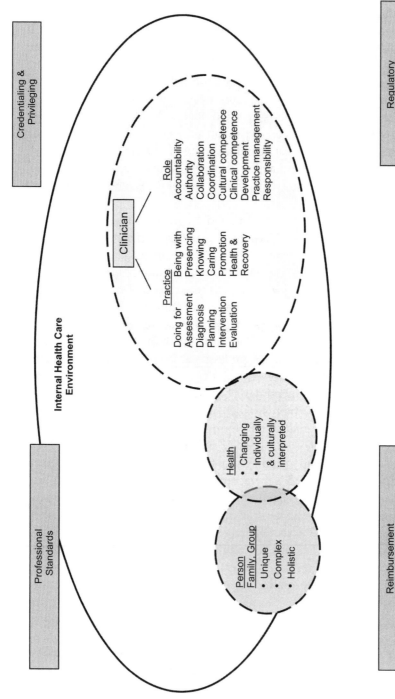

FIGURE 11.3 MGH Patient Care Delivery Model.

essential elements, including vision and values, standards of practice, narrative culture, professional development, patient-centeredness, clinical recognition and advancement, collaborative decision making, research, innovation, and entrepreneurial teamwork (see Figure 11.4).

The Professional Practice Model reflects an organizational commitment to teamwork in an effort to facilitate optimal patient care. The Professional Practice Model is an interdisciplinary model, in which each discipline articulates its contribution to professional practice. The model is the infrastructure that supports clinicians as they care for patients and influences the development of a culturally sensitive practice environment. A collaborative governance model supports clinicians and helps advance professional participation in decision making. Active participation in practice, teaching, and research occurs within all disciplines.

Staff Perceptions of the Professional Practice Environment Survey

Once the Professional Practice Model was developed, evaluating its effectiveness became an important goal and led to the creation of the first version of the Professional Practice Environment Scale. In 1998, the Staff Perceptions of the Professional Practice Environment Survey (PPE) was first administered to provide an assessment of eight organizational characteristics determined to be important to clinician satisfaction. The survey allows clinicians an opportunity to participate in setting the strategic direction for Patient Care Services, helps provide information on trends, provides feedback on established goals, and identifies opportunities to improve the environment for clinical practice. Survey data is used to identify strengths and opportunities to improve the environment of care for clinicians, patients, and families.

The original Staff Perception of the Professional Practice Environment Survey was developed as a 35-item scale designed to measure eight characteristics: autonomy, control over practice, clinician-physician relationships, cultural sensitivity, communication, teamwork, conflict-management, and internal work motivation (Table 11.1).

The organizational characteristics we chose are documented in the literature as important in determining clinician satisfaction with the professional practice environment. The survey contains questions designed to measure staff's agreement with statements about each organizational characteristic. Responses are measured on a 4-point Likert scale. Overall satisfaction in each category is measured on a 6-point Likert scale. And strategic goals are measured on a 6-point Likert scale indicating their level of importance and how well they are working. Comments can be added throughout the survey and are qualitatively analyzed and presented as themes in the final report.

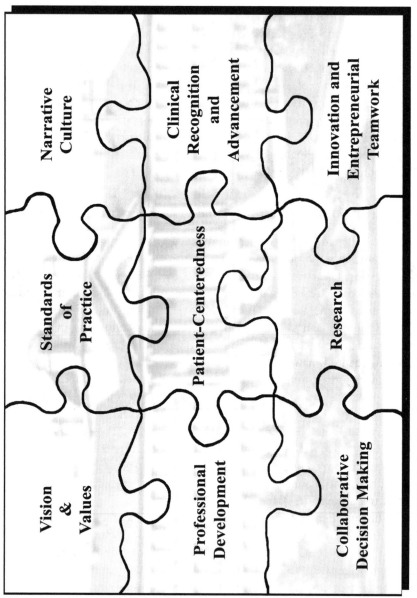

FIGURE 11.4 MGH Professional Practice Model-Components.

TABLE 11.1 Patient Care Services, Organizational Characteristics, and Definitions

Organizational characteristic	Definition	Source
Autonomy	The quality or state of being self-governing and exercising professional judgment in a timely fashion	Aiken, Sochalski, & Lake, 1997
Clinician-MD relations	Relations with physicians that facilitate exchange of important clinical information	Aiken, Sochalski, & Lake, 1997
Control over practice	Sufficient intraorganizational status to influence others and to deploy resources when necessary for good patient care	Aiken, Havens, & Sloan, 2000
Communication	The degree to which patient care information is related promptly to the people who need to be informed through open channels of communication	Shortell, Rousseau, Gillies, Devers, & Simons, 1991
Teamwork/leadership	A conscious activity aimed at achieving unity of effort in the pursuit of shared objectives	Zimmerman, Shortell, Rousseau, Duffy, Gillies, Knaus, et al., 1993
Conflict management/handling disagreements	The degree to which managing conflict is addressed using a problem-solving approach	Zimmerman et al., 1993
Internal work motivation	Self-generated motivation completely independent of external factors such as pay, supervision, and coworkers	Hackman & Oldham, 1980
Cultural sensitivity	A set of attitudes, practices, and/or policies that respects and accepts cultural differences	The Cross Cultural Health Care Program, 2000

Psychometric evaluation of the PPE (Ives Erickson et al., 2004) described the tool as a reliable and valid measure of staff perception. That means the tool measures what it was created to measure, and its findings are useful and generalizable to the whole. The tool monitors how staff perceives organizational performance at the macro (system) and micro (unit/department) levels.

Data from the Staff Perceptions Survey inform our strategic direction. Data are shared at three organizational levels: department-wide (Patient Care Services), discipline-specific, and by individual unit. One important outcome of the survey is the dialogue that ensues between managers and clinicians regarding the results of the survey. Successful strategies employed over the years include:

- sharing results at staff meetings to generate a discussion
- identifying areas for change and innovation linking specific strategies to outcomes
- understanding trends over time
- evaluating the impact of changes made based on survey results
- identifying best-practice environments

Receiving feedback from staff is important, so survey results are presented in a variety of forums. This is also an opportunity to share ideas on how to address issues identified in the survey. Realistic goals and specific interventions can be developed, implemented, and then evaluated for effectiveness over time.

LESSONS LEARNED

As we began our journey, we focused on key elements of doing well for our patients and their care providers. What we did not know was that we were preparing to become a Magnet hospital. The importance of working in a professional practice environment has been well documented since the first Magnet hospital study (McClure, Poulin, Sovie, & Wandelt, 1983). In this study, autonomy, control over practice, and collaborative relationships with physicians were identified as essential components of professional practice and critical to creating work environments that act as magnets for talented clinical staff, and indeed those were the key elements of our work.

The components reviewed above (strategic plan, patient-care delivery model, professional practice model, and staff perception survey) are interconnected and form a solid infrastructure to support nurses and other members of the health care team to do what they do best—care for patients and families and each other.

Nursing leaders should always look for opportunities to improve patient care. Patients and families are always at the center of our thinking. "What does the patient need?" is the question we need to ask. Patients need a strong nursing presence. Nurses need to be able to practice autonomously, have the appropriate resources to do their job, and have good relationships with other members of the health care team. Nurses need to be equal partners with their physician colleagues, whether at the bedside or at the planning table. Collaborative governance, our communication and decision-making structure, is vital in ensuring that the voice of clinicians at the bedside is heard.

Establishing the components of a supportive professional practice environment takes time and work and focus. But the benefits are great. Once achieved, it is important not to forget the fundamentals. It is tempting to relax discipline, forget essential routines, or ignore the rules when you feel you have achieved your goals. As Tom Peters says, you must always "stick to the knitting" so erosion of the professional practice environment doesn't occur (Peters, 2003; Peters & Waterman, 1982).

CONCLUSIONS AND IMPLICATIONS

Leadership is complex. Some of it is taught in formal settings—other aspects are learned in the moment. Nursing leadership requires focus, a personal connection to the organization and the people, and a passion for advancing the art and science of the profession.

In today's specialized world, we are often tempted to compartmentalize our lives, putting professional interests in one corner and other matters in another. With the rapid changes occurring in health care, nursing leadership can be a source of great strength. Nurses must emerge as dynamic leaders who can guide health care organizations to create healing environments for patients, families, and the health care team (Porter-O'Grady & Malloch, 2006).

Leadership is not about power or control or ego. Leadership is about meeting the challenges of our time with passion and focus. It is about living life with a purpose—a strategic purpose. The foundation of strong leadership is the ability to articulate a vision that can be embraced and understood by an increasingly diverse community. Consensus may not always be possible, but a shared vision is essential. I'm often told that staff nurses relate to me as a leader because I haven't lost sight of my identity as a nurse or my passion for nursing practice. And equally important is the ability to advocate for nursing to administrators, public policy makers, financial experts, and the media.

Understanding how to communicate in a timely, professional, and appropriate manner is a key factor in effective leadership. Some issues may require lengthy explanations for one audience, streamlined information for another, and only brief comments for another. A good leader knows how to communicate, when to communicate, what to communicate, and to whom to communicate.

Do not underestimate the importance of listening. What are patients, families, staff, and colleagues telling you? And, more importantly, what *aren't* they telling you? Becoming a good listener takes practice and attention.

All of the important lessons should be articulated in a strategic plan to translate a vision into reality. Respect from staff, colleagues, peers, and administration is necessary in achieving goals and earning the needed buy-in to deliver results. This comes from their ability to be aligned with and articulate the key messages for both today and tomorrow.

As a leader, I have always emphasized the importance of strategic planning. You have to know where you are headed and be able to motivate your team to *want* to take the journey with you. And it is just as important to be a tactical planner—to be able to identify every step the team must take in order to realize the shared vision.

REFERENCES

Aiken, L., Havens, D., & Sloane, D. (2000). The magnet nursing services recognition program: A comparison of two groups of magnet hospitals. *American Journal of Nursing, 100*(3), 26–36.

Aiken, L., Sochalski, J., & Lake, E. (1997). Studying outcomes of organizational change in health services. *Medical Care, 24*(11 Suppl.), NS6–NS18.

American Nursing Association. (2003). *Nursing's social policy statement.* Washington, DC: American Nurses Association.

Auerbach, D. I., Buerhaus, P. I., & Staiger, D. O. (2007). Better late than never: Workforce supply implications of later entry into nursing. *Health Affairs, 26*(1). pp. 178–185.

Bureau of Labor Statistics. (2003). U.S. Department of Labor. Retrieved January 24, 2008, from www.dol.gov

The Cross Cultural Health Care Program. (2000). Retrieved January 24, 2008, from www.xculture.org

Gallup News Service. (2006, December 14). *Nurses top list of most honest and ethical professions.* Retrieved January 24, 2008, from www.gallup.com

Hackman, J., & Oldham, G. (1980). *Work re-design.* Reading, MA: Addison-Wesley.

Ives Erickson, J., Duffy, M. E., Gibbons, M. P., Fitzmaurice, J., Ditomassi, M., & Jones, D. (2004). Development and psychometric evaluation of the Professional Practice Environment Scale. *Journal of Nursing Scholarship,* 3rd quarter, 279–285.

Kouzes, J. M., & Posner, B. Z. (2003). *The leadership challenge* (3rd ed.). San Francisco: Jossey-Bass.

McClure, M. L., Poulin, M. A., Sovie, M. D., & Wandelt, M. (1983). *Magnet hospitals: Attraction and retention of professional nurses.* Washington, DC: American Nurses Publishing.

Nevidjon, B., & Ives Erickson, J. (2001). The nursing shortage: Solutions for the short and long term. *Online Journal of Nursing, 6*(1), ms. 4.

Peters, T. J. (2003). *Re-imagine!—Business excellence in a disruptive age.* London: Dorling Kindersley Limited.

Peters, T. J., & Waterman, R. H. (1982). *In search of excellence: Lessons from America's best-run companies.* New York: Warner Books Edition. Retrieved January 24, 2008, from http://www.nursingworld.org/MainMenuCategories/ANAMarketplace/ANA Periodicals/OJIN/TableofContents/Volume62001/Number/January2001/Nursing Short ageSolutions.aspx

Peters, T. J. (2003). *Re-imagine!—Business excellence in a disruptive age.* London: Dorling Kindersley Limited.

Porter-O'Grady, T., & Malloch, K. (2006). *Managing for success in health care.* St. Louis, MO: Mosby.

Senge, P. (1990). *The fifth discipline: The art and practice of the learning organization.* New York: Doubleday Currency.

Shortell, S., Rousseau, D., Gillies, R., Devers, K., & Simons, T. (1991). Organizational assessment in intensive care units (ICUs): Construct development, reliability and validity of the ICU nurse-physician questionnaire. *Medical Care, 29,* 709–723.

Zimmerman, J., Shortell, S., Rousseau, D., Duffy, J., Gillies, R., Knaus, W., et al. (1993). Improving intensive care: Observations based on organizational case studies in nine intensive care units. *Critical Care Medicine, 21*(10), 1443–1551.

CHAPTER 12

People

Susan R. Lacey and Karen S. Cox

In April of 2007 Dr. Ed O'Neil, the Director for the University of California San Francisco (UCSF) Center for Health Professions, provided incredible clarity for the pervasive framework for organizational leadership within the health care industry in the center's monthly online newsletter (O'Neil, 2007). He lays out the conundrum of trying to deal with the ever-mounting pressures encountered within health care organizations by increasing and valuing management over that of leadership. Not only is this way of conducting business adding layers upon layers of additional costs; managing rather than leading will not create the new health care system for which our industry is in great need and which every major report, such as the Institute of Medicine (2001) and the Commonwealth Foundation, (2007) indicate is critical and urgent to sustain our systems of care and to improve quality outcomes for patients.

Much of the flurry of activity in health care today is centered on trying to manage not only the day-to-day operations of an organization—which is prudent—but also to manage processes and people. Nothing could be farther from what we need to be doing today than the latter. As we try and grapple with decreasing profit margins; nursing shortages; quality improvement edicts such as reporting, transparency, and pay for performance; and various other mandates and regulatory issues, the tighter we try and reign in these complexities, the more they seem to spiral out of our control, particularly since we continue to use worn-down management paths to find ways to get it right in health care. In this chapter we offer two specific touchstones for consideration as you seek ways to lead in these turbulent times. The first will parallel the work of an airline industry giant, Southwest Airlines. The second will translate how you can use the basic principles (e.g. the 14 forces) of Magnet certification even if pursuing Magnet status will never be part of your organization's future.

Each of these two either individually or in concert can create a new level of inspiration for your organization for everyone involved. Your staff awaits your leadership; in fact, they hunger for true leaders to emerge and guide them out of this health care wilderness. Further, the patients and families who enter your facility do so with a willingness to trust those you lead to care for them and with an implicit contract that in the case of their care, you will get it right.

SOUTHWEST AIRLINES: NOW, WHY DIDN'T WE THINK OF THAT?

In the past 10 years there has been a push toward looking at other industries for solutions to health care problems. Specifically, there has been enormous energy to use lessons learned from the aviation industry to increase quality outcomes, which in the case of health care translates into reducing errors and more specifically reducing death and injury. Yet there are other valuable lessons to learn from the airline industry that would serve us well as we try to satisfy the perpetual "quality soup" and "war for talent" we all seem to be stewing in today. Take the case of Southwest Airlines; the only employee-owned airline in the industry—and the one airline that continues to surpass all of the other carriers in customer service, efficiency and competitive edge both fiscally and operationally—which translates into money and safety! Now, who in the health care business is not interested in those crown jewels? If we want to improve the lives and care of our patients, we must focus on our employees. It is really that simple.

One needs only to scan the latest business section, where other airlines are regularly mentioned moving in and out of Chapter 11 protection and to note that the one airline never mentioned in these terms is Southwest Airlines. What is the lesson from Southwest that is key and applicable to a chapter on leadership in service organizations specifically related to nursing? The answer is simple; the leaders at Southwest get it. By getting it, we mean that they realize they hold a great public trust as an airline—whose business is both high risk and high volume, which sounds fundamentally like the business of health care today. But Southwest leaders do not stop at understanding this pact with their customers. They extend this thinking to include the notion that, if you take care of your employees, your employees will take care of your customers! They empower their employees to find ways to correct a problem, either real or perceived on the spot; they provide upward mobility and recognition to employees, and an environment that expects and nurtures mutual respect that is lateral and vertical; they reward innovation; and key to their success, employees reap the tangible benefits of satisfied customers in that the business model Southwest uses is based on profit sharing.

Since 1987 Southwest has consistently posted the lowest ratio of complaints per passengers boarded, and yet if you read Colleen's Corner, written by the president of Southwest Airlines in May of 2007, she indicates they understand that "we are only as good as your most recent flight with us," "that complacency could be our own worst enemy," (Colleen's Corner, 2007, p. 12) and speaks to new initiatives underway in customer service—*New* initiatives from the highest-ranking airline in customer service, what a concept!

Health care executives from time to time pay lip service to this way of thinking. There is great enthusiasm for books such as *Servant Leadership* (Greenleaf & Spears, 2002), and *Good to Great* (Collins, 2001), which are phenomenal books. In addition, health care has tried to achieve major shifts that look at process, not people, when trying to discern how a sentinel event occurred. However, when it gets to crunch time—which in many ways reflects the *daily* world of health care—we revert to the paternalism of trying to strong-arm employees into doing more with less, while being safe, and on top of this we demand our employees be nicer to improve an arbitrary score on patient satisfaction surveys. This is nothing more than trying to manage human resources in a way that contradicts human nature—treating people like commodities. So, we continue to pour new wine (new ideas and concepts such as aviation safety and servant leadership) into old vessels (hierarchical administrative structures and processes), and we wonder why things do not improve. In the words of Albert Einstein, "Insanity is doing the same thing over and over expecting different results" (Einstein, 2007).

For those of us who might say it is not realistic to use a model such as Southwest Airlines because our organizations cannot be employee-owned, this is true; however, this is but one tenet of the airline's mantra. It is more about building relationships within organizations that are built on trust and mutual respect and where innovation is praised and rewarded, not stifled and rejected. Health care organizations can create the Southwest "feel" by empowering employees to make the care experience safe and worthy of praise.

You do not have to give an employee a dividend check to make them feel like they have a stake in the organization. Recognition is relatively inexpensive, and paths to upward mobility can and should be created especially in light of our growing consumption of health care goods and services, as 77 million Baby Boomers are poised to cripple an already burdened system. Sending out for pizza when you know that a unit has had a particularly horrific shift is budget dust compared to not recognizing that staff are working through lunches and breaks to the point that a tired and exhausted seasoned nurse walks out the door and takes his or her wealth of knowledge with her. Each time a staff nurse leaves it costs the organization, on average, one year's salary to replace that nurse (estimates run between $30,000–$70,000, depending on specialty area and geographic region of the country). Look at your voluntary turnover rate (and be honest), then calculate the difference in springing for some well-deserved lunch or even fruit and cookies when your staff are working to their emotional and physical breaking points.

If you begin with the notion that to take care of your patients and families you must provide what employees need, particularly on the front lines of care, then you are on your way to a better organization already. Far too many leaders choose to take the easy and traditional path to fiscal health, by cutting the very heart of an organization's primary care providers—nursing staff. These leaders use talking points that include their brilliance in management, which have led to chart-busting productivity numbers while not reducing staff nurses, but when pushed for details they admit they have made significant cuts in support personnel, which in turn place other nonclinical functions back on the nurse, such as more secretarial and custodial work. Having a nurse who makes $25 per hour clean a room after a midnight delivery on a mother-baby unit while call lights go unanswered and medication administration gets backed up is penny-wise and pound-foolish. These cost-cutting measures are a temporary fix to a complex industry for which the end products can literally be life or death. Although this may yield a quick return, the long-term impact could be losing a patient and potentially an entire extended family's health care business for years to come. If your organization is in the position of being the only game in town, then it is especially important not to squander this unique position within your community.

As the leadership of Southwest Airlines knows, "we are only as good as your most recent flight (patient encounter) with us." If patients have a good experience without incident they are likely to tell 5 people, whereas if they have a bad experience they are likely to tell 20 people, at the grocery store and their place of worship—which is not good for business or the industry. To learn more about Southwest, we highly encourage your entire health care team from housekeeping to staff nurses to your board of directors to read *The Southwest Way: Using the Power of Relationships to Achieve High Performance,* by Jody Hoffer Gittel (2002). Then provide opportunities for individuals to answer one simple question, "How can we apply these principles to our organization?" It will enlighten and rekindle your passion about why you wanted to be a nurse and a nurse leader at the beginning.

In March of 2007, the Agency for Healthcare Research and Quality (AHRQ) released the findings from a meta-analysis of 94 observational studies conducted between 1990 and 2006, which suggests that increased nursing resources in hospitals are associated with decreased patient mortality, shorter length of stays, and lower risk of adverse events (Kane, Shamliyn, Mueller, Duval, & Wilt, 2007). It is time we shift the research question from describing the link between the numbers of nurses and patient outcomes to isolating which specific nursing actions or interventions are linked to these measurable patient outcomes (Clarke, 2007). We need no additional data to support what we should do as leaders. It is time to translate this research to the bedside by pilot-testing new and innovative ways to deliver high-quality, nurse-intensive care. If we have consistently found that more registered nurses are linked to better nursing outcomes, can we not assume that it is not simply the numbers of bodies on staff that translates into improved outcomes—but, rather *what* nursing actions these greater number of nurses are doing? This is an area of science where funding is only beginning to emerge.

We know that nurses spend roughly 20% of their time with patients. The balance of their day is primarily spent "hunting and gathering" and navigating their own system to support their practice in caring for patients who are more complex than ever before. Patients who once would have been admitted to an intensive care unit are now regularly admitted to a general medical/surgical unit and length of stays continue to decrease. Can we even imagine models of delivery where nurses actually spent 80%–90% of their time with patients? This single change alone could revolutionize what happens in the work environment for nurses, who time and time again have indicated their great desire to provide safe, quality care (Reineck, 2007). As the nursing shortage intensifies we need leaders who—in consultation with experts at the bedside, not paid external consultants—create new models of care to maximize the professional nurse's time, energy, and knowledge. The first order of business is not to form a task force of mid- or higher-level managers to discuss ad nauseum the pros and cons of the latest health care delivery fad. We should go to the source—the nurses themselves. They live and work in this world every day and are some of the most resourceful professionals in the entire workforce. They have the answers. We must ask them, but we must be willing to then *do!*

MAGNET CERTIFICATION: USING THE 14 FORCES TO RECHARGE YOUR ORGANIZATION REGARDLESS OF YOUR OFFICIAL PURSUIT

Some of you may read this section's heading and have the inclination to disregard the contents by thinking that your organization is small and not well resourced, so Magnet status is out of the question. But we encourage you to think beyond formal pursuit and focus on the fundamental principles of Magnet, which is what makes it so rich. Your organization can use the Magnet forces as part of your strategy toward attracting and retaining high-quality employees (Lacey et al., 2007).

When discussions of the Magnet certification application process are held with nurse executives, one of the most frequently cited reasons for not pursuing Magnet is that their organization has no tangible research infrastructure, nor potential for these resources. In a word search through the summary for the 14 Magnet forces the word *research* is not found. What *was* found repeatedly was support for nurses to drive their practice environment from the nursing unit up. As you look at these forces in summary below (Exhibit 12.1) see if this is not what may be occurring at your institution now, or if this is not the case, how you could create an environment that reflects these forces. If you look closely you will see considerable parallels with the Southwest Way. Again, it is all about the people. Magnet just focuses primarily on nursing service departments, and after all, isn't that why you are reading this chapter? No, your organization may never have the resources it takes to seek this formal certification, which includes application fees and volumes of manuals for review; however, the principles are fundamental to all types of organizations both in and out of health care that want to grow and prosper in today's competitive markets.

EXHIBIT 12.1 FOURTEEN FORCES

Force 1: Quality of Nursing Leadership

Knowledgeable, strong, risk-taking nurse leaders follow a well-articulated, strategic, and visionary philosophy in the day-to-day all levels of the organization, convey a strong sense of advocacy and support for the staff and for the patient. (The results of quality leadership are evident in nursing practice at the patient's side.)

Force 2: Organizational Structure

Organizational structures are generally flat, rather than tall, and decentralized decision making prevails. The organizational structure is dynamic and responsive to change. Strong nursing representation is evident in the organizational committee structure. Executive-level nursing leaders serve at the executive level of the organization. The Chief Nursing Officer typically reports directly to the Chief Executive Officer. The organization has a functioning and productive system of shared decision making.

Force 3: Management Style

Health care organization and nursing leaders create an environment supporting participation. Feedback is encouraged and valued and is incorporated from the staff at all levels of the organization. Nurses serving in leadership positions are visible, accessible, and committed to communicating effectively with staff.

(Exhibit continued on next page)

EXHIBIT 12.1 (CONTINUED)

Force 4: Personnel Policies and Programs

Salaries and benefits are competitive. Creative and flexible staffing models that support a safe and healthy work environment are used. Personnel policies are created with direct care nurse involvement. Significant opportunities for professional growth exist in administrative and clinical tracks. Personnel policies and programs support professional nursing practice, work/life balance, and the delivery of quality care.

Force 5: Professional Models of Care

There are models of care that give nurses the responsibility and authority for the provision of direct patient care. Nurses are accountable for their own practice as well as the coordination of care. The models of care (i.e., primary nursing, case management, family-centered, district, and holistic) provide for the continuity of care across the continuum. The models take into consideration patients' unique needs and provide skilled nurses and adequate resources to accomplish desired outcomes.

Force 6: Quality of Care

Quality is the systematic driving force for nursing and the organization. Nurses serving in leadership positions are responsible for providing an environment that positively influences patient outcomes. There is a pervasive perception among nurses that they provide high-quality care to patients.

Force 7: Quality Improvement

The organization has structures and processes for the measurement of quality and programs for improving the quality of care and services within the organization.

Force 8: Consultation and Resources

The health care organization provides adequate resources, support, and opportunities for the utilization of experts, particularly advanced practice nurses. In addition, the organization promotes involvement of nurses in professional organizations and among peers in the community.

Force 9: Autonomy

Autonomous nursing care is the ability of a nurse to assess and provide nursing actions as appropriate for patient care based on competence, professional expertise, and knowledge. The nurse is expected to practice autonomously,

(Exhibit continued on next page)

EXHIBIT 12.1 FOURTEEN FORCES (CONTINUED)

consistent with professional standards. Independent judgment is expected to be exercised within the context of interdisciplinary and multidisciplinary approaches to patient/resident/client care.

Force 10: Community and the Health Care Organization

Relationships are established within and among all types of health care organizations and other community organizations, to develop strong partnerships that support improved client outcomes and the health of the communities they serve.

Force 11: Nurses as Teachers

Professional nurses are involved in educational activities within the organization and community. Students from a variety of academic programs are welcomed and supported in the organization; contractual arrangements are mutually beneficial. There is a development and mentoring program for staff preceptors for all levels of students (including students, new graduates, experienced nurses, etc.). Staff in all positions serve as faculty and preceptors for students from a variety of academic programs. There is a patient education program that meets the diverse needs of patients in all of the care settings of the organization.

Force 12: Image of Nursing

The services provided by nurses are characterized as essential by other members of the health care team. Nurses are viewed as integral to the health care organization's ability to provide patient care. Nursing effectively influences system-wide processes.

Force 13: Interdisciplinary Relationships

Collaborative working relationships within and among the disciplines are valued. Mutual respect is based on the premise that all members of the health care team make essential and meaningful contributions in the achievement of clinical outcomes. Conflict management strategies are in place and are used effectively, when indicated.

Force 14: Professional Development

The health care organization values and supports the personal and professional growth and development of staff. In addition to quality orientation and in-service education addressed earlier in Force 11, Nurses as Teachers, emphasis is placed on career development services. Programs that promote formal education, professional certification, and career development are evident.

(Exhibit continued on next page)

EXHIBIT 12.1 (CONTINUED)

Competency-based clinical and leadership/management development is promoted and adequate human and fiscal resources for all professional development programs are provided.

IT'S THE LITTLE THINGS

Over the last decade we have conducted multi-site research about the work environment, asking what nurses need (Santos & Cox, 2000; Santos et al., 2003), as well as the Robert Wood Johnson Foundation's major report, *Healthcare's Human Crisis: The American Nursing Shortage* (Kimball & O'Neil, 2002). We had the pleasure of conducting focus groups with staff nurses who were asked to provide details about what would improve their ability to provide high-quality nursing care. At first, mid-level and senior nursing executives thought their requests would involve substantially more staff, which for many was an untenable proposition. But this was not the case. What nurses wanted was actually shocking, even to us. Here are some examples of what nurses were requesting.

1. additional thermometers (so they would not have to search for one when they did vital signs)
2. one additional scale (on the other end of a very long nursing unit)
3. more readily available clean linens or other basic supplies
4. their manager to stop calling them for general, nonemergent questions when they were at home trying to sleep after working all night (how inconsiderate!).
5. their nursing manager to know their name (how sad!)

Pretty astonishing, wouldn't you say? Not one single focus group (with over 30 held throughout the country) asked for more staff or a major piece of equipment. The only way you can know what your staff wants is to ask them. But please be aware, if you ask them you must be willing to listen and do. And, if you cannot do what is asked, then there needs to be a reasonable explanation for why their requests can't be granted, *coupled* with a viable alternative negotiated with them. If you fail to follow through your staff will lose faith in you as a leader, and regaining that trust will be a difficult proposition. Again, it is not always saying yes—but rather, always listening and attending to the needs of your frontline employees. When you do, remember the old adage, when you have these town hall meetings or focus groups—and, we hope you will—you have two ears and one mouth, listen twice as much as you talk!

GOING UP? WHAT'S YOUR ELEVATOR MESSAGE TO YOUR CEO?

We encourage you to discuss your nursing service leadership plans with the CEO and COO. Before you do, you must do your homework in translating what you can save the organization if you do basic things like focusing on patient care rather than nonnursing tasks. Have a plan. It is said that you should never go into a meeting with a problem, either urgent or brewing, unless you have created several legitimate solutions, hopefully created based on staff nurses' input infused with your expertise. If you have anxiety related to having these discussions, be willing to conduct a healthy self-study or a candid critique by a valued colleague on why previous requests and conversations have not gone well, then work with a coach to role play your next CEO interaction so that you have your "elevator message" down to a science. If you wanted to be a professional singer, you would not think twice about hiring a voice coach. Be diligent and methodical in your life's work. Running around trying to put out fires is rarely as productive *or successful* as good fire prevention, and, unless you seek pleasure from high anxiety, is far less enjoyable.

Consider yourself the exception. You want to learn new ways to improve your leadership not only for your own professional growth, but for the individuals who work very hard each and every day providing patient care. Individuals who do not want to change their thinking or doing enjoy the status quo. It is safe and secure and it can be highly lucrative. We are not insinuating that you should not make a good salary for what you contribute to the organization—quite the contrary. However, if you are keeping your job because you are keeping staff nurses down or in their place, then that is a different matter and you can determine that. The fact that you are reading this book and specifically this chapter means you are the exception in the league of nursing leaders. You want to gain momentum to translate your dissonance (when you know what you are experiencing is not as it should be) into a legacy of leadership. What would you rather be said about you when you move to the next professional level—(a) he/she took the money and ran, or (b) he/she left a legacy of trust and mutual respect that filtered throughout the organization to change lives for staff and most importantly for patients?

The choice is yours. We need pioneers now in nursing more than ever. Are you a nursing pioneer?

LEADING OTHERS INTO LEADERSHIP

For some of you gardening may be one of your pastimes and hobbies. The one thing you know is that simply planting bulbs in the ground and walking away will not yield the beauty of what is possible if you nurture and tend to your garden. A similar way of thinking can be applied to how you tap into potential leaders within your organization.

People come and go in leadership positions within our organizations. It is the very nature of employment. A visionary leader is one who seeks out the potential leaders around him or her. Even though they may not be ready to assume a leadership position right at the moment, you can grow, nurture and encourage them to become the leaders of the future. Nursing leaders do not have to be the best clinical experts on the unit. In fact, they may not be the best choice at all. You should seek out passionate, visionary, yet organized individuals and provide them with the organizational support they need to become good leaders. You can do this through internal mechanisms such as on-site conferences or educational sessions about leadership, or provide funds for them to participate in external conferences or the academic enterprise so they can determine if this is a path they might want to pursue. Having someone who has been developed and coached into assuming a new role within your organization if the day comes when they are needed is quite a different approach than simply finding yourself 1 day one manager down on 3 East—with no one to take his or her place. Being proactive about this growing new leaders creates an organic approach to your entire organization, which should be lively and dynamic. What an investment for your people and for your health care system!

WILL YOUR ORGANIZATION BE READY WHEN YOU ARE? TIME TO MOVE ON!

Most likely the time will come in your career where you are ready to move on to another level of leadership or you may find that the organization is no longer a match for you philosophically and you feel a need to change directions. Or in some cases you just may want to retire. If you truly care about your organization and the people you are leading you will consider this as part of the life cycle of your career trajectory and help prepare for such a transition. If you are a teacher you do not simply walk out of the classroom mid-lecture, and if you are a staff nurse you do not walk out in the middle of your shift and leave your patients and coworkers to fend for themselves. Likewise, you as a leader should have a succession plan.

Chances are you are working with intelligent and insightful nurse managers and directors. Do you see future leaders right in front of you? If so, you should be actively coaching and mentoring them to be your possible successor, even if this person does so in an interim capacity while your replacement is being sought. What a gift to give your organization and the person you have helped to aspire to a new level of responsibility.

Leadership is about working in the present with an eye on the future. What does the leadership world of nursing need now and in the long term? The answers are within you. Seize every opportunity to stretch in your thinking and application of new ideas. It certainly cannot be harmful to an entire industry sorely in need of new ideas and new ways of doing things.

REFERENCES

American Nurses Credentialing Center (2004). *Magnet recognition program application manual 2005.* Silver Spring, MD.

Clarke, S. (2007). Registered nurse staffing and patient outcomes in acute care: Looking back, pushing forward. *Medical Care, 45*(12), 1126–1128.

Colleen's Corner. (2007). Colleen Barrett, Southwest Airlines President's Corner. Customer Satisfaction. *Spirit Magazine, 16*(5), 12.

Collins, J. (2001). *Good to great.* New York: Harper Collins.

The Commonwealth Foundation. (2007). *New update of international health system comparisons: U.S. continues to lag on most performance measures, spends most on health care, least on health information technology.* Retrieved May 16, 2007, from http://www.commonwealthfund.org/newsroom/newsroom_show.htm?doc_id=482616

Einstein, A. (2007). *The quotation page.* Retrieved May 10, 2007, from www.thequotationpage.com

Gittel, J. H. (2002). *The Southwest way: Using the power of relationships to achieve high performance.* Columbus, OH: McGraw-Hill.

Greenleaf, R., & Spears, L. C. (Eds.). (2002). *Servant leadership: A journey into the nature of legitimate power and greatness.* New York: Paulist Press.

Institute of Medicine. (2001). *Crossing the quality chasm: A new health system for the 21st Century.* Washington, DC: National Academy of Science Press.

Kane, M. R., Shamliyn, T., Mueller, C., Duval, S., & Wilt, T. (2007, March). *Nursing staffing and quality of patient care.* Evidence Report/Technology Assessment No. 151 (Prepared by the Minnesota Evidence-based Practice Center under Contract

No. 290–02–0009). AHRQ Publication No. 07-E005. Rockville, MD: Agency for Healthcare Research and Quality.

Kimball, B., & O'Neil, E. (2002). *Healthcare's human crisis: The American nursing shortage*. Princeton, NJ: Robert Wood Johnson Report.

Lacey, S. R., Cox, K. S., Lorfing, K. C., Teasley, S. L., Carroll, C. A., & Sexton, K. (2007). Nursing support, workload, and intent to stay in magnet, magnet-aspiring, and non-magnet hospitals. *Journal of Nursing Administration (JONA)*, 37(4), 199–205.

O'Neil, E. (2007). *Center on managing or leading*. Retrieved May 15, 2007, from http://www.futurehealth.ucsf.edu/from_the_director_0407.html

Reineck, C. (2007). Nursing Models: A closer look. *Journal of Nursing Administration (JONA)*, 37(5), 209–211.

Santos, S. R., & Cox, K. S. (2000). Workplace adjustment and intergenerational differences between matures, boomer, and xers. *Nursing Economic$, 18*(1), 7–13.

Santos, S. R., Carroll, C. A., Cox, K. S., Teasley, S. L., Simon, S. D., Bainbridge, L., et al. (2003). Baby boomer nurses bearing the burden of care. *Journal of Nursing Administration, 33*(4), 243–250.

CHAPTER 13

Process

Gaurdia Banister

LEADERSHIP PROCESS: A JOURNEY, NOT A DESTINATION

Arthur Ashe said, "Success is a journey, not a destination. The doing is often more important than the outcome." Often organizational focus is more on outcomes and not enough on the methods and processes that will make the outcomes a reality. Success is more about the journey—the process—and less about the destination. Deciding where to go—the goal—is less difficult than getting there. A leader or anyone else is less likely to succeed if they do not have good process skills. It is the things you do along the way of life—the journey—that make goals and destinations possible. Doing the journey well almost always gets you where you want to go.

Much has been written about the concept of leadership, perhaps because most meaningful human progress has been ushered into existence by an effective leader. The success or failure of any organization or initiative is dependant in large measure on the caliber of its leadership. It is no wonder then that leadership has been scrutinized and dissected in every imaginable way in order to find the most effective leadership traits and characteristics.

According to Dr. Edward H. O'Neil, the Center for Health Professions at the University of California at San Francisco has developed a strategy for developing leaders with proven results that are built around four interrelated core leadership dimensions. The dimensions are *purpose, people, process,* and *personal* with each having an in-depth set of competencies. Considering the state of the health care delivery system, effective leadership will be essential in addressing the myriad problems facing nursing leaders today and in the future. Using a case study approach, the dimension of *process* will be examined from the perspective of addressing a key nursing and health care challenge: the nursing shortage and the lack of diversity.

Setting the Stage

The nation's nursing workforce is in crisis. Some of the causes of the current and emerging shortages of nurses are well documented: the aging population, the aging nursing workforce, declines in relative earnings, and an inability to attract diverse applicants (National Council of State Boards of Nursing, 2002). A U.S. Health and Human Services report (2002a) predicts that the nursing shortage of 6% in 2000 will grow to 12% in 2010 and then accelerate rapidly. By 2020, the nation's nursing needs will fall short by 29%.

Racial/ethnic minority populations are increasing at a much faster rate than the representation of minorities in the nursing profession. Twelve percent of the nation's nurses come from racial and ethnic minority backgrounds. While the number of minority nurses increased in the years between 1996 and 2000, these numbers have not kept up with the 30% minority rate in the general population. For example, African American registered nurses represent 4.9% of the total RN workforce and yet African Americans represent 12.1% of the general population (U.S. Department of Health and Human Services, 2002b). Between 2000 and 2020, the percentage of total patient care hours physicians spend with minority patients will rise from approximately 31% to 40% (U.S. Department of Health and Human Services, 2003). The fact that the nation's health professions have not kept pace with changing demographics may be as great a cause of disparities in health access and outcomes as the lack of health insurance. The U.S. Census Bureau data shows that America's population is growing increasingly diverse. In 1900, only one in eight Americans was of a race other than white. Today the ratio is one in four. By 2070, an estimated one in two Americans will be African American, Hispanic, Native American, or Asian /Pacific Islander (American Hospital Association, 2007).

Research indicates that U.S. racial and ethnic minorities are less likely to receive even routine medical procedures and are more likely to experience a lower quality of health care. The Institute of Medicine (IOM) report, *Unequal Treatment: Confronting Racial and Ethnic Disparities in Healthcare,* concluded that "(al)though myriad sources contribute to these disparities, some evidence suggests that bias, prejudice, and stereotyping on the part of healthcare providers may contribute to difference in care" (Smedley, Smith, & Nelson, 2002). From this alarming report, the IOM recommends many strategies, one of which is increasing the number of minority health professionals as a key strategy for eliminating health disparities.

The Sullivan Commission convened in April 2003 to serve as the focus for strategies to increase diversity in the health professions. The commission was composed of 16 leaders in health, business, higher education, law, and other fields. The Sullivan Report, *Missing Persons: Minorities in the Health Professions,* recommended a number of strategies to make education and training in the health professions more attainable and more affordable for minorities, including student scholarships versus student loans; reducing dependency on standardized tests for admission; and enhancing the role of 2-year colleges (Sullivan, 2004).

Finally, the National Advisory Council on Nurse Education and Practice (NACNEP) has identified increasing the racial/ethnic diversity of the RN workforce as one of the measures necessary to ensure the availability of a workforce appropriate to meet the nursing needs of the population and has initiated a national action agenda to address those issues. Recommendations issued from this group focused on four broad themes: education, practice, leadership, and cultural competency. The four major goals issued based on these themes are:

- Enhance the efforts to increase the recruitment, retention, and graduation of minority students.
- Promote minority nurse leadership development.
- Develop practice environments that promote diversity.
- Promote the preparation of all nurses to provide culturally competent care. (U.S. Department of Health and Human Services, 2000)

A culturally diverse workforce, that is, a workforce composed of people from varied backgrounds, is essential in the health care setting to meet the needs of the nation's diverse population. Lack of diversity not only contributes to workforce shortages, but it may contribute to poorer health care if the professionals providing care are not familiar with cultural differences. Promoting diversity is one of a health care organization's key human resource considerations, because diversity creates an environment where thoughtful decisions are based on different life experiences and perspectives and brings to the workforce a more comprehensive range of knowledge and abilities. It is this openness and ability to furnish culturally sensitive care that improves patient outcomes (Shea-Lewis, 2002).

THE INITIATIVE/CASE STUDY

Don't be afraid of the space between your dreams and reality. If you can dream it, you can make it so.

—Belva Davis

The Health Alliance—Creating Workforce Diversity initiative began as a pilot project in 2002 and continues today. It was designed to link disadvantaged youth in the District of Columbia to careers in nursing. This initiative was based on the need to develop the full potential of local youth and to help meet the critical nurse staffing needs.

In an attempt to improve the quality of health care and better serve the needs of the community, Providence Hospital, the Urban Alliance Foundation, and the University of the District of Columbia Nursing Division formed a partnership to address the common goal of providing economic opportunities to disadvantaged youth and providing a pipeline for more persons in nursing careers.

The three partners have strong histories of providing care and service to the disadvantaged populations in the District of Columbia. Providence Hospital (PH), the oldest continuously operating hospital in the nation's capital, serves a largely African American patient population. The hospital is also a Catholic facility serving the needs of the poor and underserved. More than 83% of the patients are African American. The Urban Alliance (UA) was founded in 1996 to create employment and educational opportunities for economically disadvantaged Washington, D.C. high school students. UA helps students with their first steps in the professional work experience, building partnerships with schools and the business community. The University of the District of Columbia (UDC) is an urban land-grant institution of higher learning offering quality, affordable post-secondary education to any qualified resident of the District.

This nursing career initiative was designed to recruit students, many with disadvantaged backgrounds, interested in health careers. The initiative would subsidize their educational costs, provide them with stable employment in an acute and long-term care setting, support them in their nursing studies with academic tutors and nurse preceptors, and guarantee them employment upon graduation.

The Process in Leadership: Vital Steps

It is not a question of how well each process works, the question is how well they all work together.

—Lloyd Dobens and Clare Crawford-Mason,
Thinking About Quality

Effective leadership is difficult to achieve and maintain because it requires being good at so many things. A leader must know where to go and how to get people where he or she is going. Assuming the leader can get a group or organization to the agreed upon place or goal, the ability to maintain this progress will depend on the leader's ability to continually use an appropriate level of resources while satisfaction remains among workers, leaders, and the community being served. This is a tall order. Increasingly leaders are being replaced after short tenures because satisfaction among workers, other leaders, and the served community cannot be maintained.

Purpose, people, process, and personal are four interrelated core leadership dimensions. Among them, a case can be made that a good process is the conduit through which the other leadership dimensions flow. Leadership process is more about the way you go about leading. It is the steps you take to get things done. If a leader consistently follows a thoughtful and appropriately detailed process, the organization can expect the leader to be successful in achieving the organization's goals and purpose with people that possess the right personal attributes.

In a real sense, the four interrelated core leadership dimensions are the dimensions we seek in all employees. The leader with the good process is more able to attract and satisfy employees with core leadership dimensions.

As one can imagine, there are many process skills for an effective leader to utilize well. Depending on the goal or issue, differing process skills may be required, and each process skill may have a varying relative value. For instance, a given project may require more conflict management than another. If process skills were a finite number like one thousand, the best and most effective manager would want to be reasonably good in a thousand process skills. But it is not reasonable to expect that a leader will excel in every process skill in order to be effective. However, a wide range of process skills is vital to the success of any goal or project.

The Health Alliance—Creating Workforce Diversity initiative is being used to demonstrate some of the technical process skills that the competent leader will use to accomplish organizational goals or projects. This initiative, like all initiatives, has a particular set of process skills, each with a relative value to its achievement. As this initiative is reviewed, only a few of its required process skills will be discussed. These include:

- making a relevant business case for an undertaking
- managing conflict
- working with and through systems
- using decision-making techniques
- developing and using process improvement techniques

However, by no means is this meant to imply a cookie cutter approach. One size does not fit all in the leadership process. Leadership is complex and multifaceted.

Making a Relevant Business Case

*The very essence of leadership is that you have to have vision. You can't blow
an uncertain trumpet.*

—Theodore M. Hesburgh

When the Health Alliance Program was first conceived, as the project leader, I found it relatively easy to make the business case for the initiative. The nursing shortage was in full swing and everyone knew about it. At Providence Hospital, millions of dollars were being spent on supplemental staff due to nursing vacancies. The need for increasing the diversity of nursing, particularly due to health disparities, was also well documented. Providence Hospital is a faith-based institution with a mission to serve the poor and underserved. So assisting disadvantaged youth who had dreamed of becoming registered nurses was considered a community benefit and was clearly aligned with our hospital's mission. Each of the students who would enter the program were on a track to not only improve their own personal quality of life, but also the quality of life for their families. Furthermore, in some instances, some of the students would be the first in their families to graduate from college. At that time, the cost that ranged between $3,000 and $10,000 per student per year seemed like a bargain compared to the cost of overtime and contract employees. Upon graduation the students would be obligated to work at Providence Hospital a minimum of 2 years after receiving their RN license.

However, over a period of 5 years, the business case to continue this initiative would be constantly tested. The initial pilot group of six students struggled with serious and sometimes overwhelming social, financial, emotional, employment, and academic issues. Many of the students had never held a job before. General work requirements such as coming to work on time or even showing up for work at all became a problem. Some of the students were not academically prepared for the college environment despite hours of tutoring. Each semester the students' grades would be reviewed and one or more students would receive a grade of a D or F. An entry exam was taken by each student to determine their readiness for the intensive nursing curriculum. Ninety percent of the students in the pilot group, as well as the students recruited in years two and three of the initiative, were required to take remedial courses that would extend their time in the program for 1–2 years. This program, initially designed to assist students in obtaining a 2-year associate degree, would take up to 4 or 5 years to complete in some instances. For some students, their home environment was so disruptive and dysfunctional that they could not concentrate on their studies. At least one student became homeless while participating in the program. Two students in the initial group later dropped out of the program. Multiple improvements in the selection process of students reduced the attrition rate, but it is still a concern.

For each setback, the business case to continue with the program required readjustment. This kind of program had never been tried in the metropolitan D.C. area. Doubters in management respond best to a well-documented business case. A prospective leader must always know the facts and figures that will satisfy the decision makers. The decision maker may not love the initiative, but if the facts and figures add up, he or she is less likely to reject the proposal. This is a process skill that requires great attention. There is the skill of knowing what data are necessary in presenting the most compelling business case. To garner continued support for this project, in addition to outlining the actual costs of the program, it was also effective to highlight supplemental staff costs, staff satisfaction, the impact of continued staffing vacancies on quality and patient satisfaction, and the benefit of the program to the students as well as the community at large. When expected results in the initial plan were delayed or not achieved, the business plan had to be modified and presented to maintain funding and support from the partners. Few projects are approved or continued without a good business case being presented.

Developing and Using Process Improvement Techniques

Process improvement strategies were used throughout this initiative. As the project leader, each component of the Health Alliance initiative was evaluated and reevaluated to determine the effectiveness in reaching the goal: graduate RNs. The following is a listing of the process improvement changes that were made.

- *Admission process modified:* In the beginning of the program, applicants were mainly accepted if they filled out a simple application expressing interest in the program. After several of the early students dropped out of the program, it was determined that the application process should be more selective and thoughtful. The application to apply for the Health Alliance program was restructured. Potential students are required to have (a) two letters of recommendation—one letter from a professional reference and one letter from an academic referral; (b) an official transcript from the student's high school; (c) two essays to gauge the student's writing ability, and (d) the experience of participating in a "Nurse Shadow Day" at Providence Hospital, at which the potential students spend time shadowing a nurse to see what he/she does in caring for patients. The dropout rate has been reduced.
- *Addition of pre-entry study skills and time management workshop:* Some of the students seemed to lose focus during the program. The

program was modified so that students taking remediation classes during their first semester would not carry a full load, as these are very demanding courses, especially for students who have been away from school. A training program is presented to strengthen the students study and time management skills. This was developed to help them as they prepare for the more academically challenging courses that lie ahead. Listening to students and interpreting what they were *really* saying is vital to modifying the program. Often students complain about something, but you have to know that the solution is not always going to come from where they think it will come. Effective leaders hear many concerns. The most effective leaders can translate even harshly presented concerns to broader system issues that need addressing.

- *Enhancement of a Student Project Contract:* At the beginning of the program all students were asked to sign a contract outlining the goals, requirements, and expectations of the program. The contract was revised to ensure that all program requirements and expectations were listed explicitly so that there are no questions or ambiguity. Furthermore, each component of the contract is reviewed with each student to ensure their comprehension, and then signatures are obtained. Too often, leaders act on what they believe is implied in a relationship instead of clearly stating and writing expectations. We realized that the program would have less confusion in expectations by simply writing down our expectations in more detail. Leaders should get in the habit of putting expectations in writing that are easily understood by the reader. This is a process skill that is easier said than done, as word meaning is often a source of disagreement.

- *Improvement on the communication and coordination among the project's partners and between the program partners and students:* In the beginning, the three sponsors of the program communicated through a representative from each sponsor. The representatives were individuals who had many other responsibilities. Quickly, the sponsors determined that a project coordinator would be needed to manage the initiative. A new position was created and funded, titled project coordinator. The position was introduced to serve as the link between all the project partners facilitating communication and collaboration. In addition, the project coordinator relays and explains pertinent information and/or concerns between the program partners and students. Leaders spend much of their time assessing the need for resources.

- *Increased support and individualized attention for the students:* The students struggle with a number of serious social, emotional, and academic issues. In order to be successful in the project, they needed more intensive support. To this end, a case manager was introduced to the program to provide coaching on life and job skills, and to assist with tutoring. If there is a situation outside of the case manager's realm of expertise, the case manager will find and provide information on helpful resources, or in some cases, access to a local professional such as an academic tutor or clinical therapist, to resolve the issue. This is another example of when leaders must make sure that the support structures are in place to ensure the success of the program or project.

- *Creation of a written evaluation form to monitor and record the students' progress:* Increasing the level and frequency of student evaluations was determined useful in dealing with the dropout rate for students. The students are assessed upon completion of each key step in the program timeline. Specifically, assessments are done upon completion of the 6-week Certified Nursing Assistant (CNA) course and at the end of each semester in school. A quarterly written evaluation would include a report of the student's grades and class attendance, comments and performance appraisals from the student's work nursing supervisors, and comments from the case manager assigned to each student to address any social or emotional issues or concerns. This process provides an effective mechanism for evaluation and communication of the project goals.

- *Increased skill development in the workplace:* The students were initially frustrated that they would remain employed as CNAs in a long-term care setting for their entire nursing training. A progressive employment experience was incorporated into the project that would enable students who have completed their first year of nurse training to become student nurse technicians. This position allows the student to work in the acute care facility of Providence Hospital. A leader must always be sensitive to the needs and concerns of all stakeholders.

This initiative required constant review and modification. Being good at process improvement requires good listening and communication skills, good analysis and judgment skills, and good collaboration skills. Listening to the students was sometimes difficult. Some could not communicate their concerns well. Sometimes what they talked about required interpretation to determine what was needed to resolve the situation. Because some staff were reluctant to work with this group of students because of their perceptions about the disadvantaged, great patience and effort was required to get these staff to work with the students.

It was gratifying to note positive results from program modifications. Sometimes the slightest positive result gave the programs leaders great joy. We understood that we were dealing with a population with many hurdles to overcome. There are many hurdles to overcome to improve our national health care systems. In many ways, the difficulties are greater than dealing with disadvantaged students. It can be said that the improvement of health care systems in America is one large and continuous process improvement project.

Managing Conflict

Leadership has a harder job to do than just choose sides. It must bring sides together.

—Jesse Jackson

As discussed earlier, there are three partners in this initiative, Providence Hospital, the Urban Alliance, and the University of the District of Columbia. Each partner has remained committed to the program and the program goals. However, due to the attrition rate of the students, one of the partners who was responsible for recruiting the students asked that recruitment efforts be stopped. Their board of directors had issued a mandate to them.

In retrospect, this was a logical step. My organization, Providence Hospital, was only partially affected by the attrition rate because we were not paying the students' tuition until they were accepted into the nursing program. The Urban Alliance had been picking up all of the tuition expenses for the remedial courses, and a large number of those students were not successfully moving on to the nursing curricula. The decision to stop recruiting the students caused a great deal of anxiety, frustration, uncertainty, and conflict among the partners. Furthermore, the decision by the board coincided with the award of the federally funded grant to increase the number of students that were currently enrolled in the initiative. The receipt of the award helped to validate the concept of the program, and suddenly the program's future was in jeopardy.

Managing conflict became an invaluable leadership process strategy. Several meetings were held with members of the board, finance officers, and staff from the Urban Alliance. There was a thorough review of the financing of the project. There was even a discussion during the negotiations to decline the grant award for 1 year until the issues could be resolved. A compromise was achieved because fundamentally all the partners cared deeply about the welfare of the students. We had come too far to turn back. In each meeting my role was to facilitate a discussion of the pros and cons of each decision. An environment of trust, collaboration, and cooperation was stressed. In the end, it was decided that the Urban Alliance would not recruit new students; however, our other partner, the University of the District of Columbia suggested that students from their program would be ideal candidates for the program. Most of them were from disadvantaged backgrounds, were minorities, and had already overcome many of the barriers that the students out of high school faced. This truly turned out to be a win-win situation for everyone.

Working With and Through Systems

To manage a system effectively, you might focus on the interactions of the parts rather than their behavior taken separately.

—Russell L. Ackoff

Since there were three partners, each had a different set of expectations and requirements related to their organizations. Negotiating these systems in leading this project was at times daunting, confusing, and frustrating. Frequently it felt like entering a maze and trying to determine whether the next step was up or down, to the right or to the left. Each had their own set of rules that had to be followed. In the hospital, a number of departments were involved, including human resources, finance, nursing education, patient care services, and more. With the University of the District of Columbia, there were numerous challenges with course schedules, class availability and sequencing, access to professors, and registration issues. Lastly, the Urban Alliance partner had its own set requirements and deliverables to its board members and funders. The Urban Alliance had an extremely flexible system and frequently compromised to eliminate some of the system issues. Some contentious and delicate negotiations occurred to maneuver the students through the various systems. One of the key leadership tactics was to review and discuss how the partners could work together to accomplish the goal. For instance, student selections would occur early enough to plan accordingly for workplace orientation, or in some instances a special orientation was held for the students. Several accommodations were made to assist the students in getting the appropriate class schedule, and when this was not possible alternative courses were identified to support the nursing curriculum.

Whenever differences exist between groups (organizations, departments, professions), there will usually be challenges for leaders to overcome created by those differences on the way to workplace or system change.

Using Decision-Making Techniques

Leadership should be born out of the understanding of the needs of those who would be affected by it.

—Marian Anderson

As part of the process, a meeting was held monthly with the partners to evaluate the status of the students. A report was given on each student's academic status, including information such as grade point average, test results, tutoring needs, and other academic concerns. The students' work performance was also reviewed, including tardiness, absenteeism, caregiving activities, relationship with supervisor and mentor, and more. The students' social and emotional challenges were also reviewed in great detail. Many of the students struggled with issues of low self-worth and a lack of self-confidence. Almost any setback would cause the students to doubt their ability to succeed in the program. All of the students were assigned a case manager in order to challenge these concerns head-on.

As the facilitator leading these discussions with the partners, the fate of each student's future in the program was in our hands. The decisions had to be consistent, fair, objective, and defensible. Some of these sessions were heart-wrenching. In some instances, students who were known to be talented with so much potential were released. In each meeting, the needs of each partner and the needs of each student were weighed carefully. Each partner had made commitments of financial resources, personnel, and time. In releasing a student, the emotional consequences weighed heavily.

RESULTS FROM WHAT HAS BEEN DONE

Outcomes

Since the beginning of the program, 72 students have entered the Health Alliance Program. Of that, 36 have successfully completed the certified nursing assistant program. Five students are currently enrolled in prerequisite classes in preparation for entry into the RN program. Twenty-four students are in their first or second year of nursing school and receiving excellent grades. In May 2007, the program had its first RN graduate, and she is currently studying for the National Council Licensure Examination-Registered Nurse (NCLEX). She is interested in becoming a labor and delivery nurse but has decided to complete 1 year of medical surgical nursing prior to entering into that specialty.

In order to address the high attrition rate, intensive tutoring sessions on study skills were included in the tutoring program along with test-taking skills. The partners are in the process of evaluating the current tutoring contract with regard to the improvement of academic outcomes.

The partners have also expanded their recruitment efforts to include individuals who are more mature, up to 28 years of age, and who have life skills to draw on as they prepare and progress through the program. Participants have also been recruited from the nursing program at UDC. Those individuals that would benefit from the academic and social supports provided by the Health Alliance program have been targeted. One-on-one study classes will be coordinated for those students with special study/test-taking difficulty. In addition, group classes will be offered to help students study for the required exams and NCLEX.

A new case coordinator with over 25 years experience in nursing education has been hired. Her background includes teaching nursing theory as well as clinical practice, and she has worked with students from diverse ethnic and economic backgrounds. Her management areas of expertise are wide-ranging and include program creation and management, and policy and standards development. She has a commitment to professional excellence and has a strong record of improving student retention and academic success.

We would like to note that although each student is supported on the pathway to become a registered nurse, some of those that have voluntarily dropped out or were terminated from the program have remained in the health care field as certified nursing assistants. This has met a need in the community and has helped these disadvantaged men and women secure stable employment.

In July 2005, the program received an $800,000 federally funded grant to increase enrollment in the Health Alliance–Creating Workforce Diversity initiative and to ensure that the financial resources needed to support the students are in place. Private funding has also been obtained.

PERSONAL EXPERIENCE/LESSONS LEARNED

As the project leader for the Health Alliance Initiative, there have been a number of lessons learned throughout this 5-year journey. I have been profoundly changed by my experiences in leading the Health Alliance–Creating Workforce Diversity project. One of the key leadership lessons is an acknowledgement and appreciation of the blessings and opportunities I have had. As a person of color from a disadvantaged background, I am no different from the students in our program. I was one of the lucky ones, for which I am truly grateful. In working closely with these students, it is quite apparent that they have so many barriers blocking their path to success. Many of them who either dropped out or were released from the program have potential, have talent, have character, but the obstacles are overwhelming even when given resources and support for their aspirations. In leading, there must be passion, and in this program, my passion and the passion of the partners helped us to find answers to make this program successful despite setbacks and at times challenges that seemed insurmountable.

Another important lesson is that the term *cost* must be measured more broadly than just dollars and cents. In this program, the students' lives were at stake. Their ability to achieve success in the program was tied to their ability to become contributing members to society. Reaching the goal of registered nurse not only allows them the financial resources to care for themselves and their families, but the students also become role models for others. As a member of this society and as a leader, there is an obligation to help others reach their goals and dreams.

As mentioned earlier, the first graduate received her associate degree in nursing in May 2007. It is anticipated that there will be at least 10 graduates next year, given how well the students are currently performing. The other students that are now in the pipeline are also performing well. Perseverance and patience are vital lessons in this leadership process. When you know in your gut that something is right, you must remain true to your convictions. We live in a society that worships the quick fix. Sometimes this thinking has to be suspended. One could have easily been discouraged with the number of obstacles and challenges that affected this project. While it is exciting to have finally reached some success, it is also exciting that some of the students who were released or dropped out are excited about the progress and achievements they made while in the program. Some are working certified nursing assistants or patient care technicians. They did not reach their dream this time, but in some cases they feel the accomplishment of that dream is still within their grasp.

The importance of communication as a leadership lesson cannot be minimized. Communicate, communicate, and communicate more. This project had a number of stakeholders: board members, faculty, nursing leadership, administrators, nurse mentors, tutors, grant writers, funders, patients, family members, and students, as examples. It was essential that everyone receive timely and accurate communication about the initiative. It was also important to tailor the information to each individual audience. Each stakeholder was looking through a different lens in assessing the successes and challenges of the initiative. In order to continue to garner their support, effective communication of even the failures and how the failures led to improved processes helped to solidify support.

Another leadership lesson is the importance of flexibility. When the program was initially created, the obstacles, challenges, and barriers that would be faced were not conceivable at the time. Throughout this leadership journey, there have been a number of changes, modifications, additions, and deletions to the program. The current success and sustainability of the program is due to the ability to be flexible in making changes to address the environmental conditions.

Fundamental in the leadership process is the need for constant evaluation and reevaluation. Evaluation was used systematically to assess and reassess the program outcomes and objectives. This information was vital in making changes to the program.

Sr. Irene Kraus, former chairperson of the board of the American Hospital Association, was fond of saying, "No margin, no mission" (Walker, 2005). It sounded odd coming from a nun, but cost-benefit analysis is really important. Finding the balancing point between margin and mission will remain one of the most difficult challenges for any leader. Frequently over the course of this program, the worth of the investment was discussed. The leader must consider the cost to society to have a family remain trapped by the welfare system versus giving a person a profession and a means to get out of poverty, care for their family, feel accomplished, and increase their self-esteem in the process. Perhaps the value of such initiatives is priceless!

CONCLUSIONS AND IMPLICATIONS

This initiative is really about making the life journey of individuals better while helping the community get to a destination—improved nurse staffing levels and increased diversity of the nursing staff to reduce health care disparities.

A Typical Participant in the Pilot Project

Leadership needs purpose to keep it striving to improve the process. Purpose for any program is tied to the individuals served. Monique (the name has been changed) is a student in the program. Her story gives purpose to leadership.

Monique is an 18-year-old, single mother of a 1-year-old. As a young mother, Monique faced many challenges. She grew up with a drug-addicted mother in unstable and unsafe housing conditions, and recently, her mother was evicted from their shared apartment. Without formal child care available, Monique was forced to depend on unreliable friends for child care assistance. Monique is now living out of a suitcase, staying with friends, but determined to make a better life for herself and her child. Despite these problems, Monique finished high school and joined the Health Alliance program. In July 2004, she completed a CNA course at Providence Hospital and passed her certification exam. She began work at Carroll Manor and enrolled in UDC taking remedial classes. She is working at Carroll Manor as a CNA and is achieving A's and B's in her UDC coursework. Urban Alliance staff is helping Monique find suitable and affordable child care and safe housing.

The Program's First Graduate

Shanel DeBruce, the first graduate of the program, said,

> Choosing a career path has been very difficult, but I have known for quite some time that I would enjoy working in a health care environment. I take pleasure in caring for those who need medical and/or physical attention, especially mothers and their newborns. For that reason, I decided that I would pursue a career in nursing. . . . Getting into a program that will accommodate my needs so perfectly is my calling to become an excellent nurse, and that is why the Health Alliance Nursing Program has caught my interest. . . . I am very determined to become a nurse and I have also become fixed on the idea, so I know there is nothing that will stop me from achieving this goal. . . . As a result of being involved in the program I have a source of guidance. I feel that I am being pushed to achieve my goals and me having the extra push is what I need to succeed. In the past few months, I have learned that when I find myself in need of help that I should not be afraid to ask.

There is comfort when the people served including our patients give testimony that speaks to the worthiness of our leadership efforts. The ultimate success or failure of this initiative is dependant on effective leadership to maintain the interest and achievement of the students and the support of the partners. The life stories of the students provide one incentive to lead. Improving the quality of health care through improved staffing and reducing health care disparities provides another. Process skills give the leader a good chance at a successful journey.

REFERENCES

The American Hospital Association. (2007). *Protecting and improving care for patients and communities: Racial and ethnic diversity and eliminating disparities in care.*

National Council of State Boards of Nursing. (2002). *Education issues: The nursing and nursing faculty shortage.* Retrieved January 3, 2008, from http://www.ncsbn.org

Shea-Lewis, A. (2002, January). Workforce diversity in healthcare. *Journal of Nursing Administration, 32*(1), 6–7.

Smedley, B., Smith, A., & Nelson, A. (2002, March). *Unequal treatment: Confronting racial and ethnic disparities in healthcare.* A report from the Institute of Medicine, Board on Health Sciences Policy.

Sullivan, L. W. (2004). *Missing persons: Minorities in the health professions.* A report of the Sullivan Commission on Diversity in the Healthcare Workforce.

U.S. Department of Health and Human Services, Bureau of Health Professions, National Center for Health Workforce Analysis. (2002a, July). *Projected supply, demand, and shortages of registered nurses: 2000–2020.* Retrieved January 4, 2008, from ftp://ftp.hrsa.gov/bhpr/workforce/rnsupplyanddemand2002.pdf

U.S. Department of Health and Human Services, Health Resources and Service Administration, Bureau of Health Professions, Division of Nursing. (2002b, February). *The registered nurse population, findings from the national sample survey of registered nurses.* Retrieved January 4, 2008, from http://bhpr.hrsa.gov/ healthworkforce/reports/nursing/samplesurvey00/default.htm

U.S. Department of Health and Human Services, Health Resources and Service Administration, Bureau of Health Professions, Division of Nursing. (2003, Spring). *Changing demographics: Implications for physicians, nurses, and other health workers. A report from the National Center for Workforce Analysis.* Retrieved January 4, 2008, from http://bhpr.hrsa.gov/healthworkforce/reports/changing demo/default.htm

U.S. Department of Health and Human Services, Health Resources and Services Administration. National Advisory Council on Nurse Education and Practice. (2000). *A national agenda for nursing workforce racial/ethnic diversity.* Retrieved January 4, 2008, from http://bhpr.hrsa.gov/nursing/NACNEP/reports/first/default.htm

Walker, G. (2005, September). No margin revisited. *Homecare Magazine.* Retrieved January 4, 2008, from http://homecaremag.com/mag/medical_no_margin_revisited/

CHAPTER 14

Process

Valentina Gokenbach

The concept of process within the realm of leadership should not be confused with management processes that are functional activities enacted to complete work. Within the context of a leadership discussion, management processes take on a new meaning and incorporate the depth and breadth of leadership skill and strategy that lace through the components of the process to bring achievement of goals to a higher level of success. For example, a management process such as the creation of a budget can be improved when leadership skill and finesse is applied. This could be through the inclusion of staff at the point of service or the exploration of input from individuals from departments or industries outside the organization. This new intelligence could provide valuable insight as well as improve engagement and support of the budget in development. The creation of a new service in a health care organization known as Safety City USA is an example of processes that through applied leadership resulted in a wildly successful program that has become the centerpiece for community outreach.

ISSUES

Several issues within the environment provided the impetus for the creation of Safety City USA. These included a community need for safety programming, regulatory requirements, and an increase in competition coupled with a decrease in market share. A discussion of the issues follows.

Community Need for Safety Programming

In the United States, unintentional injury remains the number one killer of children. According to National Safe Kids, it is estimated that as many as 90% of unintentional injuries can be prevented. During the summer of 2004, more than 2.4 million emergency room visits by children age 14 and younger in the United States were due to unintentional injury (Centers for Disease Control and Prevention, 2006), and 2,143 children died (National Vital Statistics System, 2007).

A child's death or injury is a terrible tragedy for the family and the community. Perhaps less well known is the economic toll unintentional injury exacts on society. In 2000, unintentional injuries and deaths of children ages 0 to 14 cost society $58 billion in medical bills, in lost wages of the children's caregivers, and in the future productivity of the children who died prematurely (Miller et al., 2005).

Nearly 60% of total child unintentional injury and deaths in this time period involved drowning, biking, falls, motor vehicle occupant activities, and pedestrian incidents (Safe Kids Worldwide, 2007). While these statistics are significant and staggering, they only account for a percentage of the total number of unintentional injuries per year. Each year, approximately 1,000 children under the age of 12 die because of fire and almost 8,000 are seriously injured. In addition, approximately 8,000 youngsters are seriously injured or killed in motor vehicle crashes nationwide. It is estimated that 90% of these injuries are preventable.

The state of Michigan has a particular problem with injury in comparison to other states. Michigan has shown the least amount of improvement in the prevention of accidental injury and deaths. Unfortunately, Michigan ranks in the bottom half of the United States (30th) in unintentional injury deaths that occur in May–August for children ages 0–14. Michigan's death rate is 4.32 deaths per 100,000 (2000–2004). This is above the national death rate of 3.67 deaths per 100,000 for the same time period (Safe Kids Worldwide, 2007). (See Figure 14.1.)

It is not known whether this is due in part to a lack of adequate programming or the lack of consistent, funded programming. Many agencies such as the fire departments and police departments have attempted safety fairs to improve the knowledge base of the community; however, there is no guarantee that the capture rate is enough to make a noticeable difference in outcomes. School systems have also attempted to include safety programming, but without a defined curriculum that is often left to the individual teacher to develop and include. There is even less of a focus within this community on injury prevention in the senior population. Prevention of these tragedies is the goal of Safety City USA and the reason it was created.

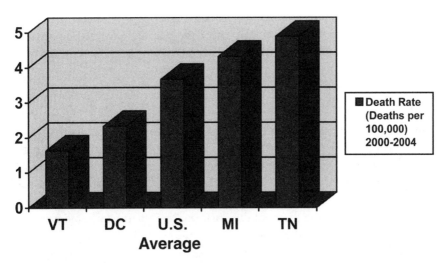

FIGURE 14.1a The death rate for accidents and trauma in Michigan ranks very high in comparison to other states.

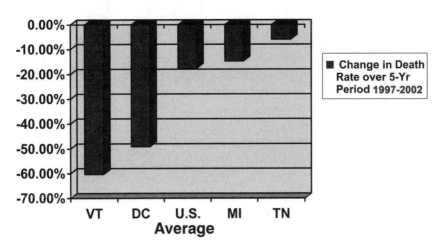

FIGURE 14.1b Michigan has been unsuccessful in reducing death rates related to accidents and trauma.

The implementation of a program such as Safety City USA would provide a systematic approach to safety education and training and provide a methodology that could reach all of the targeted children from potentially all schools in the southwest region of the state. This fixed site facility would serve as a destination site for the provision of safety programming for all age groups. Over time, it is the goal to continue to expand the knowledge base of the community as new students and citizens attend courses.

Regulatory Requirements

Currently, the hospital within this case study is the only accredited Level 1 trauma center in the county. The American College of Surgeons (ACS) continues to increase the requirements of community education in the areas of injury prevention and safety as part of the ACS Level 1 designation. Review of the current educational offerings revealed a robust focus on community education; however, the desire of the organization was to establish a program that was unsurpassed in the industry. The creation and inclusion of a program such as Safety City USA would certainly more than achieve this lofty goal.

Competition for Health Care Services

The hospital is feeling the pressure of a changing market. Weakening of the Certificate of Need laws in the state, coupled with population shifts, have allowed for the over-bedding and expansion of health care facilities in direct competition for the same patient population. A decrease in market share of 3.3% was realized during the calendar years of 2005 and 2006. It became clear that creative programming targeted to capture new market shares would be needed to increase exposure and advertising of the organization. It is well documented that females are the predominant decision makers in regard to the management of health-related issues in the family.

A program such as Safety City USA could accomplish these goals through preventative programs dedicated to saving the lives of children. The plan was to provide hospital information for all the children to take home following their experience at Safety City. This information, coupled with a positive life experience could begin a positive relationship with the parents, leading to future use of the hospital and services.

THE STORY OF SAFETY CITY USA

Safety City USA is a freestanding interactive learning center designed to provide prevention programs targeted at the reduction of injury in all age groups. Through the use of both traditional classroom education as well as hands-on practice, participants are educated about safety-related injuries and prevention strategies. Kids get to learn how to escape from a burning building, they learn about the dangers of strangers; they learn how to protect themselves from other hazards and also how to get help if necessary. Programs also are available to the elderly population, new parents, and anyone who would like to learn about lifesaving or safety. The goal of Safety City USA is to help individuals, from little children to seniors, make safer choices and learn to protect themselves. All programs are designed to be age-specific and can be customized to the needs of the particular school or community.

Educational programs are presented by nurses, firemen, and policemen, which also helps to maintain the credibility of the material presented. Classes offered at Safety City USA include senior safety, self-defense, Internet safety, certified sitter classes, protect your babies, animal and pet safety, CPR, family and friends, stranger danger, fire safety, good touch and bad touch, suicide prevention, hazards of drunk driving, and drug awareness: what every parent should know. During daytime hours school-age children can participate in field trips with curriculum aimed at fire prevention, home safety, and bike safety. During evening and weekend hours particular Scout troops and community groups can experience the program after school. Children can even celebrate their birthday parties while learning how to keep themselves safe. A comprehensive week-long summer camp program is also available, which is focused on summer hazards such as weather and water safety.

Inception of Safety City USA

The inception of Safety City USA began with the interest of a group of nurses from the Emergency Center and Trauma divisions, who presented a unique concept based on a trauma prevention program in Ontario, Canada. This facility was a freestanding, interactive learning center funded by the Canadian government, designed to teach kids about safety. It was a requirement that all Canadian students attend programs at Safety Town at key points during their grade school and high school education. After visiting Safety Town, a local firefighter was the catalyst behind the Safety City USA program. Based on his experiences in the field, he felt that he wanted to make a difference in the lives of others by attempting to prevent unnecessary injury and death. Through tears he told compelling stories of how he had watched too many children die unnecessarily, all of which could have been prevented. This was his life's mission, but he needed a partner to help share the vision and make a program like this a reality. It became instantly apparent that this was not only a project that would be nice to do, but also a program that could positively impact the community in a profound way.

Advantages of the Program

Apart from the obvious and profound opportunity to save lives and improve the quality of life for the community, many other advantages were apparent. This program would provide a unique opportunity for the hospital to partner with other community agencies, including the fire and police departments as well as local government. This alignment would improve political capital for the hospital in future endeavors as well as provide positive exposure and marketing of the hospital.

Barriers

Money was the greatest barrier. Reducing margins and limited capital budgets prevented the funding of extraneous, unbudgeted projects, especially in the middle of a budget year at a time when the organization was performing below budgeted projections. It was clear that in order to proceed, there would need to be extremely creative approaches to finding capital and accomplishing the work needed to build a facility.

Space was another barrier. The hospital campus was already congested, with every inch of space accounted for and a waiting list for the creation of other projects. It was also the goal to attempt to build a facility off-site that looked more like a destination location for fun activities rather than a sterile hospital environment. Unfortunately an off-site location would be expensive and possibly cost-prohibitive.

Last, there were varying degrees of support from individuals in the organization who found it difficult to conceptualize the program and realize the potential, especially in light of economic pressures. The response from the hospital director was very supportive in concept although it was clear that there would be limited funding if any. Rather than dampen spirits, these barriers represented tremendous personal challenges and growth opportunities. It became a personal goal to overcome the barriers and to build Safety City USA for the greater good of the community.

LEADERSHIP PROCESSES

Leadership processes begin in the mind of the leader far before the execution of the process begins. The leader must have a clear vision of the goal and be able to articulate that vision to the team. This requires that the leader reflect and develop a comprehensive plan to communicate along with the identification of personal thoughts and feelings that could contribute either positively or negatively to the progress (Murphy, 1996a). Within the context of Safety City USA the components of the plan included the creation of a compelling vision and mission, the development of a strong team, identification of funding, and developing plans to address facility, program development, marketing, and staffing.

Development of the Mission and Vision

Jeffries (1996) stated that in order to capture the hearts of a team, the vision and mission need to have a spiritual quality, and the vision and mission need to be clear to the leader, who then has the responsibility of transferring the passion to the team. A project such as Safety City USA lends itself to the creation and transference of a spiritual vision and mission. A draft of the vision and mission was crafted for presentation to the working team at the first meeting. In order to empower the team and increase the level of engagement, the plan was to present the ideas in draft form and allow the team members to decide on the final statements. The following mission and vision are the result of the work of the team following the infusion of the ideas of the leader.

The Mission

The mission of Safety City USA is to significantly reduce death and injury in children and adults, secondary to unnecessary accidents and trauma, and concurrently improve the quality of life for all.

The Vision

It is the vision that Safety City USA will be the leading injury prevention program in Michigan, providing safety education to over 295,000 individuals on an annual basis and providing the benchmark for prevention of injuries and death in the state. This will be accomplished through the use of interactive educational experiences in a fun and warm learning environment.

Establishment of the Team

No leader can work in isolation to achieve any goal without the support of an effective team. "The term team implies a strong, cohesive, complementary group of people who pull together in support of the leader's vision and aspiration"

(Katzenbach, 1998, p. 4). The belief in this statement alone does not ensure success of the team. Although there are many critical success factors necessary for a team to succeed, the centerpiece is an effective collection of team members with complementary skills and organizational responsibilities. In regard to leadership process as it relates to team building, this is the critical step. As the leader possesses a grasp of self, they also must understand the power of others and that power in relation to the critical needs of the project.

As the leader of this initiative, it was critical for me to first of all identify individuals that might share a passion for a project such as this. Individuals were chosen for their past work experiences that clearly displayed an interest in giving to others. Several members of the team led particular charity walks and supported philanthropic opportunities, which demonstrated the joy of personal giving. There would certainly be a good degree of personal commitment to this project.

Members of the team were also selected for their expertise and authority in particular areas necessary for the completion of Safety City USA. These individuals represented the hospital as well as the community organizations. Disciplines included the fire chief, the assistant fire chief along with the fireman who presented the project, representation from the police department, hospital administration, two managers from the buildings and facilities department, the trauma coordinator, and the surgical chief of trauma services, trauma educator, several representatives from the public relations areas and the foundation, and leaders from the rehabilitation department. It was believed that this team would be able to address all of the internal (within the hospital) and external (within the community) issues as they surfaced. Once the team was established, work began in five major areas of focus, including operations, facility planning, program development, marketing, and philanthropy.

Operations

One of the first steps to the creation of a program or service is the development of the strategic plan. It is relatively easy for a leader to perform a routine task such as this independently, with some help from the marketing department or Web sites. To infuse leadership into the process, asking for insight from the team on the document provided for greater alignment as well as improved the potential for engagement. The development team of Safety City USA was included in many components of the strategic plan.

The financial pro forma was created with the help of the finance department. Several analyses were conducted to identify the break-even point as well as the price point for programs. Once the financial pro forma was created, the development team was asked to provide insight into selection of the most reasonable volume target. This strategy could serve the leader in two important ways. First of all, the team members feel valued that their input is critical to decision making; however, even more important is the collaborative effort and motivation to achieve the goals identified by the team.

Following the opening of Safety City USA, the team remained engaged in the financial success of the organization through the monthly review of the financial statements. Deficits were identified, along with strategies to modify programming and achieve financial targets. This approach provided a proactive methodology for the maintenance of a positive bottom line.

A critical decision to be made by any leader is to ensure that the management of a department or program continues under the direction of individuals who are engaged in the project and care about the outcome. Without the emotional connection to a department, given financial pressures, it becomes easy for programs to be eliminated. With the passion inherent in this program, it was clear that the manager and associated parent department needed to care. Oversight and management structure were established with several goals in mind. It was important to the success of the project to align Safety City USA within the domain of a department that valued the initiative. With this outcome in mind, Safety City USA was to report to the trauma coordinator within the Department of Surgery, who was also on the development team, with a matrix relationship to the chief nurse executive. The close alliance with the trauma department provided a liaison between the trauma physicians, the emergency staff, and the prehospital providers such as EMS and the police department.

Last, within the realm of operations, the notion of staffing was an easier decision. Since there was no funding for staffing positions, there would be no permanent, hired staff, and all programs would need to be taught on a volunteer basis. The team was also included in the brainstorming as to how to handle the necessary staffing needs. It was decided that scheduling could be conducted via the established physician referral line through a dedicated phone number that triggered a script written for Safety City USA. Since the facility is located off-site in a retail mall, on-site presence for tours and programs was more problematic. The trauma coordinator decided to physically move her secretary into the site to provide visibility through the day. The goal ultimately was to hire the appropriate staffing as demand increased and revenues were sufficient to support salaries.

Facility

Without funding, this barrier seemed the most unachievable of all. Perseverance and a true commitment to the creation of the program with the intent to save lives became the driving mantra that kept the team moving. The facility representatives on the team were the magicians through these challenges. With luck, a small storefront became available in the retail mall owned by the hospital. The director of the facility was approached with the concept and a reasonable rent and cost structure was agreed upon.

The next barrier was construction, and without any funding it seemed impossible to achieve. The team developed a plan to approach several local business leaders who wanted to become part of this wonderful endeavor with the opportunity to be recognized through sponsorship and naming opportunities in the facility. For example, a local interior design shop built the kitchen and was recognized by a large brass plaque bearing the name of the company for all guests to see. The park area was named for a donor who provided significant funding. A sponsorship wall is also in the plans for the near future that will be proudly displayed at the entrance for all who helped build Safety City USA. A total of 68 local companies worked in various capacities for a period of 3 months to bring the project to fruition. The collaboration and coordination was nothing but amazing. This was clearly another example of sharing the vision and engaging a community. (See Figure 14.2.)

The acquisition of furniture and equipment would also need to be accomplished without available funding. A list of necessary items and furniture was developed and publicized to the hospital staff for donations. Every item on the list was secured through donations. Local furniture stores also found out about the needs through some of the contractors and offered to outfit the facility. Audiovisual equipment was both donated and purchased through foundation money.

There would also be other services necessary to maintain the facility and operations of Safety City USA, including maintenance, security, and catering. Sharing the vision of Safety City USA with these departments quickly engaged their services. Several members from these departments were added to the ongoing governance committee.

Program Development

Program development was one of the easier, more enjoyable exercises for Safety City USA. A task force of the development team was identified for their expertise in the area of education and programming and charged with the development of a philosophy of education and creation of appropriate classes. The overall philosophy surrounded the vision to teach all citizens about safety, with the goal of decreasing injury and death and improving quality of life in a proactive way. With this in mind, programs were developed for school children at three times through the course of their primary education. Age-appropriate

FIGURE 14.2 68 companies and hundreds of volunteers gave of their time and materials to build Safety City USA.

programming was developed to meet the learning needs of the particular age group. These include the very young (ages 5–7), middle school (ages 10–12) and teenagers early in the high school years (grades 9–10). This programming would also ensure consistent attendance at Safety City USA because schedules could be created for the schools several years in advance with the expectation of educating the upcoming, matriculating classes. The team also selected the type of educational programming and the related learning tracks identified for presentation.

The senior population was also considered a target for potential programs, as well as other adults. Demographic data showed an aging population in the adjacent community that could benefit from this initiative. This approach would optimize the utilization of the facility and help to generate the necessary revenues to maintain the program.

Last, weekend birthday parties and summer camps were identified as potential programs that would serve as a method of reaching a greater target audience and increase revenue and utilization. Programs for special populations were also developed to provide inclusion of all potential learners. It was an incredible experience to watch the pride and self-confidence of the first handicapped child to successfully escape through the window of a simulated burning bedroom to safety.

The team presented their proposal to the larger project team for input and suggestions. In relationship to the leadership approach to this process, once again the team was empowered to create the product and then valued for their input. This synergistic approach allowed for the development of an attractive array of offerings but also provided for a focus on the community and consumer value. In a discussion about results-based leadership, Ulrich, Zenger, and Smallwood (1999) identify the need to begin thinking about what the consumer would find valuable and develop programs and products in a way to please them and not the organization.

Philanthropy

Gunther, McGrath, and Keil (2007) proposed that a great degree of the failure of new business ventures or elimination of new programs is related to the under-estimation of costs and the resulting under-funding. It is the responsibility of the leader to plan for worst-case scenarios and to develop strategies to support new programs until they become successful. This also needs to be done without the introduction of doubt that would undermine the positive outlook of the team. In response to Safety City USA, the back-up funding source would be philanthropy. This was easily a program that appealed to the community and had a potential draw for funding. To help with this strategy, a member of the foundation was included in the development team to help with cultivation of donors, writing of grants, and presentation of the concepts to the appropriate audiences. In this case, money was raised to support the program for 2 years through lean revenue periods during the start-up phase. Money could be transferred from the restricted fund account to meet the deficits on the operational side. Money was also secured for scholarships for children who could not afford the modest entry fee for the programs. Another benefit to the focus on philanthropy was the increased visibility to the community.

Marketing and Promotions

As there was no money for program development, there was certainly no money for formal marketing. The marketing experts on the team were able to develop a comprehensive marketing strategy that capitalized on press releases and media opportunities. Safety City USA was utilized by the media as a backdrop for every news story that focused on community and safety topics. Logos and flyers were developed in the hospital for local distribution through schools, community groups, and organizations. The most effective marketing approach was the development of a "road show" concept, whereby team members would present at school board meetings and teacher gatherings. This strategy was achieved through creative, visionary thinking that focused in on the specific target markets that would be the most likely to benefit from the programs.

There were also many events to celebrate the opening of Safety City USA, which included political figures, local leadership, hospital leadership, and the education community and members of the fire and police departments. A special thank-you event was also hosted for all of the contributing business owners and workers.

Status of Program

Safety City USA opened its doors on January 2, 2007 and is a tremendous success. Although far from projected revenue targets, the number of children visiting the programs has more than doubled every month. Analysis of the progress demonstrated the greatest interest in the school programs and special groups such as Boy and Girl Scouts. The birthday parties have not been very successful, but another effort at marketing is planned to pique the interest of this program. Summer camps had initially low numbers but continued to increase, resulting in enough attendees to run the program.

The increased interest in Safety City USA (see Figure 14.3 at the end of this chapter) has led to the need for customized programs. This has been handled in a modular way, with classes being arranged to meet the needs of special groups. Senior programs are now in development along with evening adult courses. The certified baby-sitting class continues to be a success.

The governance board has begun to look for a larger facility that could be operational by the year 2010. Several local community groups have expressed interest in partnering with Safety City USA. Joint venturing will depend on the amount of land available and the funding to build a new facility.

LESSONS LEARNED

All leadership processes provide invaluable learning experiences if evaluated by the leader. Learning opportunities are present regardless of the results of the program or process; however, it is the level of emotional intelligence within the leader that allows for the internalization of the wisdom (Murphy, 1996b). In regard to leadership lessons learned, this was personally a tremendous growth opportunity in several areas.

Risk Taking

This project was a risk for the organization, which translates into a risk for the leader and the team advocating for the project. It would have been easier and safer to embrace the safety training concept with the fire and police departments and offer some classes and staff to teach the classes in the hospital or the affiliating organizations. Instead, making the commitment to take the risk to build an entire facility in support of a new concept made this project all-encompassing and real. The personal outcome was an increase in self-confidence and a sense of accomplishment and pride for all involved.

The Power of a Vision

Safety City USA would not be a reality without a strong vision of the outcome. In this case, the power of the vision united, excited, and motivated the group. It also reinforced the belief that if you set your mind to a target and look at sights and opportunities of a much higher order in the universe, it becomes easy to achieve. This is what fueled the determination of the group to persevere through all the tough times and disappointments along the way.

Sharpening of Operational Skills

The execution of an interesting program such as this, which reached beyond the hospital walls to the community, provided an opportunity to sharpen operational skills that may be applied differently in various organizations. The issues of policy and procedure within community organizations are very different from those of the hospital. It was challenging to navigate the strategic course while engaging the community partners. In addition, the focus on philanthropy was new for many members of the team.

The Magic of Synergy

Selecting the team and building a team are processes, but what surfaces as a tremendous lesson was experiencing the magic of synergy and how the synergy unlocked the passion within the team members. This team of phenomenal loving and caring people ranked personally as the most inspiring and successful team throughout the course of 35 years in leadership positions. All members became one and shared the same dream and desire to work tirelessly toward the accomplishment of this goal on such a grand scale. The team members spent many hours on weekends and off-shifts to complete the construction, cleanup, and necessary work. These team members requested to remain together to become the oversight committee to guide the progress of Safety City USA. The team's focus has changed to fund-raising and program expansion. Many friendships have also been created throughout this experience. The level of support and collaboration between the fire and police departments, community leaders, and local business owners has also improved.

The Importance of Giving of Self

The greatest lesson learned as a leader is the notion that life is not about the leader, it is about what the leader can do to help others. Helping others, whether it is through giving to others, mentoring, supporting, or coaching, is what transcends the leader and the team. Once leaders begin to let go of torturous self-interest and ego, there is nothing that cannot be achieved. This experience has forever transformed the lives of the team in many ways, but it has especially transformed the life of the leader in what has been learned about personal self and the power of transformational leadership.

CONCLUSION

The story of Safety City USA is clearly a salient example of a nurse-led initiative that despite multiple challenges rose to a level of success and status

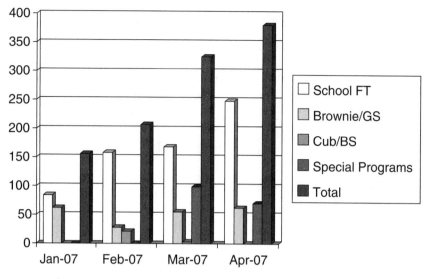

FIGURE 14.3 Number of program attendees

that could not have been anticipated. Nurse leaders, however, face many inherent barriers to achieving status equal to those of other leaders in the organization. Perhaps this is due to the primarily female nursing population or academic preparation that is largely different from the business world. Regardless of the reasons, it is the responsibility of nurse leaders to accept challenges, take risks, and personally believe in themselves as the gateway to achieving success. After all, once you have dedicated your life to saving the lives of others, everything else pales in comparison to the value of that commitment.

REFERENCES

Centers for Disease Control and Prevention. (2006). *Web-based injury statistics query and reporting system*. Retrieved January 11, 2006, from http://www.cdc.gov/ncipc/wisqars

Gunther McGrath, R. & Keil, T. (2007, May). The value captor's process: Getting the most out of your joint ventures. *Harvard Business Review, 12*(5), 128–136.

Jeffries, E. (1996). *The heart of leadership: How to inspire, encourage and motivate people to follow you*. Dubuque, ID: Kendall Hunt.

Katzenbach, J. (1998). *Teams at the top: Unleashing the potential of both teams and individual leaders*. Boston: Harvard Business School Press.

Miller, T., Finklestein, A., Zaloshnja, E., & Hendrie, D. (2005). The cost of child and adolescent injuries and the savings from prevention. In K. Liller (ed.), *Injury prevention for children and adolescents: Research, practice and advocacy* (pp. 15–64). Washington, DC: American Public Health Association.

Murphy, E. (1996a). *Leadership IQ: The groundbreaking program to develop and improve our leadership ability.* New York: John Wiley & Sons.

Murphy, E. (1996b). *Leadership IQ: The personal development process based on a scientific study of a new generation of leaders.* New York: John Wiley & Sons.

National Vital Statistics System. (2007). *2004 mortality data.* Hyattsville, MD: National Center for Health Statistics.

Safe Kids Worldwide. (2007, May). *U.S. Summer Safety Ranking Report.* Retrieved June 10, 2007, from https://www.safekids.org/

Ulrich, D., Zenger, J., & Smallwood, N. (1999). *Results based leadership.* Boston: Harvard Business School Press.

CHAPTER 15

Personal

Patricia Reid Ponte

Leading an organization or program of patient care in one of today's health care settings—be it a hospital, ambulatory clinic, rehabilitation center, nursing home, or palliative care or hospice facility—is a tremendous honor that is full of challenges and opportunities for creativity. With their executive colleagues, nurse leaders in such roles impact social, economic, political, and personal dimensions of the lives of the many people who work in the organization or are served by it. As one of the institution's leaders and a member of its senior executive team, the nurse leader shares accountability for the organization's operational viability and role within the community. As the head of a practice discipline, the nurse leader is responsible for the creation of a practice environment that assures excellence, compassion, and respect for all who are served by the health care organization and for the professional and support staff it employs.

Based on my experiences as a nurse leader in a comprehensive cancer center and multiple professional organizations, I believe there are four areas that must command a nurse leader's full attention and energies. I call these a nurse leader's key commitments, because nurses leading service organizations must commit their time, knowledge, and energies to making each of them a priority and championing them within the organization. These key commitments include: (a) implementing patient- and family-centered care and having it define the way care and services are delivered; (b) assuring interdisciplinary collaboration within a respectful, inclusive, transparent, and blame-free culture, (c) instilling a philosophy that promotes continuous improvement and the use of technology to support practice, and (d) making leadership development a priority for all professional staff who hold leadership positions within the organization.

Nurse leaders in service organizations must also cultivate personal leadership competencies that allow them to lead successfully and find joy and challenge in the process. These competencies include developing a disciplined approach to self-knowledge, one that is achieved through personal values clarification, introspection, and continuous self-improvement; cultivating the ability to foster trust within work teams and the organization as a whole; and learning to integrate personal and professional life commitments. Nurse leaders who master these competencies find they not only lead successfully, but also continue to grow and remain open to new ideas and opportunities.

In this chapter I describe the elements of the four key commitments and examine the personal competencies that nurse leaders must master to lead successfully.

KEY COMMITMENTS FOR NURSE LEADERS IN THE SERVICE SECTOR

Commitment to Patient- and Family-Centered Care

Depending on the way it is interpreted, patient- and family-centered care has the power to transform the way organizations operate and meet the needs of those they serve. In organizations that are truly committed to implementing it as a model of care, patients and families are valued as partners in all domains of the organization, and the provider–patient relationship is marked by social equity, transparency, and joint decision making. In these organizations, patients and family members work side-by-side with administrators and clinician leaders, helping establish the organization's priorities, collaborating on decisions about the care environment, and participating in initiatives to improve care and service delivery. New employees are educated about the elements of patient- and family-centered practice during orientation, and job descriptions, performance reviews, peer review processes, and supervisory guidance are imbued with clearly articulated expectations regarding the behaviors, norms, and values that assure patient- and family-centered care in day-to-day practice. The organization's priorities include strategies to continuously improve the delivery of patient- and family-centered care, and the board of trustees knows what it means and expects senior officers and managers to provide supports to assure its ongoing implementation.

In organizations where the commitment to patient- and family-centered care is minimal, the term simply becomes words in the organization's philosophy or mission or values statement. Were you to look closely at such organizations, you would likely find they are missing strategic priorities to operationally define what patient- and family-centered care means, behavioral standards or expectations to guide interactions with patients and families, and governance structures or activities to assure that the perspective of patients and families is represented in decision making and that patients and families are treated as partners in care planning and delivery.

Creating an organization that has patient- and family-centered care at its core must be a key commitment of every nurse leader in the service sector. It is not a solo act, however. Rather, it requires the commitment and energies of leaders at every level. Its implementation cannot be assigned to a single individual as a nursing leadership project, nor can it be assigned to the realm of a single department, like social work or patient advocacy. Instead, all members of the senior clinical and administrative teams, along with the board of trustees, must embrace patient- and family-centered care wholeheartedly and directly participate in its implementation.

When is an organization ready to fully commit to patient- and family-centered care? In general, organizations are ready after their senior leaders have studied the concepts that underlie this model of care and have a vision of what it would take to make it a best practice for their organization. Visiting organizations that have truly implemented it, reviewing the literature to understand what it means in theory and practice, and recruiting leaders or consultants who have guided its implementation in other settings are all approaches that leaders can use to jump-start the introduction of patient- and family-centered care within their organization. Nurse leaders play a key role in this process and must champion the model and use their leadership position to assure it takes hold as a strategic priority, for without having patient- and family-centered care firmly embedded, high-quality, safe patient care is extremely difficult to achieve.

As a first step toward implementing a patient- and family-centered organization, the executive leadership team and the board of trustees must explicitly communicate their intent to have the model become the way the organization conducts its business. Next, the chief nursing officer, chief executive or operations officer, chief medical officer, and others in comparable positions must collectively and consistently develop strategies, operational structures, and processes that make patient- and family-centeredness tangible to others in the organization.

One early strategy involves identifying patients and/or family members who are interested in participating in specific organizational initiatives, such as policy development, program implementation, or building or renovation projects. With the guidance and support of the senior triad (i.e., the CNO,

CMO and COO/CEO), having patients and family members participate in these processes makes it clear to all involved that the patients and/or family members add invaluable information and perspectives.

A good second step toward implementing patient- and family-centered care involves the formation of a patient and family advisory council or other similar forum. Such a group should consist primarily of patient and family volunteers, who chair the group and serve as members. It is imperative that the executive triad be included as full voting members—consistently attending council meetings and actively participating in the council's decision-making and priority-setting activities. Their involvement signals the organization's commitment to the formation of partnerships among patients, families, organizational leaders, and staff, and is crucial for the successful evolution of a patient- and family-centered organization (Connor, Reid Ponte, & Conway, 2002; Dana-Farber Cancer Institute, 2006; Ponte, 2004).

Commitment to Interdisciplinary Collaboration Within a Respectful, Inclusive, Transparent, and Blame-Free Culture

The work of planning and delivering high-quality, safe, and effective patient- and family-centered care is by definition an interdisciplinary process. Good leadership is no longer considered a solo act; rather, it demands a commitment to leading in partnership with others. For interdisciplinary leadership to be successful, however, executive leaders must develop a joint understanding of what it is, and agree on the areas of responsibilities that are shared and those in which accountability rests with one member of the group.

An organization truly committed to interdisciplinary leadership and governance typically has a leadership triad at its highest level that consists of its most senior nurse, physician, and administrator. Other physician-nurse-administrator triads provide joint leadership at the service and unit level. This type of leadership structure typically strengthens decision making around priority setting, resource allocation, improvement efforts, and the practice environment, because it assures that the perspectives and needs of all constituents are equally valued and represented at the table. The effectiveness of each triad, however, rests in its members' ability to jointly and equally develop the mission, strategies, business practices, and care commitments of the areas it oversees, and to clearly decide which aspects of management and oversight rest within the domain of each individual leader.

While using leadership triads to lead and manage clinical practices, services, and organizations helps assure a more collaborative environment, it requires a disciplined approach to decision making and priority setting. Developing and maintaining such an approach is hard work that requires careful planning and consideration, as well as the time and commitment of leaders at every level. Strategies that facilitate shared decision making and promote inclusiveness can make the process easier. Four of these strategies—framing the issue for better decision making, collaborative practice agreements, attaining diverse perspectives through transparency and inclusiveness, and promoting a culture of accountability rather than blame—are explained in the next section (Ponte, Gross, Winer, Connaughton, and Hassinger, 2007; Ponte, 2004; Reid Ponte, 2005).

Collaborative Leadership Agreements—A Methodology for Proactive Relationship Planning and Accountability

When leaders come together to lead an organization, a service, a team, or a project, they often come with a belief that leading together will naturally fall into place—after all, they are each good, strong leaders with plenty of experience. Often, however, collaborative leadership does not happen so seamlessly or effortlessly, and in many cases, it does not happen at all. To be successful, leadership dyads and triads must take a proactive approach toward defining collaborative leadership methods and develop a framework for shared planning, decision making, priority setting, and when applicable, day-to-day management. Exhibit 15.1 highlights issues that should be addressed as soon as a leadership dyad or triad is formed. Resolving these issues at the start of the leadership relationship and revisiting them periodically thereafter assures that each member of the dyad/triad holds the same expectations regarding shared and individual accountabilities, roles, management processes, and outcomes.

Nurse leaders who are members of leadership dyads/triads are well positioned to introduce and champion the use of leadership agreements or other methods to specify shared accountabilities and leadership processes. Addressing these and other issues proactively helps leaders avoid making decisions based on assumptions that are not held by everyone and prevents missteps in communication that compromise collaboration and create confusion among staff.

Framing Issues for Better Decision Making

Before involving others in a discussion about care, resources, or priorities, leaders of an interdisciplinary management team must first work together to plan a strategy to guide the discussion. A key element of this strategy involves framing the issue, since posing a dilemma or problem to a large group for decision making can be a waste of time if the issue is not well-articulated. Leadership teams may find the following eight steps helpful when framing an issue for a broad group of constituents (Ponte, 2004, p. 483)[1]:

EXHIBIT 15.1 PLANNING FOR COLLABORATIVE LEADERSHIP

1. Determine the appropriate membership of the leadership dyad or triad. Examples include:
   a. Physician-Nurse-Administrator
   b. Medical Oncologist-Surgical Oncologist-Radiation Oncologist
   c. Physician-Nurse
   d. Pharmacist-Physician
   e. Social Worker-Nurse
   f. Social Worker-Physician
   g. Administrator-Clinician
   h. Administrator-Administrator
   i. Clinician-Patient-Family Member
2. Determine the domain of accountability that is shared by the leadership team (e.g., clinical services, a clinical practice, a unit or floor, a program or a project, a care plan)
3. Identify each leader's unique domains of accountability (e.g., accountability for one or more specific disciplines, roles, parts of the program, or other functions)
4. Determine decision-making parameters: consensus versus majority vote versus one member of the dyad/triad holds ultimate accountability and decision-making power (due to the organizational structure). Parameters will vary with each dyad/triad.
5. If the team agrees that decisions must be made through consensus, determine steps to be taken if an impasse occurs.
6. Determine how the team will communicate with one another:
   a. Establish a routine meeting schedule and meeting location
   b. Plan meeting agendas in advance
   c. Agree on how, when, and where to establish priorities
   d. Determine how team members will communicate about issues that warrant immediate communication (via paging, phone call, or a face-to-face short encounter)
   e. E-mail guidelines for communicating with one another
7. Determine how the dyad/triad will communicate to others
   a. Process for sending e-mails, memos, and letters from the leadership dyad/triad. Determine when it is appropriate for one member of the dyad/triad to communicate independently about a shared domain of accountability

(Exhibit continued on next page)

EXHIBIT 15.1 (CONTINUED)

   b. How will meetings be conducted? Which meetings will be co-chaired and which will be chaired separately?
   c. Define how contact with the media will be handled.
8. Determine timelines for all facets of shared work
9. Identify metrics that will be used to monitor the effectiveness of the dyad/triad
10. Define how the dyad/triad will be evaluated and which groups/individuals will be asked to provide feedback (e.g., staff, peers, supervisors)

---

1. *Create the context:* Why has the problem come to the leaders? Why is it important now?
2. *Determine the assumptions:* What do we believe to be true about the problem or issue?
3. *Describe the criteria that must be met:* What must be solved? What aspects are beyond the scope of the current discussion?
4. *Identify principles to guide the decision:* The principles should clarify values and provide a frame for decision making. For example, the leadership team might assert that the discussion and decision should satisfy the following: ensure a patient- and family-centered outcome; involve the perspective of frontline staff; reflect a systems approach, principles of a fair and just culture, and teamwork; improve the work environment; and support diversity.
5. *Present straw models for consideration:* What are some possible solutions or approaches? Presenting straw models gives the group something to respond to, can spark constructive debate, and often adds efficiency to the process.
6. *Define metrics that will demonstrate sustained improvement or resolution:* Be clear from the onset of the process about what measures will demonstrate improvement over time and how data collection and analysis will be resourced.
7. *Define a time period for reflection:* Group members need time to consider their decision before making a final commitment. Be clear about the time interval that is being allotted for reflection, however, so that procrastination does not occur.
8. *Identify leaders and accountability for implementation:* Identifying accountability for implementing a decision or plan is a critical piece of framing the issue and is essential to good group process and teamwork. This step includes defining an implementation timeline and clarifying responsibility for monitoring progress and outcomes.

Attaining Diverse Perspectives Through Transparency and Inclusiveness

As noted earlier, interdisciplinary leadership models foster an environment that encourages collaboration and the sharing of ideas and perspectives. Such an environment is also fostered by transparency in decision making, in which the processes used to make decisions are clearly defined and the input of staff at all levels is welcomed. Committing to transparency as a behavioral standard takes courage and discipline on the part of organizational leaders. It often starts with creating a governance structure that is participative and inclusive, and that assures that the diverse perspectives of all staff are heard and help shape organizational priorities, strategies, and operations.

Listening intently to staff, patients, and families is a leadership skill that does not come naturally to many leaders, particularly those who believe that a more important aspect of leadership is public speaking and learning to respond verbally to staff, patients, families, and other leaders. Some leaders feel staff often complain without cause; others believe that as leaders they should have the answers and that only they know what is best. As a result, the importance of listening is often underestimated and the skill of listening intently is never developed.

Whenever staff become upset or concerned about an issue, leaders must take the time to stop and listen and not assume that staff are fabricating the problem or simply trying to be difficult. Taking time to listen requires discipline. It helps if a forum is already in place that allows staff to routinely interact with leaders at the unit, service, and organizational level. Shared governance structures that allow professional staff to lead in partnership with organizational leaders, and encourage support staff to participate in the development of policies and processes impacting the practice environment also help assure good listening and facilitate dialogue that promotes transparency and the sharing of diverse perspectives.

Promoting a Culture of Accountability Rather Than Blame

Nurse leaders in the service sector must champion the adoption of a fair and just culture within their organizations. This means removing the phenomenon of blaming individuals when mistakes happen, replacing it with a systems-based approach to understanding risk and error, and developing systems that assure accountability at the individual, program, and system levels. Committing to a fair and just culture, or one that promotes accountability rather than blame, also involves designing and implementing a set of principles and behavioral standards for managers, professional staff, and leaders to follow in their interactions with staff, patients, and families. These principles should be drawn from the science of systems thinking, error mitigation, and safety.

One of the behavioral standards must address the need for respect and compassion. Principles of a fair and just culture cannot be introduced into an organization unless there is a commitment by senior executives and boards of trustees that everyone served by the organization and those who work in it feel respected in every interaction. For some individuals, the concepts of respect and compassion are elusive and/or completely opposite from the way they have been socialized as individuals and professionals. Their first impulse when a mistake happens is to find someone to blame—a reaction that unfortunately is part of our societal culture and that is viewed by many as normal. Creating a process to replace this with one that promotes an environment of accountability and respect can transform an organization.

Organizations that embark on the journey toward establishing a fair and just culture can start by following these 5 steps: (a) develop an understanding that removing blame does not absolve individual or organizational accountability; (b) commit to respect as a prevailing value of the organization; (c) create principles of a fair and just culture that are experienced from the bottom up (see Exhibit 15.2 for an example of principles adopted by the author's organization); (d) assure that executive leaders and board members understand and support the principles and live the behavioral standards of respect (this includes educating leaders about when to apply the methodology of a root cause analysis); and (e) measure the effects of the new principles continuously over time (Connor et al., 2007).

Moving toward such a culture not only strengthens the relationship between the organization and its staff, but also has a profound effect on patient safety and the quality of care that is provided to patients and families.

Commitment to a Philosophy That Promotes Continuous Improvement and the Use of Technology to Support Practice

Driving an organization's mission requires a solid understanding of best practices in systems thinking and a commitment to continuous improvement and learning. Identifying and analyzing problems and creating sustained improvements requires highly specialized knowledge and skills in the areas of industrial engineering, human factors analysis, process improvement methodologies, team leadership, and other related bodies of knowledge. The technical and cognitive skill set needed to analyze systems and processes and then improve them is not learned through experience, nor does it come naturally to most clinical and administrative leaders. For this reason, leaders who are accountable for patient care practices and programs require the support of a cadre of experts in process improvement as they unearth and examine the

---

EXHIBIT 15.2 DANA-FARBER CANCER INSTITUTE— PRINCIPLES OF A FAIR AND JUST CULTURE

Background

It is inevitable that people will make mistakes or experience misunderstandings in any work environment. When events occur that cause harm or have the potential to cause harm to patients or staff members, or that place the Institute at legal, financial or ethical risk, a choice exists: to learn or to blame. Dana-Farber Cancer Institute (DFCI) is committed to creating a work environment that emphasizes learning rather than blame.

Dana-Farber Cancer Institute recognizes the complexity and interdependence of the work environment in all aspects of its operations, including patient care, clinical operations, research, support services and administration. The intent is to promote an atmosphere where any employee can openly discuss errors of commission or omission, process improvements, and/or systems corrections without the fear of reprisal.

It is well documented that most errors, whether or not they cause harm, are due to breakdowns in organizational systems; however, when an error takes place, individual culprits are often sought. Blaming individuals creates a culture of fear and defensiveness that diminishes both learning and the capacity to constantly improve systems.

Most errors take place within systems that themselves contribute to the error. In spite of this, it is difficult to create an institutional culture that integrates the understanding that systems failures are the root cause of most errors. Learning from errors often points to beneficial changes in systems and management processes as well as in individual behavior.

In the context of promoting a fair and just culture, what does it mean? A fair and just culture means giving constructive feedback and critical analysis in skillful ways, doing assessments that are based on facts, and having respect for the complexity of the situation. It also means providing fair-minded treatment, having productive conversations, and creating effective structures that help people reveal their errors and help the organization learn from them. A fair and just culture does *not* mean non-accountable, nor does it mean an avoidance of critique or assessment of competence. Rather, when incompetence or sub-standard performance is revealed after careful collection of facts, and/or there is reckless or willful violation of policies or negligent behavior, corrective or disciplinary action may be appropriate.

Applying these principles creates an opportunity to enact the core values of the Dana-Farber Cancer Institute. In order to have the greatest impact and

(Exhibit continued on next page)

EXHIBIT 15.2 (CONTINUED)

achieve the highest level of excellence, staff must be able to speak up about problems, errors, conflicts and misunderstandings in an environment where it is the shared goal to identify and discuss problems with curiosity and respect. To achieve excellence, unwanted or unexpected outcomes and inefficiencies of practice must be used as the basis for a learning process. Respect must be shown to all people at every level of the organization.

PRINCIPLES OF A FAIR AND JUST CULTURE

1. DFCI strives to create a learning environment and a workplace that support the core values of impact, excellence, respect/compassion and discovery in every aspect of work at the Institute.
2. DFCI supports the efforts of every individual to deliver the best work possible. When errors are made and/or misunderstandings occur, the Institute strives to establish accountability in the context of the system in which they occurred.
   - *We commit to creating an institutional work environment that is least likely to cause or support error.*
   - *We are proactive about identifying system flaws.*
3. DFCI commits to holding individuals accountable for their own performance in accordance with their job responsibilities and the DFCI core values. However, individuals should not carry the burden for system flaws over which they had no control.
4. DFCI promotes open interdisciplinary discussion of untoward events (errors, mistakes, misunderstandings or system failures resulting in harm, potential harm or adverse outcome) by all who work, visit or are cared for at the Institute.
   - *We commit to developing and maintaining easily available and simple processes to discuss untoward events.*
   - *We commit to eliciting different points of view to identify sources of untoward events and to use the information to improve the working and care environment.*
   - *We commit to fostering an interdisciplinary teamwork approach to the analysis of untoward events and to the actions taken to address them.*
   - *We believe that individuals are responsible for surfacing untoward events and for contributing to the elimination of system flaws.*
   - *We commit to analyzing episodes of institutional or patient harm or potential harm in an unbiased fashion to best determine the contributions of system and individual factors.*

(Exhibit continued on next page)

EXHIBIT 15.2 DANA-FARBER CANCER INSTITUTE—
PRINCIPLES OF A FAIR AND JUST CULTURE (CONTINUED)

- *We seek solutions that promote simplification and standardization wherever possible.*

5. DFCI acts to improve all areas of the workplace by implementing changes based on our analysis of problems and potential or actual harm.
   - *We know that actions designed to address the root causes of untoward events will improve the effectiveness of our work environment and the safety of care. We commit to identifying and assigning responsibility for implementing those actions to specific individuals or groups.*
   - *We commit to developing timely and effective follow-up and an effective organizational culture through education and systems for ensuring on-going competency.*

6. DFCI commits to a culture of inclusion and education.
   - *We commit to fostering a culture that is concerned with safety in research, clinical care and administration through continuous education, proactive interventions and safety-based leadership.*
   - *We believe that patient input is indispensable to the delivery of safe care and we commit to promoting patient and family participation.*

7. DFCI will assess our success in promoting a learning environment by evaluating our willingness to communicate openly and by the improvements we achieve.
   - *We commit to monitoring actions and attitudes for their effectiveness in supporting a culture of safety and modifying actions as needed.*

Principles adapted with permission from Allan Frankel, MD, and the patient safety leaders at Partner Healthcare System. Source: Frankel, A., Gandhi, T.K., and Bates, D.D.W. "Improving patient safety across a large integrated health care delivery system." (2003). International Journal for Quality in Health Care, 15 (Suppl. 1), 31–40.

myriad complex systems and processes that require monitoring and continuous improvement and work to stay abreast of technology changes and advances in systems of care.

Over the last two decades, health care leaders have begun to appreciate the critical role that technology can play in improving processes and assuring safe environments. Robust information systems applications, medical device technologies, and ergonomic equipment help increase the efficiency and safety of patient care and of those who deliver it. The adoption of systems and technologies that support practice must proceed as rapidly as possible in all health services sectors, particularly in organizations that provide direct care to patients and families. Although capital dollar constraints demand that health care organizations continually triage and prioritize their purchases, certain technologies should be at the top of every hospital's list. These include technologies that streamline and improve the safety of medication administration, equipment tracking devices, equipment that offers ergonomic advantages to care providers, and technologies that support long-distance care and communication.

Commitment to Leadership Development

Developing knowledge and leadership skills is by necessity a continuous, ongoing process. Nurse leaders in the service sector who make continuous learning a priority for themselves and for nurses on their leadership teams often find that complex problems, decisions, and initiatives are effectively addressed, and that the principles of collaboration, transparency, and inclusiveness gradually become the organizational norm.

Given the unique culture, climate, and structural attributes of each institution, the first step in designing a plan for leadership development for a team or an organization is to define principles or expectations for organizational behavior. Over the past few years, I have worked with the leaders of the patient care services department at my institution to identify the following principles:

- Communication is open and transparent.
- Different opinions are respected.
- Every voice is valued.
- Leaders are dedicated to serving the greater good, not personal ambition.
- Accountability is built into every decision (i.e., determine who is accountable for what).

These principles are based on a framework developed by noted anthropologist Angeles Arrien (2005). The framework describes essential character traits for living and leading in a collective and is based on archetypal anthropological evidence. Our efforts to apply our principles of organizational behavior to our interactions were facilitated by two executive coaches, who worked with the leadership team collectively and individually as challenging situations arose. The coaches emphasized the importance of incorporating honesty, courage, respect, authenticity, and compassion into our relationships and interactions with others. They also emphasized the importance of self-reflection and of asking the question, "Why does a particular situation challenge me, and do I have any blind spots?"

The coaches also provided us with a methodology for engaging in encounters involving challenging, difficult, or conflict-laden situations. The methodology helps leaders prepare for difficult conversations by identifying key principles and steps. For example, the methodology instructs leaders to begin difficult conversations with a succinct and clear statement of "what is at the heart of the matter" and to describe how the other person's behavior impacts them. In addition, before the end of the interaction, the leader should describe agreements that were reached as a result of the conversation. These principles, as described by Connaughton and Hassinger (2007), have helped members of the entire leadership team become more effective in dealing with conflict and/or troubling situations and behaviors.

Having a common lexicon for managing relationships and the inevitable conflicts and challenges that relationships consistently pose not only helps team members develop their leadership skills and abilities, but also enhances the team's influence on the organization as a whole.

PERSONAL LEADERSHIP COMPETENCIES

Competency 1. Gaining self-knowledge through a disciplined approach involving personal values clarification, introspection, and continuous self-improvement

Effective leaders are constantly striving to be better at what they do. This involves, at the minimum, developing awareness and the habit of self-reflection. The first step in the journey to self-knowledge, continuous self-improvement, and ongoing personal leadership development involves identifying your personal values. Understanding what is important to you and why not only helps you identify your personal goals, but also helps you recognize strengths and talents that can help you achieve them. Leaders who understand their own talents and propensities also learn to appreciate where they need help and how to surround themselves with people who have complementary strengths.

Recognizing talents that you lack is also critical. In *First Break All the Rules,* Buckingham and Coffman (1999) note that areas of "non-talent" are most often manifested by skills or cognitive areas that pose a struggle for the individual. A non-talent only becomes a weakness when a person is in a role where success depends on excelling in the non-talent area. For example, a non-talent in public speaking is of little consequence in and of itself. It becomes a weakness only if you are in a role where public speaking is critical to your success. Leaders who find themselves in such a position must make a conscious effort to attain competency in the area of non-talent. Often, this means seeking the help of a colleague, friend, partner, or coach who can help you recognize your talents and non-talents and develop a plan to increase your effectiveness in areas critical to your success.

Gaining self-knowledge requires commitment and an ability to access your own internal as well as external resources. Sharing your commitment and stating it publicly to your team or with those in your household can help you stay the course. Explicitly declaring your desire and commitment to improve and focus on an issue, acquire knowledge, practice new skills, and seek feedback will help you be successful since you and those around you will better understand what you are doing and why.

My own experiences with seeking self-knowledge offer an illustration of its benefits. Following an annual executive coaching session, I became acutely aware of some of my strengths and weaknesses. I realized that one of my inherent strengths is setting a vision and describing a theoretical end-point, but I was weak in providing clear and focused direction and support at the specific, operational level. I also realized I have a tendency toward inclusiveness and consensus—a wonderful characteristic, but one that if left unchecked can compromise the timeliness of decision making and result in procrastination and ineffective leadership. I committed to begin working with an executive coach to better understand my strengths, talents, and areas of weakness, and to develop a plan to improve and monitor my behaviors. The insights I gained and the action plan I developed are shared in Table 15.1. Naming my weaknesses, developing an action plan to address them, and documenting my progress helped me remain aware of my personal development goals and of the steps I needed to take to achieve them.

Competency 2. Creating trust within a collective

A successful leader is a trusted leader. As a first step toward establishing trust, nurse leaders must take time to assess whether trust exists within their teams. As Stephen M. R. Covey (2006, p. 46) notes, "trust means *confidence,* and the opposite of trust—distrust—means *suspicion.*" When distrust is at play, members of a team continuously direct their energies toward determining motives and arranging safety nets to protect themselves from the fallout of the leader's actions. This is an extremely corrosive team dynamic and will inevitably result in ineffectiveness and apathy.

Nurse leaders must also engage in self-reflection to determine whether they are acting in a consistent and congruent manner, an essential element of integrity. Covey suggests individuals can bolster their integrity by taking the following steps: make and keep commitments to yourself; stand for something; be open; clarify your intent internally and with others—(i.e., your motives, agendas, and behaviors) (Covey, 2006).

To develop trust within their work teams, nurse leaders must also take time to obtain team members' perceptions of their leadership abilities and style, including whether they have established a rapport with their team members and are "in synch" with them. Daniel Goleman (2006, p. 85) describes such rapport as "social intelligence." Like others, he believes individuals can develop greater social intelligence over time.

TABLE 15.1   Author's Annual Coaching Grid, September 2003

My Strength	Potential Pitfall	Action	Progress—3 Months
• Inclusiveness	• Over-process, deadline slips	• Make a conscious choice regarding boundaries—that is, who gives input, who makes decisions, time frame. Finally, trust self	Decided to create a small work team to solve a complex issue
• Thoroughness	• Indecisiveness	• Create process with clear objectives and time line	Using a more disciplined approach to writing and sharing work plans
• High degree of intuition/radar	• Don't trust self without data	• Consciously note what I sense, and act decisively	When I perceive something, validate it more routinely
• Compassion	• Enabler of dysfunction in others· • Inadequate delegation of work leading to exhaustion	• Act decisively in face of conflict; stay centered; be willing to disengage • Raise the bar of expectations for others with clarity; trust they will push back if necessary	Have been more attentive to my authentic reactions and my responses to situations at work and have begun sharing these compassionately with my coworkers and staff
• Determination/ self-confidence in ability to solve problems	• Cannot fix everything; entanglement with others	• Stay centered and aware of boundaries, what is mine, what is not. "Know when to fold 'em"	I am handing off issues to others and more clearly articulating what I expect
• Stamina/ resilience	• Over-commitment to activities	• Use a disciplined approach to saying yes and no to new work; eliminate work not in alignment with core mission	Am clearer about what I prioritize and why and then proceed with perseverance
• Humility	• Missed opportunities to lead powerfully	• Understand the difference between humility and leadership	Have continued to be humble but not holding back

Competency 3. Integrating personal and professional life commitments.

A key competency for nurse leaders involves developing a methodology or approach to healthy living. This competency requires a commitment to staying up-to-date with knowledge and science pertaining to physical, mental, and spiritual health, organizational behavior, and approaches to managing the priorities, opportunities, and challenges of a professional leadership role. Some of the methods that I have found helpful in managing my personal and professional commitments are described in more detail below.

Personal Health—A Model for Balancing the Physical, Mental, and Spiritual Domains of Health

Nurse leaders can use different frameworks to guide their efforts to improve who they are and what they do. A framework I have found particularly helpful is based on proactively assessing and redefining my commitment to my physical, mental, and spiritual health. Over the years, I have realized that unless I pay attention to each of these dimensions, my performance in every sector of my life suffers and the joy and satisfaction I experience is diminished.

While most people share similar definitions of physical and mental health, the definition of spiritual health varies across individuals. Many people agree, however, that tending to the spiritual dimension of health is critical to their overall well-being. A related area involves understanding and managing one's own energy and using it selectively and smartly to meet demands. Loehr and Schwarts (2003, p. 4) note that "Energy, not time is the fundamental currency of high performance." They suggest that only when we are fully engaged do we perform at our best. To be at our best, we must draw on four related sources of personal energy: physical, emotional, mental, and spiritual. Just as we build physical capacity through disciplined training, repetition, and strengthening routines, we can also strengthen our emotional, spiritual, and mental capacities by continually nurturing and stretching our abilities in these areas.

Nurse leaders who avail themselves of the support and guidance of coaches or psychological and spiritual counselors, and who engage in physical training, are more likely to realize who they are, where they are in life, and where they want and need to go. Being open to evolving as a person and leader, and always moving toward a sense of personal mastery as defined by Peter Senge (1990), helps leaders develop a habit of self-reflection and build a foundation of personal integrity and authenticity. Experience alone is insufficient to build this foundation; however, it can provide an invaluable context for self-reflection and learning and help leaders acquire self-knowledge. This is illustrated in the next case study.

Case Study 15.1: Stopping Dead in My Tracks

After finishing my last meeting, I commented to my executive assistant, Deborah, that the day had gone well, and that I was looking forward to attending an event that evening with my husband, Bill. Before I could pick up the phone to call Bill, my cell phone rang. Bill was on the other end and greeted me with the words, "Luke has been shot in the head."

Thinking I heard him incorrectly, I said, "What do you mean?" "Luke has been shot," he repeated. "I just arrived at his house to get Matt [our son] and found that something terrible has happened. They're putting Luke in the ambulance now and they say he's heading to the medical center. Get here quick."

I immediately thought there must have been some kind of accident. Luke had somehow been shot, but he must be okay, I thought. It couldn't be too bad. I knew I needed to get home, but before I left I wanted to contact the nurse leaders at the hospital Luke was headed for. I knew them well and wanted to tell them that a friend, a 17-year-old boy who might be in terrible condition would be arriving shortly, and to ask them to please do everything possible to help him. I quickly called to Deborah, "Call Diane at the medical center and get me a cab. Tell them it's urgent. Matt's best friend has been shot; I don't know how and why, but I need to get back home. Matt is okay."

Our town is only 8 miles from my place of work. On a good day and with little traffic, I can get home within 20 minutes. After hearing what happened, the taxi driver broke my commuting record. I arrived at Luke's house to find his mother, Sally, a wonderful friend, arriving at the same time. I quickly discovered that Luke was already in an ambulance and on his way to the emergency room.

Over a very short time, I began to unravel what happened. Luke had gotten a gun from a locked gun cabinet, taken it to his room, and shot himself in the head. He was apparently still alive in the emergency room, and his mom and dad, Sally and Joe, wanted desperately to get there. But there was so much going on that it was hard to sort out what to do first. The police were still there; Luke's older brother, grandparents, uncles, and aunts needed to be contacted; and most importantly, Luke's younger brother, who had found Luke, needed support. Finally, we agreed that Joe and Sally and I would leave immediately for the hospital, and Bill would follow with Luke's brothers once his older brother arrived.

On the way to the hospital, Joe and Sally and I agonized, prayed out loud, cried, and hoped for the impossible. When we arrived, it became clear that Luke was essentially dead, but because of the bullet's path, he would live until taken off the ventilator. A compassionate, young neurosurgeon spoke to us before we saw Luke and told us there truly was no hope. Sally immediately said, "We want to donate his organs." Her focus and generosity in the face of personal tragedy took my breath away.

The next 6 hours were surreal. As I stood beside Sally and Joe and looked down at Luke lying on the stretcher, I sometimes talked to myself out loud, saying again and again, "How can this be? It can't be real." The nursing staff and social workers stood nearby throughout this time and skillfully addressed all of our concerns and questions. Luke's hands were warm and his face was peaceful, as if he were sleeping, but he was not there, nor would he ever be again.

Throughout this time, my mind often turned to worrying about my son, Matt, who by all accounts was now aware that something terrible had happened. He and his friends, who had always been welcomed by Luke's family and spent hours at their house, finally understood that Luke had tried to kill himself. What they didn't know was that he had been successful. For the next day or two they thought that perhaps Luke would get better and survive. Instead, the process of stopping the ventilator and waiting for donor procurement processes to occur were underway. Eleven days after the shooting, Luke was buried.

Throughout those 2 weeks and for the next year and a half, we were all in agony about Luke's suicide and constantly recalled our lives and decisions before and after that tragic moment. We continually asked ourselves whether any of us—if only we had been more educated, more attentive, more definitive, or more compassionate—could have averted this terrible outcome.

In time, several things became clear to me—some immediately and some later. As I thought back on other tragedies and losses that I and others have experienced, I realized that none of them had hit me with the force of this tragedy, even though some, like the 9/11 terrorist attack, had been so much more damaging to humankind. This loss, however, had stopped me dead in my tracks. I did not return to work for 2 weeks. I was focused solely on what was happening with Matthew, my son Jon, Bill, Luke's mom, dad, brothers, friends, relatives, and the community. I simply hunkered down into the most terrible place, but one where I knew I needed to be.

This tragedy and loss has taught me much about personal leadership at work and at home, about clarity of purpose in my personal and professional life, and about what I value most in life. I learned, first, that you cannot anticipate what might come your way in terms of loss or challenge, but if you survive, you will clearly be stronger because of it, especially if you seek the help of a coach or counselor and are open to learning and improving who you are.

Second, I learned that my relationship with my husband trumped all else, including my relationship with our sons. That is, Bill and I pledged that in spite of whatever might happen, the primacy of our relationship would give us the strength to forge through anything and to be helpful to others. Third, this tragedy helped me learn to value the time I spend with those I love and care about. I learned the value of simply sitting beside my teenage son, even if we don't converse. What is important, I began to realize, is making the time, taking the time, and focusing on the person I am with. I had never spent time this way before. I do now, routinely. Fourth, I learned much about mental health and depression. Before Luke's death, I thought I knew a lot about mental health, just because I was a health professional and must have absorbed it through osmosis. In reality, I did not know the signs and symptoms of teenage depression. I do now. I also understand the importance of learning about health issues that might affect those around me.

Perhaps one of the most important things I learned is to stop when I begin to feel role overload, role strain, or simply overdone one way or another in either my personal or professional life. I understand now that the schedule I follow on a day-to-day basis is primarily contrived by the decisions I make, and that at any given time, I can decide to stop, not do something, do something different, or simply change my mind. The first act in this deliberative process is to stop and determine the consequences of proceeding or not, then weigh the impact of a new path and make a conscious choice to do it or not. Since having this realization, I have learned it is okay to change plans at the last minute, to decide not to attend a meeting, to golf with my husband and brother-in-law instead of working on a chapter that is due in a week, to go to bed early instead of staying up with company when I am on vacation, to not work on a day I return from the West Coast on the "Red Eye," and to make an appointment with my trainer instead of going to a professional meeting. These decisions never come easily or without careful consideration and the necessary communication, but I venture to say I have become a more successful leader and person since I've learned to make them.

This tragedy also gave me insight into how I react to anxiety and frustration. Through it I learned that I own my own reactions and that something as simple as breathing deeply can help me control them. I now make a point of practicing deep breathing routinely, particularly when I anticipate needing to respond or react to a stressful situation. I've learned that how I react is totally up to me, and that I have the power within myself to be the best I can be and to help others do the same. When I am at my best, I now realize, others are more likely to be as well.

Finally, I have learned that I have the strength to weather any future loss—of a person, of freedom, or of my own health. During the agonizing months after Luke died, I came to realize that if my family and I could endure the pain that we experienced when we lost Luke, we could handle anything that comes our way, even the loss of one another. Although it might feel impossible on many levels, we know we have done it once and would be able to do it again. This clarity allows each of us to make the most of each moment and to know deep in our hearts that we are strong and capable. Now, when the phone rings and I hear Matthew on the other end saying "Mom," and then hesitating, I still hold my breath, but the fear that once was there in the months following Luke's death has dissipated and has been replaced with the knowledge that I will be able to deal with whatever he will say.

Professional Health—A Methodology for Balancing Role Responsibilities With Professional Commitments

A key competency for nurse leaders is the ability to methodically and proactively integrate one's personal and professional commitments, priorities, and goals. Nurse leaders who are invigorated by challenging assignments and prominent roles must find a way to assure they do not accept positions and projects that will ultimately collide in time, space, or energy. Although learning to integrate competing commitments is an essential skill for nurse leaders if they intend to lead productive and joyful lives, doing it well does not necessarily come naturally, but instead requires thought, skill, and commitment.

While the demands and expectations that come with some commitments are unforeseen, most are blatantly obvious at the outset. It is essential that leaders take time at the start of any new opportunity to identify what it will require and to assess their ability to maintain the required energy, commitment, and focus. Leaders should also ask themselves whether the opportunity demands skills—such as public speaking—that lie outside their areas of strength, and to consider whether they want to decline the opportunity or want to use it as a way of stretching themselves by doing something that is not comfortable or easy.

Over the years, I have learned the value of carefully considering the opportunities that come my way and evaluating how they match my interests, talents, and the time I have available. One example of this occurred last year when I was invited to accept a nomination to become a Magnet commissioner for the American Nurses Credentialing Center (ANCC). In considering the nomination, I had to decide whether I would be able to take on this new responsibility and do it justice while still fulfilling my other roles.

To place my decision in context, I need to go back to an earlier time when I was asked to join the board of the Massachusetts Organization of Nurse Executives (MONE). I had been a MONE member for years and had long aspired to become a board member; however, the invitation to join the MONE board came at a time when I was thinking about moving into a higher-level position at work. After some deliberation, in which I evaluated whether I could handle both challenges, I decided that the opportunity offered by MONE was manageable and made sense from a number of perspectives, and I accepted the invitation. While serving as a board member over the next 5 years, I also assumed the role of CNO at a comprehensive cancer center, completed a Robert Wood Johnson (RWJ) Nurse Executive fellowship, and became a fellow of the American Academy of Nursing. At the end of the 5 years, I also became president-elect of MONE.

I found myself reflecting on these earlier activities as I considered the Magnet commissioner nomination. I realized my accomplishments of the previous 5 years not only complemented one another, but also created a synergy that had resulted in my being offered another incredible opportunity. (A wonderful colleague, who I had met during my RWJ fellowship, had recommended me as a candidate for the ANCC Magnet commission seat.) Since the position as Magnet commissioner carries a 4-year commitment, however, I needed to carefully consider whether I would be able to fulfill a commissioner's responsibilities, should my candidacy be accepted, while also meeting the obligations of my other roles. I knew that during the 4 years, I would also maintain my role as a senior executive at the cancer center, and during one of the years, would be president of MONE, another rigorous and time-consuming role.

My deliberations were aided by a formal decision-making methodology that I often use. The methodology is described in Exhibit 15.3 and consists of a simple tool that forces me to consider and weigh the implications of

---

EXHIBIT 15.3 DECIDING WHETHER TO ACCEPT A PROFESSIONAL OPPORTUNITY

Directions: Criteria for deciding whether to accept an opportunity are listed below. Each criterion is weighted from least important (1) to most important (3). The weight is noted in parentheses at the end of each statement:

- Advances and is synergistic with current role and work priorities (3)
- Adds to personal growth and development or to those who directly report to you (1)
- Highlights organization, positioning it positively in the community (2)
- Realistically manageable from time management perspective (3)

(*Exhibit continued on next page*)

EXHIBIT 15.3 (CONTINUED)

- Frequency of the opportunity to engage (1)
- Financially feasible at personal and/or organizational level (2)
- Matches your own talents, interests, and strengths (3)
    1. Think about each criterion in relation to the opportunity you have been presented and assign it a score of 0, 1, 2, or 3. A score of zero means the criterion is not applicable to the opportunity or your decision-making processes; a score of 3 suggests the criterion should weigh heavily in your decision.
    2. For each criterion, multiply the score you assign by the weight to obtain an item score.
    3. Sum the item scores to obtain an overall score. The higher the overall score, the more compelling the opportunity. The range of possible overall scores is 0 to 45. A score of 0–15 is considered low, 15–30 is moderate, and 31–45 is high.

The following example illustrates how a particular opportunity would be scored:

Criteria	Weight	Your Score	Item Score
Advances and is synergistic with current role and work priorities	3	3	9
Adds to personal growth and development or to those who directly report to you	1	3	3
Highlights organization, positioning it positively in the community	2	1	2
Realistically manageable from time management perspective	3	2	6
Frequency of the opportunity to engage	1	3	3
Financially feasible at personal and/or organizational level	2	1	2
Matches your own talents, interests, and strengths	3	3	9
OVERALL SCORE			**34**

my decisions. After applying this methodology and consulting with my colleagues, family, and friends, and with my boss, the CEO of the cancer center, I decided to accept the nomination to the ANCC commission. My nomination was ultimately accepted by the ANCC board.

At present, I am about 1 month away from passing the gavel of the MONE presidency to my capable successor and I have just completed a year as a Magnet commissioner. We have also had an incredible year at our comprehensive cancer center. I believe I made the right decision when I accepted the nomination to be a Magnet commissioner, because the role has enriched me personally and has allowed me to gain experience that enhances my performance in other roles. Although you would need to ask my family, peers, colleagues, and boss for their perceptions of my performance during the past year, I believe I have been able to lead well within each of my professional domains and have contributed significantly and positively in all of the professional arenas I operate in as well as within my family. The decision-making methodology I used when making the decision is one I continue to draw on whenever I am asked to take on a new role or to significantly expand my responsibilities.

SUMMARY

My aim in writing this chapter was to provide nurse leaders with an appreciation of the critical goals, competencies, and commitments that come with being a leader in the service sector. In addition to creating organizations that are patient- and family-centered, and that prize interdisciplinary collaboration, transparency, continuous improvement, and leadership development, nurse leaders must develop self-knowledge and learn to integrate their personal and professional commitments if they are to be truly successful and find joy in their personal and professional lives.

NOTE

1. From "Nurse-physician co-leadership: A model of interdisciplinary practice governance," by Patricia Reid Ponte, 2004, *Journal of Nursing Administration, 34,* p. 483. Copyright 2004 by the *Journal of Nursing Administration.* Reprinted with permission.

REFERENCES

Arrien, A. (2005). *The second half of life. Opening the eight gates of wisdom.* Boulder, CO: Sounds True, Inc.

Buckingham, M., & Coffman, C. (1999). *First break all the rules—What the world's greatest managers do differently.* New York: Simon & Schuster.

Connaughton, M. J., & Hassinger, J. (2007). Leadership character: Antidote to organizational fatigue. *Journal of Nursing Administration, 37,* 464–470.

Connor, M., Duncombe, D., Barclay, E., Bartel, S., Borden, C., Gross, E., et al. (2007). Creating a fair and just culture: One institution's path toward organizational change. *Joint Commission Journal on Quality and Patient Safety, 33*(8), 617–624.

Connor, M., Reid Ponte, P., & Conway, J. (2002). Multidisciplinary approaches to patient safety. *Nursing Clinics of North America, 14,* 359–367.

Covey, S.M.R. (2006). *The speed of trust—The one thing that changes everything.* New York: Simon & Schuster.

Dana Farber Cancer Institute. (2006). *Implementing Dana Farber Cancer Institute Patient Safety Rounds in your organization—A toolkit.* Boston: Dana Farber Cancer Institute.

Goleman, D. (2006). *Social intelligence—The new science of social relationships.* New York: Bantam Dell Publishing Group.

Loehr, J., & Schwarts, T. (2003). *The power of full engagement.* New York: Free Press.

Ponte, P. R. (2004). Nurse-physician co-leadership: A model of interdisciplinary practice governance. *Journal of Nursing Administration, 34,* 481–484.

Ponte, P. R., Conlin, G., Conway, J. B., Grant, S., Medeiros, C., Nies, J., et al. (2003). Making patient-centered care come alive: Achieving full integration of the patient's perspective. *Journal of Nursing Administration, 33,* 82–90.

Ponte, P. R., Gross, A. H., Winer, E., Connaughton, M. J., & Hassinger, J. (2007). Implementing an interdisciplinary governance model in a comprehensive cancer center. *Oncology Nursing Forum, 34,* 611–616.

Reid Ponte, P. (2005). Nursing: Strengthening a critical hospital resource. In Association and the American College of Healthcare Executives (Eds.), *Futurescan: Healthcare trends and implications: 2006–2011* (pp. 37–40). Chicago: Health Administration Press.

Senge, P. (1990). *The fifth discipline—The art and science of the learning organization.* New York: Doubleday.

Index

Nursing Leadership

A Concise Encyclopedia

Editor-in-Chief:
Harriet R. Feldman, PhD, RN, FAAN

Associate Editors:
Marilyn Jaffe-Ruiz, EdD, RN
Margaret L. McClure, RN, EdD, FAAN
Martha J. Greenberg, PhD, RN
Thomas D. Smith, MS, RN, CNAA, BC
M. Janice Nelson, EdD, RN
Angela Barron McBride, PhD, RN, FAAN
G. Rumay Alexander, EdD, RN

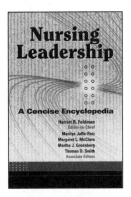

"We are delighted to introduce this book to a new generation of readers. The challenges in nursing, as well as in health care, have never been greater. The need for resources such as this text is profound."
—From the Foreword by **Joanne Disch**, PhD, RN, FAAN, School of Nursing, University of Minnesota
and **Kathleen Dracup**, DNSc, FNP, RN, FAAN, School of Nursing, University of California, San Francisco

Nursing Leadership: A Concise Encyclopedia is a manageable, one-volume reference that describes and defines the field of nursing leadership. The Encyclopedia will provide students, faculty, nurse managers, executives, and others with a comprehensive resource for information about the range of knowledge and roles encompassed by the term "nursing leadership." It details the contributions of key nursing leaders, the knowledge base and traits of leadership, skills and models on which leadership is based, the regulatory environment of health care, the range of practice settings and roles, and the design of quality outcomes.

The editors and contributors to this essential reference comprise some of the best-known and influential leaders in the nursing field. This book will be a cherished resource for leaders and future leaders in health care.

2008 · 576pp · hardcover · 978-0-8261-0258-4

11 West 42nd Street, New York, NY 10036-8002 • Fax: 212-941-7842
Order Toll-Free: 877-687-7476 • Order Online: www.springerpub.com

Management and Leadership in Nursing and Health Care

An Experiential Approach, 2nd Edition

Elaine La Monica Rigolosi, EdD, JD, FAAN

"What sets Dr. Elaine La Monica Rigolosi's newest edition of her well written book above the rest...[is that] she draws on such masters of organizational and communication theory as Hersey and Blanchard, Argyris, Maslow, and Hertzberg. Too often, in a rush to mention the latest and the newest, authors leave out some of the best because they are considered 'passe'....Dr. Rigolosi's case studies and exercises smack of realism. Reviewing them, the reader can imagine him or herself in what sometimes feels like the cauldron of a modern health-care setting. For theory, practice, old masters, latest research, easy to read, thoughtful, and practical this book has it all. Dr. Rigolosi believes learning is a lifelong experience....Through her book, she makes learning accessible."

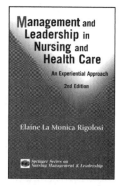

—**Harriet Forman,** EdD, RN, CNAA
Formerly Executive Director of *Nursing Spectrum*

This book presents the basics of leadership and management for nurses—what is essential in order to effectively motivate and educate individuals to achieve the set goals of a group, team, or organization in health care. The basic components of management and leadership theory are described, such as effective communication, analyzing a problem, conflict resolution, and time management. Extensive simulation exercises provide learners with an opportunity to observe, experience, and carry out new behaviors in a safe environment. The book and exercises are designed for use in both self-learning and classroom environments.

2005 · 432pp · hardcover · 978-0-8261-2525-5

11 West 42nd Street, New York, NY 10036-8002 • **Fax: 212-941-7842**
Order Toll-Free: 877-687-7476 • **Order Online: www.springerpub.com**

SPRINGER / PUBLISHING COMPANY

Leadership and Management Skills for Long-Term Care

Eileen M. Sullivan-Marx, PhD, RNC, FAAN
Deanna Gray-Miceli, DNSc, APRN, Editors

While the scope of long-term-care settings has expanded from nursing homes and home care agencies to assisted living facilities and community-based health services, the training for nurses, managers and administrators, medical directors, and other professionals who work in these facilities is often fragmented. This book was developed to fill a widely recognized gap in the management and leadership skills of RNs needed to improve the quality of long-term care. The book is based around learning modules in leadership and management competencies that were site-tested in three

types of long-term-care settings and revised based on the resulting feedback. Several of the nurse experts involved in the project contribute to this book.

The leadership modules cover team building, communication, power and negotiation, change theory and process, management direction and design, and management that moves from conflict to collaboration. Two additional modules cover cultural competence and principles of teaching and learning related to adult education in the long-term-care environment. Together, these skills will enhance the nurse's ability to build and interact with the geriatric care team, resolve conflict, negotiate for solutions, develop collaboration, and teach and mentor nurses and nursing assistants.

Key Features of this book:

- Addresses the gap in RN preparation in leadership and management skills in long-term-care settings
- Easy-to-use modules suitable for self-learning or group training
- Modules include pre- and post-tests, learning objectives, case studies, and materials for hand-outs

2008 · 200 pp · 978-0-8261-5993-9

11 West 42nd Street, New York, NY 10036-8002 • Fax: 212-941-7842
Order Toll-Free: 877-687-7476 • Order Online: www.springerpub.com